IDENTITY FORMATION, YOUTH, AND DEVELOPMENT

The concept of identity is one of the most important ideas the social sciences have investigated in recent years, yet no introductory textbooks are available to those who want to gain a sense of this burgeoning field. The first of its kind, this text provides an introduction to the scientific study of identity formation, with a focus on youth development. The analyses of the problems and prospects faced by contemporary young people in forming identities are placed in the context of societies that themselves are in transition, further complicating identity formation and the interrelated processes of self-development and moral-ethical reasoning.

In order to sort through what is now a vast literature on the various aspects of human identity, this book introduces the Simplified Identity Formation Theory. This theory cuts through much of the academic jargon that limits the accessibility of this promising field, and builds an understanding of human identity from first principles. Part I outlines the philosophical and theoretical roots of the "identity question," explores different historical and cultural contexts, and provides a framework for studying the multifaceted nature of contemporary identity formation. Part II examines related forms of human development, focusing on perspective-taking and moral reasoning, and how these are related to ethics and forms of agency. Part III completes the book by examining the scientific evidence concerning identity formation in various societal contexts, along with the interventions that can be undertaken to foster optimal development. A robust website also accompanies this text, containing everything from flashcards to a study guide for students, and an instructor's manual to PowerPoint presentations for instructors.

James E. Côté is a Professor of Sociology at The University of Western Ontario. He is the founding editor of *Identity: An International Journal of Theory and Research*, Associate Editor of the *Journal of Adolescence*, and the author or co-author of nine other books.

Charles G. Levine is an Associate Professor of Sociology at The University of Western Ontario. He has .... ce Kohlberg, *Moral Stages: A Current* ....

"Côté and Levine adeptly manage to place the field of identity theory and research into a psychosocial historical context that gives the reader new insights into the developmental task of identity formation, in a manner that is accessible to all."
—Steven L. Berman, Ph.D., Associate Professor, Psychology Department, University of Central Florida and President, Society for Research on Identity Formation, USA

"Identity is the integrating principle that makes sense of human existence but its study has tended to be fragmented and incomplete. Côté and Levine make a major breakthrough with their holistic view of human development in which identity and identity capital have a central place."
—John Bynner, Ph.D., Emeritus Professor, Institute of Education, University College London, UK

"Professors Côté and Levine provide a masterfully erudite, creative, and singularly important integration of the multidisciplinary roots of the concept of identity, and offer a new and significant frame for future research through their Simplified Identity Formation Theory (SIFT). This is an invaluable book that is destined to become required reading for all scholars and students seeking to understand, and to advance knowledge about, identity development among youth."
—Richard M. Lerner, Ph.D., Bergstrom Chair in Applied Developmental Science and Director, Institute for Applied Research in Youth Development, Tufts University, USA

"Côté and Levine are at their best when they describe identity issues in the college years and in the transition to career from college. An audience of undergraduates, worried about what will come of themselves, feeling both uncertain and guilty at failing to do as well as they should have, will much appreciate the parts of the book that let them know that they are not alone."
—Daphna Oyserman, Ph.D., Dean's Professor of Psychology, University of Southern California, USA

"This book integrates multiple perspectives on identity development with the sociological and psychological study of youth, and frames identity within the constraints of social and historical contexts. The emphasis on the interplay of agency and structure is extremely valuable, especially within a cross-cultural lens. Côté and Levine provide a roadmap for studying identity within the complex modern world."
—Seth J. Schwartz, Ph.D., Professor of Public Health Sciences, Leonard M. Miller School of Medicine, University of Miami and President-Elect, Society for the Study of Emerging Adulthood, USA

IDENTITY FORMATION, YOUTH, AND DEVELOPMENT

A Simplified Approach

James E. Côté and Charles G. Levine

Psychology Press
Taylor & Francis Group
NEW YORK AND LONDON

First published 2016
by Psychology Press
711 Third Avenue, New York, NY 10017

and by Psychology Press
27 Church Road, Hove, East Sussex BN3 2FA

*Psychology Press is an imprint of the Taylor & Francis Group,
an informa business*

Library of Congress Cataloging-in-Publication Data
Côté, James, E.
    Identity formation, youth, and development : a simplified approach / by
James E. Côté and Charles G. Levine.
        pages cm
    Includes bibliographical references and index.
    1. Identity (Psychology)   2. Identity (Psychology)—Social
aspects.   3. Developmental psychology.   I. Levine, Charles (Charles G.)
II. Title.
    BF697.C673 2015
    155.2—dc23
    2015000002

ISBN: 978-1-84872-673-4 (hbk)
ISBN: 978-1-84872-674-1 (pbk)
ISBN: 978-0-203-76704-7 (ebk)

Typeset in Bembo
by Apex CoVantage, LLC

Printed and bound by CPI Group (UK) Ltd, Croydon, CR0 4YY

BRIEF CONTENTS

TABLE OF CONTENTS

PREFACE

Questions about human identity—perceptions of belonging, distinction, and continuity—have been asked throughout the ages. Historically speaking, however, the opportunity to ask these questions is somewhat of a luxury, arising when people are free from subsistence conditions where they are constantly concerned about keeping a roof over their heads and having enough food to last them until the next hunt or growing season. Throughout most of its history, the human species has struggled to meet its basic survival needs. Only when these fundamental needs are met do people have the luxury of pondering more abstract and philosophical questions about their existence. By most accounts, this luxury was typically available to the powerful and wealthy, and those under their protection and patronage. For the common folk, religions typically provided ready-made answers about these questions at a personal level; at the same time, societies were rigidly structured to unequivocally tell people "who they were" at a social level. It is only recently that a significant portion of humankind has been able to accumulate enough security-providing wealth—primarily in the West in the period called **late-modernity**—that these issues of identity have become more general concerns among the populace.

Paradoxically, this "modern" freedom to ponder questions of identity has not been a universally positive experience. In fact, just the opposite has occurred for many people. As recently as the 1950s, circumstances in the West had reached the point where the historical period was declared to be the "age of identity anxiety." It was at this historical juncture—following two soul-crushing world wars but in a period of unprecedented affluence—that the masses were confronted with the personal task of forming major aspects of their identities that had hitherto been settled for them largely by religion or ascribed by their class-based societies.

In the decades to follow, the shackles of other forms of identity ascription, such as race/ethnicity, gender, and sexuality, were the object of mass reflection and revolt.

Since that time, the concept of identity has been one of the most discussed and researched ideas in the social sciences and humanities, taking it from the philosophical realm into the scientific and political realms. The scientific literature suggests that at the same time that identity formation and identity maintenance have become more challenging, they have also become promising. On the one hand, identity formation has changed in significant ways, with many young people now making their *own way* to adulthood in many respects. On the other hand, identity maintenance has become more of a preoccupation among the adult-aged population, especially as the traditional statuses of key social identities have been contested and placed in opposition to others, as in the cases of racism, sexism, and homophobia. Consequently, even as some people are successfully forging viable new adult identities, others are floundering in the face of these challenges. In other words, in the current era, we are witnessing both adaptions in forging and maintaining adult identities and a proliferation of identity-related problems and even pathologies.

The magnitude of these problems, and the importance of adapting to current societal conditions in a thoughtful manner, has prompted us to write this book. Our hope is to help people—especially those making the transition to adulthood—to better understand the difficulties and complexities of identity formation as an important component of human development. In selecting material for this book, we focused especially on the issues of moral and personal responsibility facing people in their relations with family and friends, coping with educational and work requirements, and finding a place in society as fully functioning, contributing members. In addition to presenting a theory with which to understand identity-related prospects and problems, we show some ways in which the theory can be applied. In doing so, we are providing the first introduction to this field for those wishing to understand various identity issues at both theoretical and practical levels, but without much of the technical jargon that makes reading this literature difficult for those who are encountering it for the first time. We thus hope we have presented the best ideas culled from this field in ways that are conceptually accessible to nonspecialists.

In order to sort through what is now a vast literature on the various aspects of human identity, we have developed the Simplified Identity Formation Theory (SIFT) and present it for the first time in this book. SIFT is intended primarily to introduce newcomers to the field. At the same time, we hope that it shows experts who take a variety of very different approaches how these diverse approaches are related in a number of ways. As we have noted in the previous edition of this book written for expert audiences, *Identity Formation, Agency and Culture: A Social Psychological Synthesis* (2002, Erlbaum), there is a need for a taxonomy that provides a common language with which academics of various persuasions can speak to each other and share their insights. We contribute to this taxonomy by suggesting a simplified language that speaks to the "forest" rather than the "trees." Much of the current literature being published in this area involves investigations of the fine points (the trees), but without an overall sense of how these points fit together at broader levels (the forest). Accordingly, in addition to a simplified terminology, we also do not belabor the many controversies and disputes in the identity studies field, including at the junctures of the scientific, philosophical, and political approaches, as we did in the previous edition written for expert audiences. When important debates are relevant to a point at hand, we mention them and give references to them but move on in terms of how we have resolved them in our work. Belaboring debates would take us from a general to a specialized audience and to the thrust and parry of academic disputes. This writing strategy is defensible not only on the grounds of clarity, but also because of our decades-long experience with this field. We both began studying identity formation in the 1970s, so are well versed in the various approaches that have been taken in the field over the past half-century. Ours is also a broad and accommodating approach that draws on several disciplines, especially psychology and sociology, as opposed to being single-minded and partisan.

The Plan of This Book

The primary value of this book is that it synthesizes a vast literature that has hitherto been partitioned into various sub-specialties that characterize identity studies. As valuable as this literature is, these sub-specialties are often fragmented and isolated from one another, leaving the identity studies field lacking: a unifying, multidimensional taxonomy, a consensus about underlying assumptions, and an accord concerning how to translate those assumptions into a coherent body of empirical work. To address this problem, we filter the relevant material through a multidimensional lens that draws on a range of research traditions and methods.

The style with which we approach this goal involves (a) "picking out" the range of possible approaches and ideas from which to draw, (b) "pushing along" the ones that best meet our overall goal, and then (c) later "picking up" those preferred approaches and ideas for elaboration and integration with other preferred approaches and ideas. This style of "sweeping" ideas along to pick them up later is useful, but also necessary, given the complexity of the literature and the fact that there is a necessary sequence in which ideas need to be presented in order to be properly understood.

We have divided this book into three parts that build on each other.

Part I comprises three chapters that outline the philosophical and theoretical roots of the "identity question," with Chapter 1 examining the roots of the theoretical approaches that have provided definitions of the key concepts in use today, Chapter 2 exploring models of how identity formation is experienced in different historical and cultural contexts, including its problematic forms in current

societies, and Chapter 3 then reviewing the developmental social-psychological framework for studying the multifaceted nature of identity formation.

In Part II, we "sweep along" the ideas "picked up" from Part I, examining how identity formation is an important component of other forms of human development. Chapter 4 examines how identity formation is related to the development of perspective taking and moral reasoning, and thus how both are related to the development of an "ethical awareness." Chapter 5 shifts to the concept of agency, showing how and why proactive forms of identity formation have become functional in contemporary Western societies. The idea of proactivity may suggest to some people that it is always important for people to act as independent—even selfish—agents in their lives, but in conjunction with the preceding chapter, Chapter 5 shows how this is a misconception about the potentials of identity formation, especially when identity is viewed in moral-ethical terms. With these considerations in mind, Chapter 6 presents original work on **identity capital**, illustrating a model that helps to understand how people can adapt proactively and ethically to contemporary late-modern societies.

Part III then shifts our attention to applications of the underlying social-scientific theories to the now-prolonged transition to adulthood, first as they apply to developmental processes in general (Chapter 7), then to the various contexts that influence identity formation (Chapter 8), and finally to ways in which identity formation can be optimized through individual efforts and interventions and counseling (Chapter 9). These chapters build the case regarding optimal types of identity formation, that is, how people can maximize their inner potentials by finding interpersonal and social contexts in which these potentials can be brought out and nurtured relationally. Chapter 9 also wraps up the lessons learned from the Simplified Theory of Identity Formation and examines several promising avenues for expanding our knowledge of the current challenges to identity formation.

We invite the reader to take the intellectual journey we provide in this book, promising that by the journey's end she or he will be more informed about the problems and prospects of human identity and its formation. For those who are new to this area, we hope they will find enough inspiration here to further their intellectual curiosity as well as to apply to their personal lives some of the principles we elaborate. And we encourage experts to take up the task we have begun of developing a formal theory of identity formation that is of intellectual and practical significance in addressing the basic conditions of human existence represented by the concept of identity and its formation.

Finally, a few comments are in order about our referencing format and use of the terms that are central to the SIFT. In order to maximize the flow of the text, we avoid distracting in-text author/date references that are customary in many social science texts. Instead, we put referencing information in endnotes, and we have intentionally limited the number of sources cited to keep the endnotes clearer. We do this especially when we are updating information from our previous edition of this book, which contains more extensive referencing for those who want to examine various sources in more detail. Much of the material in this new edition is a synthesis of material from our previous edition, so unless there are references to others works, readers can assume that we are drawing on the previous edition to produce the new simplified theory. In addition, we highlight concepts in several ways. Terms that are central to the SIFT are presented in bold, defined in the text following their first use, and are then succinctly defined in the glossary at the end of the book. Terms that are in general use in the social sciences are presented in italics. These generic scientific terms are defined in the text when they are first used and all are indexed to help readers find instances where we use these terms in other places in the book. Because these terms are in general usage in the social sciences, if readers do not feel that our explanations are full enough, they can easily look them up in Google searches, and Wikipedia usually provides an adequate introductory definition and illustrations of usages of these concepts. Finally, we follow the APA (6th edition, pp. 91–92) convention with respect to putting certain words and phrases in quotations. If these quotation instances are not directly attributed to a source with a page number in an endnote, readers can assume that our first use is a special temporary "coining" because a more precise, conventional word cannot be found.

PART I

Philosophical and Conceptual Roots of the Identity Question

1

FROM AGELESS QUESTIONS TO CURRENT THEORIES

"At his best, man is the noblest of all animals; separated from law and justice he is the worst."

Aristotle (384–322 BC)[1]

As noted in the preface, the posing of questions about human identity has a long history, dating at least to antiquity. In the above epigraph, Aristotle observed how human beings benefit from being "social animals" (in today's language), a characteristic involving the types of **identity formation** examined in this book. We know about various ruminations over the possible associations between human nature and human identity mainly from the written records left by philosophers, clerics, and academics, all of whom had the luxury of engaging in these reflections and recording them in ways that would be preserved through the millennia. Presumably, throughout human history, physical survival was a paramount concern, trumping more philosophical concerns. During periods of affluence over the ages, however, as in ancient Greece and the European Enlightenment, those who were not preoccupied with their basic *physical* needs could ponder a new set of needs— *psychological* ones. Over the past century or so in the West (and apparently in many other affluent cultures), more and more of the population has similarly been freed of the necessity of spending most of their time, energy, and attention on physical necessities, and they too have turned to reflecting on their psychological needs.

Currently, these two sets of needs have become intertwined. That is, physical wellbeing has become increasingly contingent upon people's ability to develop the psychological, or mental, capacities necessary to process information about their place in society, both in their present lives and in their possible futures.[2] This is in part because physical wellbeing has increasingly depended on the mental abilities and interpersonal skills necessary to establish the roles people play as to those around us throughout our lives; and that we could not exist physically or psychologically without these connections. Not coincidentally, this is also a basic principle of Buddhism, dating back some 2,500 years. The Buddha (circa 563–483 BC) stressed the point that people who believe they have a "self" that is completely separate from others are fooling themselves, and indeed will experience forms of suffering as a result (see box 1.1).

BOX 1.1 BUDDHIST VIEWS OF SELF AND EGO

Many of the Buddhist teachings that have been translated for Westerners stress a disdain for the "ego" and "self," suggesting that people must eradicate these ideas from their minds if they are to find happiness. Unfortunately, language can be very limiting in conveying complex ideas. In this case, writers tend to use the terms "self," "ego," and "identity" in their generic senses and not in more scientific ways. Social scientists often use these words to designate the basic mental processes that people use to direct their behaviors. Even the most enlightened Buddhist must employ certain mental processes to practice meditation, mindfulness, and the many other thought-driven exercises that are central to this religion/philosophy. In fact, as we see later in this book, Erik Erikson designated *ego strength* to represent these mental processes of self-control. What Buddhists appear to have in mind when giving their warnings are the forms of selfishness and egotism that cause suffering to people and those around them. Indeed, as anyone who has attempted to learn how to mediate will know, it takes a tremendous amount of *self-control* to limit our conscious thought processes and presumably experience reality independent of ourselves.

Given that religious leaders have cautioned people about selfishness for millennia, we cannot attribute egotism solely to contemporary Western culture with its high degrees of individualism. In fact, many religions discourage forms of selfishness, as in the Ten Commandments of Judaism and the Seven Deadly Sins of Christianity. In Buddhism, a similar set of "sins" is identified in the Precepts and Non-Virtuous Actions associated with karma. Still, there is much wisdom in Buddhist teachings that can benefit Westerners, and others, who have developed too many "selfish attachments" to their thoughts, emotions, possessions, and so forth. For example, Buddhist teachings can be interpreted in Western terms as rejecting the "hubristic self" associated with the Seven Deadly Sins, and in favor of nurturing a humble, compassionate, loving self that is free from egocentric attachments—a self that the mind can control and can reflexively view with detachment.[7]

Differentiation of people from each other at both the individual and group levels can be considered the second principle of human identity. It may seem paradoxical, but the differentiation principle follows from the integration one.

As humans formed cooperative groups, they needed to protect themselves from other groups that were in turn protecting themselves. Because resources were scarce, intergroup conflicts over the control and consumption of these resources were very common. Humans thus appear to have developed a built-in mistrust of other humans. From this mistrust, we have a legacy of in-group/out-group thought and behavior patterns; once based on threats to physical survival, these patterns morphed into perceptions of psychological vulnerability and danger. For example, it is not uncommon for young people who live in conditions of afflu-ence to suffer anxieties and traumas serious enough to lead them to contemplate or commit suicide because of how they perceive others' opinions of them. Cur-rent concerns about cyber-bullying and "social media suicides" bear out how fragile people can be, even as all of their physical and survival needs are met. Pre-vious generations handled such challenges by reminding themselves of the adage that "sticks and stones will break my bones, but names will never hurt me." Today, name-calling has taken on an importance unheard of in the past.

Within groups, although sociability is paramount, each individual still has a unique set of experiences and needs; as the saying goes, "we come into the world alone and leave the world alone." Although we are connected to others relationally, we still experience physical and psychological pain and pleasure as individuals, and everyone has distinct, albeit interdependent, roles to play. For instance, the person with the headache is the one actually feeling the pain, even if information about this pain is shared with another person and that person is sympathetic. At the same time, people must differentiate themselves from their parents to some extent as they mature, even as parents provide care. Parents cannot play their children's adult roles for them; in fact, there appears to be a new set of psychological problems emerging as "helicopter parents" try to control their adult children's lives by micro-managing their lives and in the process infantilizing them. As similar as people may be within an in-group, each person often has distinctive interests, and those dis-tinctive interests can create conflicts. A key problem thus emerges in establishing a balance between integration (sameness) and differentiation (distinction)—between shared interests and personal interests. See box 1.2 for an approach that examines the balance people seek in establishing a sense "distinctiveness" that is "optimal" for them, given their own identity-integration needs.

BOX 1.2   THE EQUILIBRIUM BETWEEN INTEGRATION AND DIFFERENTIATION

Marilynn Brewer proposed that people's sense of identity "is derived from the opposing forces of two universal human motives—the need for inclusion and assimilation, on the one hand, and the need for differentiation from others on the other." Brewer's *optimal distinctiveness theory* is based in part on assump-tions about human evolution, similar to those identified in the present chapter with respect to the first principles of human identity. She argues that humans are innately motivated to have functional relationships with a group, and "the larger and more inclusive the grouping, the more this motive is satisfied."[8] However, at a certain point the need for inclusion becomes satisfied and, before the assimilation might feel overwhelming, the need for differentiation activates. If the inclusiveness into a group *decreases* for a person, the differentiation need becomes less pressing as the assimilation need becomes more active again. Thus, when either need is experienced as deprived, people will make efforts to restore a balance of optimal distinctiveness with which they are comfortable. Equilibrium will be sought between the sense of "we" vs. "I"— integration with, and differentiation from, others.[9]

Research has empirically supported this theory in terms of laboratory manipulations of these needs and in analyses of people experiencing competing geopolitical group influences, as when Hong Kong was ceded back to China in the 1990s. Interestingly, in contexts where their in-group is perceived as threatened, people are willing to reduce their need for distinctiveness, and even set aside their own self-esteem needs to emphasize their support for that group.[10]

Finally, **continuity** is the third basic principle of human identity. Even as we are members of a group (integration) with specific personal qualities (differentiation), a sense of identity requires experiencing these attributes over time, with memories from the past making the present meaningful, and a meaningful present providing the basis for a purposeful future. Throughout much of human history, members of well-functioning groups/societies had this sense of continuity provided for them by merit of the continuing existence of their in-group and the security associated with each person's contributing and ascribed roles in that group. A sense of continuity, consequently, would not normally have been a problem for most people, and certainly not a problem that required personal reflection or that could even be addressed through personal reflection (i.e., there was little choice in roles, so ruminating over them would have been pointless and even dysfunctional).

Following optimal distinctiveness theory (box 1.2) as well as the proposed three enduring principles of human identity, figure 1.2 illustrates how an optimal balance between integration and differentiation can influence a sense of continuity. As noted earlier, the equilibrium that is optimal for a person is highly contextual. At both the micro and macro levels. Some cultures emphasize integration far more than differentiation, and following the macro cultural pattern at hand may provide the best support for the sense of continuity for most people. However, aspects of people's lives can vary, allowing for more differentiation under certain

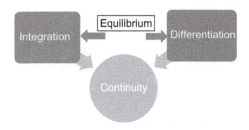

FIGURE 1.2 An optimal balance between integration and differentiation can support continuity.

circumstances, and following these micro, situational opportunities can also be supportive of the sense of continuity. Thus, in certain aspects of people's lives, blending in may be most adaptive, while in other aspects of their lives standing out may be so. For example, being fully integrated into a faith community can provide strong support for feelings of continuity, yet that same person may benefit from standing out from that community in terms of special talents or roles, as in the cases of athletic and artistic abilities, or occupational and leadership positions.

However, in Western societies, many collective–integrative sources of continuity are no longer guaranteed and have not been for some time. Using the social scientific literature as a guide, there were ruminations published about deficits in the sense of continuity in the late 1800s, and by the mid-1900s literature was growing to account for the "problem of identity" in Western societies. First came theories of mass society, then postmodern society, and more recently late-modern society. Although there are important differences among these theories, they have in common a concern with the growing preoccupation of people with inadequacies in their sense of present meaning and future *purpose in life*—two crucial anchors of a sense of personal continuity. Importantly, all of these theories locate this problem of continuity with a breakdown in traditions that securely *included* people in communities (integration) while providing people with recognized roles in those communities that allowed them to make their *distinctive contributions* to those communities (differentiation).

It is a basic premise of the SIFT that for any historical era, sources of identity, as well as many of the problems people experience in the sense of identity, can be traced to these three basic principles. Thus, we argue that it is common for people in contemporary Western societies to experience problems, especially during the transition to adulthood, with fitting into a community (integration), finding a distinctive niche for themselves in that community (differentiation), and therefore developing senses of present meaning and future purpose (continuity). Accordingly, these three basic principles of human identity provide a starting point for a scientific understanding of identity formation by pointing out the socio-historical and trans-contextual sources of identity and its disruption. However, identity formation involves further individual-level processes that are developmental in nature. Our elaboration of these developmental processes begins in the next section, and continues throughout the remainder of the book.

The Self and Its Development

Writings reflecting on the nature of the self can be traced to Enlightenment philosophers such as Immanuel Kant (1724–1804), who distinguished between the self as an experience and the self as a source of cognitive activity. The *experiencing self* is "in the moment" while the *cognitive self* steps out of the moment to engage in contextual reflections. These self-reflections can be about: our relationships with other people, how we think those people view us, and our place in society. Previously, René Descartes (1596–1650) had proposed a solution to a timeless problem of human existence—how do we know we exist?—with the famous adage, "I think, therefore I am." One way to understand Descartes's adage is in terms of a cognitive self ("I think") and an experiencing self ("I am").

In the late 1800s, philosophical thinking about the nature of self influenced the scientific discipline of psychological, as seen for example in the pioneering work of William James, and later Charles Horton Cooley and G.H. Mead.[11] James and Mead emphasized a distinction between the *I* and the *me* aspects of the self (i.e., the impulsive/creative aspects of experience and the controlling/regulatory aspects, respectively, a distinction echoing ideas about the experiencing and cognitive aspects of the self). At the same time, Cooley is noted for his famous metaphor, the "looking glass self," which spawned a great deal of investigation about *self-esteem* and *reflected appraisal* and their associations with various strategies of *self-presentation*.[12]

These lines of thought eventually morphed into *symbolic interactionism*, a theory that continues to be influential today in work on the self. This theory proposes that *interactions* among people are mediated by *symbols* (language and gestures), and that these "symbolic interactions" form and shape the self. Symbolic interactionists argue that people monitor their own behaviors and those of others to give meaning to the day-to-day happenings in their lives. In doing so, people observe the actions and reactions of other people toward themselves, and then incorporate these observations into mental (self) structures about "who they are," in the process forming **self-concepts**. For example, those who perceive that others regard them as attractive or smart may come to define themselves as such. People then use these self-concepts to direct their current and future conduct. Through these self-referential social activities, a "repertoire of selves" takes shape that is specific to each person, which can be empirically studied in terms of self-concepts that are distinguishable in terms of their salience in an overall hierarchy.

In G.H. Mead's version of symbolic interactionism, the development of the self takes place through three stages. The first stage is "pre-symbolic" and need not concern us. In the second stage, when young children acquire a sufficient vocabulary to begin naming the people and objects they observe, they begin to play-act roles. In this *play stage*, they might pretend to be a parent, firefighter, or teacher in this play-acting. In this way, they practice *perspective taking* (i.e., *taking the roles of others* whom they have observed), and are thus able to reflect upon how these others behave in a variety of roles and situations. From these experiences, children can reflect on themselves as "objects" with specific qualities and capacities—that is, they can now imagine how other people view them. During this stage, the basis of behavior moves from mere imitation to more reflexive self-direction and takes on more cognitive functions.[13]

In the third stage, the *game stage*, children develop more general and unified conceptions of themselves as they learn to simultaneously take the roles of multiple others. For example, in a game of baseball a child might alternate roles between batter and pitcher, and in the process learn to appreciate the importance of the other players on the field. As this is experienced, children imagine how those in the other roles think about their actions. Consequently, children learn to imagine themselves in terms of other children's perspectives toward them. By appreciating the interrelations of a set of roles rather than one isolated role, children develop a generalized conception of what is expected of them (i.e., what the rules are) and how others will react to them in the context of these expectations.

These experiences are *developmental* in several respects, contributing to the growth and differentiation of the young person's awareness and understanding of the world and his or her place in it. These developmental experiences contribute to the formation of the young person's *self-concept hierarchy*, with each self-concept varying in salience in this hierarchy and providing varying degrees of self-esteem. In this way, everyone has certain role- and situation-specific self-concepts that vary along a positive–negative continuum of self-esteem. This distinction between self-concept and self-esteem is important to bear in mind: Self-concept is a qualitative category (e.g., "I am a baseball player"), while self-esteem is a variable assessment of self-concept (e.g., "I am a good/average/poor baseball player").[14]

During ordinary, daily activities, self-concept and self-esteem are influenced by the young person's relationships with *significant others*. Significant others are those who are well-known to people and whose attitudes and opinions affect their lives. They include family members and friends as well as persons of high prestige, like teachers and celebrities. People are motivated to impress these others in certain ways, and engage in a number of techniques to manage how these others perceive them.

Through social activities with significant others, children come to learn how to conceive of *generalized others* in addition to single, specific others. Generalized others constitute abstractions of groups of significant others—for example, the entire baseball team in addition to individual players. Eventually, children's perceptions of generalized others represent their ideas of what is expected of them in terms of social norms, providing a unified basis for self-reference. The basis for identity formation is thus laid, as is the potential for developing more advanced moral reasoning competencies, because the young person can conceive of and reflect on both his/her place in the world as well as the responsibilities associated with that place. Both of these cognitive processes are enabled because of the ability to take the perspective of the other, or more simply perspective taking.

A more recent approach, *self psychology*, has built upon symbolic interactionism, focusing on the distinction between the self "as knower" and the self "as known," the two aspects of self-knowledge that interested earlier philosophers and social psychologists. This field has generated research concerning the *executive functions* of the self[15] and **self-efficacy**. Self-efficacy is the sense that one's actions can produce certain predictable outcomes.[16] It involves beliefs about what one can do, rather than a judgment about the positive or negative nature of one's physical or personal characteristics. The bulk of this research confirms that people's beliefs regarding whether they can influence events in their lives are important in reaching higher levels of competence and performance.[17] These beliefs can produce certain outcomes because they influence whether someone thinks optimistically or pessimistically about those outcomes, and thus whether that person seeks courses of action that are self-enhancing or self-hindering.[18] In this way, self-efficacy involves self-regulation in dealing with goal challenges and outcome expectations. Those who are more self-efficacious will choose to undertake more difficult challenges requiring more effort, will persevere longer in the face of difficulties, and are more likely to take failures as motivating rather than demoralizing. A strong sense of self-efficacy can thus inoculate people from stress, anxiety, and depression, and provide resiliency in difficult situations.[19]

Symbolic interactionism and self psychology do not provide theories of development beyond childhood, so are of limited use in understanding identity formation during the transition to adulthood, especially as affected by the conditions of contemporary Western societies, the focus of this book. Instead, they focus on the ways in which people are socialized into roles after the self is developed, and how self-esteem and self-efficacy affect behavior. Thus, they are not age-based, developmental approaches. However, with its emphasis on perspective taking, symbolic interactionism has influenced theories of moral development, which we discuss in Chapter 4. In addition, self psychology is useful in understanding **personal agency**, a concept discussed throughout the remainder of this book. At the same time, in spite of the great amount of attention that has been given to understanding the self and its development, there are still problems in this field in developing an agreed-upon definition of the self that is easily operationalized. Box 1.3 highlights some of these problems.

BOX 1.3 PROBLEMS IN AGREEING ON A DEFINITION OF THE SELF

Some readers may have found it difficult to gain a full grasp of exactly what is meant by the "self," even in the scientific literature. Well, they are not alone. The experts also have trouble. For example, the founding editor of the journal *Self and Identity*, Mark Leary, expressed his frustration in his final editorial when stepping down from the position. He hoped that future submissions to the journal would be more careful in what was ascribed to the "self," because, in reviewing myriad manuscripts during his tenure as editor, the term "has been used in so many different ways that it is not only difficult to know precisely what a particular writer means by it, [that he] sometimes . . . despair[ed] that it means anything at all."[20]

Similarly, the *International Society for Self and Identity* posted for a time on its website a brief definition, admitting that there is no "widely accepted definition or description of the self." A "best attempt" was offered, however, characterizing it as follows: "The human self is a self-organizing, interactive system of thoughts, feelings, and motives that characterizes an individual. It gives rise to an enduring experience of physical and psychological existence—a phenomenological sense of constancy and predictability. The self is reflexive and dynamic in nature: responsive yet stable." This source went on to reflect that "skeptics might argue that the description fails to resolve, even address . . . fundamental issues . . . and they would be correct. Yet the description captures what we know about the activity of the self from decades of scientific inquiry and, in that sense, provides a credible, if not complete, account of it."[21]

We concur with these concerns about problems with defining the "self," a concept that has been bandied about for ages, resulting in "contamination" by generic uses. Consequently, we have favored an emphasis on an Eriksonian approach in formulating the SIFT, because its concepts are more clearly defined, even if as controversial.

Identity and Its Formation

Scientific theories of identity formation have been influenced by the previously discussed philosophical and theoretical conceptions of the self, but have been more directly influenced by the *psychoanalytic* thinking of the early to mid-1900s, especially by the life works of Sigmund Freud and his daughter Anna, and their student Erik Erikson. In Freudian theory, the human mind consists of three major components, or agencies. The instincts and drives with which humans are born form a major portion of the physiologically based *id*. The id is impulsive, selfish, and pleasure seeking. It is also a source of psychic energies, such as aggressive and sexual urges, that can be expressed or repressed. According to this theory, the *ego* begins to emerge early in childhood as the id encounters obstacles to its impulse-gratifications, usually from parents, but also from the infant's own helplessness in dealing with its environment.[22]

For children, the ego represents those mental processes used to achieve satisfactions by overcoming the constraints, and accepting the opportunities, of its immediate environment. As children mature, these ego processes become more cognitively complex, giving children unique attributes that stem from their own ideas, beliefs, memories, hopes, and fears. The ego's interactions with the world are guided by the *reality principle*: ideas initially associated with impulse-gratification are modified into actions that are purposeful and planful in the real world, depending on actual opportunities, and therefore become crucial to the types of self-regulation necessary for functional ego development, and thus personal agency.

Building on the Freudian tradition, Erikson proposed a differentiated and positive view of the ego and its functions, pioneering the field of *ego psychology*.[23] Erikson designated the ego as the most "active" structure of the personality, which performs the **synthetic functions** of the personality (i.e., the mental processes with which realty is understood by the person) as well as the **executive functions** (i.e., the mental processes that produce behaviors). Put more simply in "input-output" terms, the ego is the "knower" and the "doer" of mental operations, synthesizing (incoming) information as a basis for executing (outgoing) behaviors. The ego is in these ways potentially agentic, and therefore proactive, having similar properties of the self proposed by self-psychology theorists with respect to the executive functions of the self and self-efficacy.

The third component of personality—the *superego*—corresponds to what is generally called the conscience. Children acquire the values and norms of their culture largely by internalizing their parents' sense of right and wrong. These internalizations then guide the ego of the maturing child in reconciling id impulses with the limitations and requirements of culture and society. The superego can thus become important in stimulating children to think about issues of morality and ethics and is an important resource for developing more complex forms of perspective taking.

Erikson also built upon the Freudian tradition by proposing that the ego develops greater complexity over the entire life span. One of his major contributions is an eight-stage description of psychosocial development. Childhood comprises stages in which four ego (or agentic) strengths can be acquired that are important for later development in adolescence and adulthood: the capacities for trust, autonomy, initiative, and industry. During adolescence and early adulthood, the developmental (stage) challenge becomes building a sense of direction and purpose with which to adopt long-term goals and commitments as a basis for an adult identity.[24] The developmental challenge of this fifth stage involves three interrelated components:

- a subjective/psychological component—forming the sense of continuity rooted in a purpose in life—**ego identity**;
- a personal component—constructing and adopting behavioral styles that differentiate individuals—**personal identity**; and
- a social component—finding and assuming recognized roles and statuses within a community—**social identity**.[25]

Coordinating and stabilizing these three components can be problematic for many people in modern Western societies for a variety of reasons discussed throughout this book. Generally, problems can involve experiencing a sense of **identity confusion** and an **identity crisis**.[26] Erikson argued that these problems were less common and more muted in traditional societies, which ascribed identities to their members. Contemporary Western societies, however, engage in far less identity ascription and have fewer collectivist norms than they did in their "traditional period," so there are increased *individual risks* for people in their personal lives—in this case, the risks include aggravated identity confusion and a prolonged period of crisis in which their sense of identity is in flux. These risks are explored throughout this book and dealt with in more detail in the next chapter.

Finally, in anticipating the material in Part II of this book, it is important to note that these five stages are crucially linked with adult development by providing the agentic capacities needed to be a functioning adult member of society. During the sixth stage, young adults face the challenge of developing a sense of *intimacy* (versus isolation), while during the seventh stage mature adults face the problem of nurturing a sense of *generativity* or caring for others, instead of being drawn into a sense of self-absorption and stagnation. In the last stage, usually entered in old age, individuals must evaluate and come to terms with the overall quality of their lives. Here the major alternatives are the senses of *integrity* vs. despair, with a sense of *wisdom* nurturing a sense of integrity over despair. Considered together, the eight stages in Erikson's model represent accumulated developmental capacities; better resolutions of earlier stages facilitate better resolutions of later stages. Moreover, understanding the endpoint of life-cycle development as "wisdom" helps to identify the waypoints earlier in life that can lead people toward wisdom in old age or away from it to despair. It is within this context that we can appreciate the importance of the ego strengths gained with earlier stage resolutions, along with the capacities for higher-order perspective taking and moral reasoning.

Differential Dimensions of Identity and Self-Development

The concepts of self and identity are multidimensional. They therefore have multiple definitions, depending on the level of analysis. Accordingly, it is useful to provide a table that specifies the three dimensions of each concept, while showing how identity formation differs from self-development in terms of *process, structure*, and *content* (figure 1.3).

	Identity	*Self*
Process: Continuity and change	**Ego Identity:** The sense of continuity over time and across contexts	**Self-Awareness:** The monitoring and appraisal of how one is perceived by others
Content: Aspects that continue/change	**Social Roles:** Based on personal identifications and shared values, which form the basis of enduring commitments that are internalized as being "part" of the person	**Self-Concepts:** Ideas and feelings about oneself pertaining to various spheres social functioning, such as family, school, and peer group
Structure: Organization of contents	**Role Repertoires:** An arrangement of roles in terms of perceived importance (salience) and openness to change (permeability)	**Self-Concept Hierarchies:** An arrangement of self-concepts into self-schema based on their perceived importance in the person's life in various contexts

FIGURE 1.3 The dimensions of self and identity compared.

Process. **Ego identity** denotes the *sameness and continuity* of psychological functioning as observed in people's interpersonal behavior and commitments to roles, values, and beliefs. In Erikson's work, the *sense* of sameness and continuity is identified as the fundamental process underlying the overall sense of identity, including personal and social identities: people with a strong sense of ego identity experience themselves as being the same person over time and in various contexts, making it possible for them to exhibit stable behavior patterns and to consistently endorse a set of values and beliefs, to set goals, and to maintain commitments (i.e., personal and social identities are stable, rather than in flux). For example, people with a poor sense of temporal-spatial continuity lack a sense of future purpose and thus have a difficult time forming goals in the first place, because they have a hard time projecting themselves into the future. And if they do form some goals, they have a difficult time meeting them, because their sense of priorities shifts with their fluctuating sense of themselves. In contrast, people with a strong sense of personal continuity can formulate goals more easily and are more likely to maintain and meet them because they have a strong sense of purpose in life. To provide a concrete example, what a person with a strong sense of continuity states her goals are in, say, January are likely to still be her goals in June and she will reach them within a reasonable and appropriate time frame: if Jane says in January that she will learn a new language, in June this would still be her goal and she would thereafter make reasonable progress in achieving competency in that language.

The process aspect of *the self* comprises of the capacity for the conscious, reflexive awareness of one's being in relation to others. The mental processes involve the monitoring of one's behaviors (actions) and the reactions of others to those behaviors during interactions, and appraising the meanings of those actions and reactions. These monitoring and appraising processes are mediated by people's other mental capacities, such as *self-monitoring*, and their senses of self-esteem and self-efficacy.

Content and Structure. The continuity and change of ego identity processes can be observed in the social roles people play. This continuity and change is especially evident as people move through the life course, from childhood, through adolescence, and then into adulthood. The roles people play often form a "unit relation" with the person: others define people in terms of the roles they play in life (e.g., student, parent, lawyer) and people internalize these definitions. These roles are arranged by the person and the significant others in their lives in terms of how important they are at a given point in their lives (e.g., a student role may be salient in adolescence and early adulthood, but the parent role salient in adulthood). Some roles are also more open to change than others. For example, the student role is more amendable than the parent role.

The continuity and change of self-processes can be observed in the self-concepts supporting people's self-awareness. These self-concepts are linked to social roles, and generally people develop self-concepts for each important area of functioning in their lives. Self-concepts thus form, for example, in terms of family, school, and work roles, and become structured in hierarchies that change over time based on their changing importance over the life course as social roles change.

Developmentally, social roles provide support for both ego identity and self-awareness processes. Social roles can change dramatically over time, stimulating adjustments in identity and self configurations. Normative—or typical—development in contemporary Western societies entails a broadening of young persons' self-awareness in relation to the social environments they experience. As the radius of social involvements expands, the breadth of awareness of that world expands, and these experiences are filtered through people's ego/self capacities in terms of their current stage of development in each area.

As a general principle, when people of any age are "in" a given stage, or period of life, optimally trying to master its challenges, they are the "subject" of that stage and therefore find it difficult to separate their internal experiences of the world from the world itself. When they move to a more advanced stage, or life period, they are more capable of treating themselves as "objects" in relation to their previous experiences, and can therefore reflect more complexly on their relationships to people in their lives, especially in terms of principles that apply beyond immediate, concrete experiences. This is an advanced form of personal **agency** that comes with age and experience and is important for identity formation and self-regulation.

Those who are agentic—or proactive—in their development tend to expand their radius of involvements in, and understandings of, their social world more

quickly and effectively, and tend to have more positive and optimal outcomes in their role transitions to adulthood. However, as with other personality attributes, agency or proactivity is a capacity that varies from person to person, and therefore cannot be assumed to exist in the same degree in all people. And, as with all personal attributes, it is in certain ways dependent on the unique experiences of each person's biography and learning history during childhood and thereafter. From an Eriksonian perspective, experiences that nurture the development of the ego strengths linked with each stage are especially important for the development of agentic capacities. Proactivity is found in people who are willing to explore and experiment in setting goals and making commitments, and who have the ego capacities to do so effectively. These explorations can in turn enhance the sense of *reflexivity* associated with learning how to treat oneself as an object when reasoning about one's place in the world and the rules/principles defining that place.

Optimal development in mainstream Western societies involves forms of **identity-based agency** that enable people to cope with more complex and demanding circumstances as they become more involved in the social world, expanding their range of potential experiences—their social radius. People's ability to regulate and manage their own behavior (differentiation) is key to developing and meeting goals (continuity) and maintaining connections in the workplace and wider community (integration).

Conclusion: A Hindu Folktale

The studies of the self, and its development, and identity, and its formation, have been undertaken from a variety of perspectives. These perspectives are often based on different assumptions, as in the contrast between symbolic interactionism and ego psychology. Indeed, they have operated in virtual isolation from one another, producing separate literatures, with little cross-referencing between the two. To help us understand this fragmentation, an analogy provided by a Hindu folktale is helpful.

In this tale, three blind men are walking along a trail and encounter a huge object blocking their way. Using only their tactile senses, each attempts to conclude what the object is. The first blind man, feeling only a tail, insists that the object is a rope; the second, feeling only a trunk, contends that it is a snake; the third man, touching only a leg, asserts that it is a tree. Each man believes that he has *the* correct description of that object, and as they argue over whether it is a rope, a snake, or a tree, the elephant walks away. The lesson is that none of the three men were wrong, nor were any right, in any absolute way. Each had a point that made some sense, though it was based on an incomplete examination of the animal/elephant, and was therefore only partially formulated. However, had they taken the time to compare their perceptions instead of arguing on the basis of limited information, they may have collectively arrived at the conclusion that they were dealing with an elephant.

The lesson here is that each of us needs to be mindful when telling each other what we think something like "identity" is and how it should be understood. We must also listen to what the other has to say. Mindful of the Hindu folk lesson, our starting point in this book, then, is that "identity" is not simply one thing that can be fully understood from only one vantage point, which is why the SIFT treats "identity" as multidimensional and adopts multiple perspectives in understanding those dimensions.

2

CULTURE AND HISTORY

How Current Experiences Differ From the Past

"[In the 1800s] the goal was achievement, not adjustment; the young were taught to work, not to socialize. Popularity was not important, but strength of character was essential. Nobody worried about rigidity of character; it was supposed to be rigid. If it were flexible you couldn't count on it. Change of character was desirable only for the wicked."

Allen Wheelis[1]

As noted in the Preface and Chapter 1, for most of human history, forming an adult identity was by most accounts a relatively straightforward process, and this did not change until quite recently—about two centuries ago. These are only two of the hundreds of centuries in which *Homo sapiens* lived in groups. The current era is therefore but a mere blip in the time scale of human history. The common folk throughout human history simply assumed the social roles that had been adopted by their parents, grandparents, great-grandparents, and so on through countless generations. These social roles also provided a ready-made purpose in life, whether people liked it or not. Those who did not accept their lot in life might have been banished from their community or punished in some way. Of course, those born into positions of authority and power, or those from wealthy backgrounds, may have had more choice in the latitude of their social roles. Still, in some of these traditional cultures, restrictive social customs and the narrow range of roles available in their rudimentary economies may have limited even the options of the powerful and wealthy.

These historical conditions are crucial reference points from which to understand the prospects and problems of identity formation in contemporary Western societies. People's identities are no longer as rigidly dictated by ascribed roles or even cultural norms, which have shifted from being duty-based to choice-based in many instances. Consequently, forming identities has become more of an individual responsibility—part of the **individualization process**. Westerners have adapted to the individualization process in a variety of ways. On the one hand, as choice has replaced obligation as the basis of self-definition in many aspects of life, some people have found this increased choice to be liberating, allowing for the formation of various new identities and for more flexibility in older identities. Consequently, more developmental opportunities have become available. On the other hand, choice-based identity formation can be a difficult, precarious, and solitary process for which other people are unprepared. These people may miss many of the new developmental opportunities.

So, whereas identity formation was not a matter of individual choice for most people throughout most of human history, a sense of belonging was more certain, and problems associated with finding a place in society would not have been common. In this historical sense, humans have not been accustomed to living in societies where they are continually confronted with high levels of choice over fundamental matters of personal meaning and purpose. It is in this context that we can appreciate the great challenges that humans living in contemporary societies face in their formation of viable identities. In other words, the process of forming an adult identity that provides a secure sense of purpose in life has become dramatically different for most people in Western societies, catching many unprepared. Thus, there is a *cultural lag*, with many people not having the individual means to cope with myriad choices and to forge their own purpose in life.

In the present era, then, many people welcome the opportunity to be the "architects of their own identities"[2] as they engage in the individualization of their life course, in part because of the sense of personal liberation and fulfillment this can produce. Conversely, many others are not so happy with having to assume the responsibility for making numerous life-altering choices, especially when they have little information and guidance as to the long-term consequences of those choices. For example, available role models for adult identities do not always help in the transition to adulthood, because many such models are ambiguous or irrelevant to the circumstances of recent cohorts. Forming occupational identities presents particular challenges for most people in recent cohorts, and their parents can often only provide minimal guidance, encouraging them with vague advice such as "get a university degree," but with little sense of where this degree will lead them. In fact, difficulties with these individualized identity-formation processes are now so widespread that many "identity problems" can now be considered "normal" in many respects.

These "new normal" difficulties include people being unsure about what they believe in or what to do for a living, being uncommitted to any course of future action beyond the next hedonistic gratification, and leaving themselves open to political and financial manipulation. At the same time, many of those who in the past might have guided them—their parents—are unaware that they should pass a sense of meaning on to their children, because the parents themselves do not have well-synthesized identities. Problems in identity formation may thus be passed on intergenerationally. In these cases, young people can lack a sense of self-definition and purpose rooted in a local community of significant others, a condition that has been a fundamental source of a sense of belonging throughout human history.

As this new normal has taken root, even the types of identity formation that were once considered "pathological" may no longer be seen as seriously harmful to the person or community. For example, the American Psychiatric Association (APA) not too long ago recommended diagnosing certain difficulties in identity formation as an "identity disorder." However, it subsequently redefined the same difficulties in making choices and commitments as an "identity problem." This shift can be seen in comparing the psychiatric handbooks DSM-III[3] and DSM-IV.[4] In the most current version of this manual (DSM-5),[5] neither diagnosis is mentioned. Apparently, the APA task force on DSM-IV[6] relegated identity disorder to identity problem out of concerns about the potential problems of pathologizing what had become "normal" developmental problems, symptoms of which might be classified as related anxiety and depression disorders. However, some identity formation researchers suggest that this diagnostic modification took attention away from what had become a serious problem for many young people.[7] They believe that dropping the identity problem classification altogether in the latest DSM further exacerbates the inattention to this problem. We see in Chapter 7 how these researchers have begun empirically investigating the distress that many people can experience during critical periods of identity formation.

Likewise, we are just beginning to understand the identity-formation problems that are related to borderline personality disorder and dissociative identity disorder. These disorders are often tolerated in communities and/or misdiagnosed when a person seeks medical assistance. It will clearly take some time before Westerners come to grips with the individualization of identity formation and the important issues associated with this major change in how the human species understands itself. Later in this chapter we return to this issue. More generally, a goal of this book is to illuminate these issues, hopefully advancing our understanding of problematic types of identity formation.

Our point here is not to glorify traditional societies, but rather to use them as a point of comparison for understanding contemporary identity problems. Indeed, traditional societies had their own problems, including widespread poverty, shorter life spans, uncontrollable epidemics, poor medical knowledge, and the like. Clearly, we are not calling for a return to these societies, nor are we saying that current Western societies are all bad. However, as humans have solved certain problems of survival, new unanticipated problems associated with adapting to these improved conditions have emerged, including how to deal with greater latitude of choice. Box 2.1 provides a political philosophy-based perspective concerning how conditions in current Western societies have contributed to the individualization of identity formation.

BOX 2.1 ECONOMIC INDIVIDUALISM AND IDENTITY FORMATION

Currently, Western societies are influenced by ideologies that define *the individual* as the *basic unit* of society. As basic units, in principle at least, individuals are defined as equal to each other, and as possessing certain inalienable rights of citizenship that the State should not violate. This ideology of individualism promotes citizens as economic agents of self-interest as well as persons with psychological needs and capacities. In achieving this form of *personhood*, individuals are seen to have a schedule of development enabling them to engage in purposive and responsible action, especially in managing their own economic efforts. With this ideology of individualism, then, the person has an obligation to be instrumentally self-directed in relation to the economic system. The term *economic individualism* captures this standard of "rational" behavior to which people are held.[8]

This ideology has affected the life course of many people in terms of processes of individualization that are marked by a weakening of the person's ties to social collectivities, such as the extended family and local community, especially among those living in secular society (i.e., without a family or ethnic-group community that provides religious ties). The individualistic ideology has affected the formation of adult identities by creating a secular process through which people must decide largely for themselves what values and beliefs to hold, what societal roles to adopt, and how their life course will unfold in terms of social commitments, such as family formation and occupational attainment.

Within this individualistic cultural context, social scientific research has found that higher levels of personal agency are empirically associated with better life-course outcomes. This form of agency represents a functional adaption necessary for social inclusion under conditions where traditional cultural norms are absent, ambiguous, or in conflict, but emerging norms are based on individual choice and self-regulation. Although it is clear to us that human-developmental strengths are influenced by the cultural contexts in which the individual is defined, in describing adaptions to economic individualism in this book, readers should be clear that we are not endorsing this political ideology as an ultimate societal goal. Indeed, there is much to criticize in how some societies have adopted this philosophy as part of their public policy frameworks, leaving many people at a serious economic disadvantage. We have provided such critiques in other publications; for example, with a political economy critique of *neoliberalism*.[9] In Chapter 4, we comment on the implications of this political philosophy for moral identities and the problem of alienated identities.

Socio-Historical Variations in Identity Formation

In this section, we present a model to propose a way of understanding how identity formation has changed in Western societies as they have evolved through three very broad phases. This socio-historical model is based on the *developmental contextual* assumption that social contexts have dramatic impacts on how humans develop, in this case how they form their identities. The impacts of socio-historical change are analyzed in terms of the three types/levels of identity defined in the previous chapter: ego, personal, and social identity. Figure 2.1 illustrates a cross tabulation of these concepts, with the three types of identity represented at three broad socio-historical periods. Accordingly, this model provides a typology representing fundamental differences in how humans form adult identities in three broad historical eras.

The top portion of figure 2.1 identifies the three broad historical periods of macro-structural social change that characterize what many sociologists believe accounts for what has happened over the past several centuries among Western societies. The distinction between **premodern** and **early-modern** society constitutes a widely accepted distinction between agrarian and industrial societies. The premodern period stretches back through to human prehistory to include earlier tribal and later agrarian-type societies. In Western societies, the transformation to early-modern societies was largely completed during the 19th century as countries industrialized, throwing traditional forms of social organization into disarray (e.g., with the decline of the extended family and rise of the nuclear family). In Western countries, this disruptive transformation began in the early to mid-1800s and lasted into the mid-1900s. Our primary concern throughout this book is on how this disruption in social norms impacts identity formation, particularly during the transition to adulthood.

Level of Identity	Historical Era		
	Premodern → (Tribal Through Agrarian)	**Early Modern →** (Industrial)	**Late Modern** (Post-Industrial)
Social Identity (Position in Society)	Ascribed at birth →	Accomplished through effort→	Managed by choices*
Personal Identity (Behavioral Style)	Tradition/Other-oriented →	Individuated/Inner-oriented →	Individualized/ Image-oriented*
Ego Identity (Sense of Purpose and Continuity)	Adopted from traditions →	Constructed from opportunities →	Discovered through experiences*

* Functional identity formation in late-modern societies requires strategic responses at these three developmental levels. These responses are more effective when they are proactive rather than passive or default. The Identity Capital Model discussed in Chapter 6 provides a theory that explains the elements of these strategic adaptations.

FIGURE 2.1 Identity formation in socio–historical context.

The distinction between early modern and **late-modern society** is more nuanced, with each describing "degrees" of *modernity*, both of which differ "in kind" from premodernity. During early modernity, industrial production became a defining feature of social relations, displacing the traditional forms of social relations in premodernity. The late-modern period refers to the type of industrial-capitalist societies that evolved in the second half of the 20th century. In figure 2.1, we settle with the term *post-industrial* to describe this most recent phase, but that term is somewhat of a misnomer because a sizable segment of the population is still involved in industrial production.[10]

Most importantly, though, the term "late modern" is distinguished from "early modern" in order to describe several important developments that have affected adult-identity formation processes and content:

- the transformation, and in some cases disintegration, of certain institutions that once provided the norms for the stable bases for social identities (some of these institutions date back to premodernity, such as religion);
- a movement from production roles as a defining feature of social identities to the conspicuous consumption of goods and services as status symbols that provide a basis for the contents of personal identities, with the fashioning of personal identities based on these symbols becoming more important than establishing social identities for many if not most people;
- the rise of information and computer technologies that have supplanted or transformed many jobs, thereby extending the time needed for occupational identity formation in the growing number of instances where more educational credentials have been required to gain employment; and
- the advent of a society in which a large proportion of the population experiences day-to-day life in impersonal, urban environments, where there is a high degree of casual contact with "strangers"—others with whom there are few enduring emotional bonds supportive of ego and personal identities.

The impact of each of the three socio-historical periods on the three levels of identity is now discussed in turn.

Social Identities

In this framework, social-identity formation differs in each type of society, as shown in figure 2.1. In premodern societies, primary social identities tend to be *ascribed* at birth based on sex, ethnicity, and the position of one's parents in a status hierarchy. In early-modern societies, the pattern is increasingly that social identities are *accomplished* through individual efforts for those people freed from the ascriptive constraints of premodernity (note that the degree of freedom from ascription varies by social identity). In late-modern societies, where ascriptive processes have diminished even more for more people, social identities need to be *managed* on the basis of choices made about the extent of identification with primary social identities, such as gender, ethnicity, and social class, as well as about choices made regarding the secondary social identities formed throughout life (e.g., student, parent, adult, and those associated with specific occupations).

These key terms can be defined as follows:

- ascribed—assigned on the basis of some inherited status;
- accomplished—based on one's own efforts and abilities; and
- managed—reflexively and strategically fitting oneself into a community of "strangers" by meeting their approval through the creation of the right impressions.[11]

In other words, in premodern societies, social identities are largely determined by essentialist assumptions of innateness, such as race/ethnicity and gender, and inherited attributes such as parent's social status. People are largely "born into" their social identities. However, in early-modern societies, as systems of ascription breakdown and status becomes more a matter of contest, social identities can be increasingly based on personal accomplishment and material attainment. It is important to stress, however, that although it is widely believed in Western societies that economic attainments are based on one's efforts, skills, and achievements, independent of one's presumed "innateness" and inherited statuses, the research on social-class reproduction shows that this is not always the case.[12] Finally, in late-modern societies, one's presumed characteristics and prior accomplishments may carry little weight in giving people legitimacy in the wide variety of social settings. Instead, people often need to make more strategic choices about how to fit themselves into preferred communities, which are often populated by "strangers." A ready example of this can be found in the competition of university graduates from middle-class backgrounds for jobs, the resulting high level of underemployment, and the increasing level of credentials they need to get ahead in the "job queue."[13] Being "middle class" does not carry the advantages it once did; nor does being "upper class" automatically confer the same privileges as in the past.

In late-modern societies, therefore, social identities are much more precarious than ever before. As opposed to being a birthright, or a sinecured social achievement, one's legitimacy can be continually called into question. In order to find a social location to begin with, one often has to convince a community of strangers that one is worthy of their company, and this acceptance can be challenged virtually at any moment. Individuals now have to manage their lives by strategically finding their place or places, often repeatedly, over their life course. In contrast to the past, it is common for people to move through a series of educational settings, jobs and careers, romantic relationships and marriages, and neighborhoods and urban settings, possibly gaining and losing acceptance a number of times. Accordingly, identity formation is now much more of a lifelong challenge. Even though the identity stage is still a crucial period for establishing adult social identities, these identities may need to be subsequently reformulated in adulthood.

Personal Identities

Personal identity refers to interpersonal behavioral styles that have been shaped by a person's actual life experiences and learning history. In a sense, personal identity conveys the culmination of an individual's "biography of everyday life" at a given point in time. At the level of interaction (i.e., the interpersonal world where societies and individuals "meet"), corresponding personal identities are largely *tradition/other-oriented*, next *individuated/inner-oriented*, and subsequently *individualized/image-oriented* in the three types of societies, respectively:

- the tradition/other-oriented identity is based on an unreflexive acceptance of others' appraisals and expectations, which produces a conformist and mechanical blending into a community;
- the individuated/inner-oriented identity emerges from the creation of distinctive personal styles and role repertoires by which people's biographies lead to an organic integration into a community; and
- the individualized/image-oriented identity is a more reflexive creation of images projected in various ways (dress, possessions, leisure activities) to impress and/or meet the approval of a community of significant and generalized others, gaining the person access to that community.

In late modernity, personal identities can be even more precarious than in the past because the standards of acceptable behavior can continually change. As a result, people tend to experiment with various ways of presenting themselves, and change their appearances and *identity displays* regularly to meet changing trends, fads, and fashions.[14] Much day-to-day interaction is with acquaintances who do not know each other's biography and with strangers who may not care about biographical information, all of whom may never see each other again. What is important in each emergent situation is how immediate circumstances are managed, and this is most easily done through *role playing* and *impression management*, often producing fabricated appearances, status displays, and affected speech and conversation. Consequently, in many situations, of paramount importance are the *images* one projects, rather than the substance of what's behind those images. Box 2.2 provides a brief summary of the Dramaturgical Model that Erving Goffman developed to describe how people manage their personal identities in the modern era.

BOX 2.2   GOFFMAN'S DRAMATURGICAL MODEL: "ALL THE WORLD IS A STAGE"

The sociologist Erving Goffman (1922–1982) developed the Dramaturgical Model to describe how people manage impressions of themselves—engage in *self-presentations*—in a variety of ordinary and novel situations, including those in which people manage discrediting information about themselves. Three assumptions govern this symbolic interactionist model of personal and social identity management: (1) social life is akin to a staged event, (2) people go to great lengths to present staged performances, and (3) these performances often contain elements of deception, either by omission (hiding something) or commission (pretending something). In other words, life is like a theatre, replete with scripts, but people must often improvise to shape their own characters. Goffman went to great lengths in analyzing various types of performances to reveal how they represent strategies of *impression management*. For example, people attempt to influence *the definition of the situation* to further their own ends, they project *personal fronts* using various "props" (e.g., speech patterns, costumes, and conspicuous consumption/possessions), and they segregate audiences in terms of a front stage, where performances take place, and a back stage, where they can "let their hair down" and practice further performances. The management of *stigmatized identities* requires special performances, including *role distancing*, in which the message is conveyed that what one appears to be doing (a role self) is not who one really is (the real self).[15]

Goffman is considered one of the most influential social scientists of the 20th century. When he wrote his best-known books in the mid-20th century, they created quite a stir. At the beginning of the 21st century, some people may question how surprising these claims are, given the socio-historical changes since Goffman proposed his model and how contrived many things now seem to be, especially in a world mediated by numerous technologies that create and distort realities. The self-enhancing and identity-disguising technologies used on a daily basis include social media such as Facebook, where people can become obsessed with impressing "friends" they have never met and would not care to interact with if they did meet face to face. The documentary *Generation Like* provides a good illustration and analysis of these recent trends.[16]

These contrived, interactive performances, of course, are standard fare among the most recent generations raised during the late-modern era, especially since the 1950s, but they stand in stark contrast to the prevailing norms of early-modernity. The passage from Allen Wheelis's 1958 book *The Quest for Identity* presented at the beginning of this chapter highlights this contrast between current circumstances and the early modern emphasis on stability and reliability—commonly referred to as character—especially in the following portions: "Nobody worried about rigidity of character; it was supposed to be rigid. If it were flexible you couldn't count on it."

Forty years later, Richard Sennett followed a similar line of thought in *The Corrosion of Character: The Personal Consequences of Work in the New Capitalism*. He argued that economic conditions that require high degrees of flexibility make it difficult for people to maintain a sense of personal character. He noted that the traditional meaning of character dating back to antiquity involved "the ethical value we place on our desires and on our relations to others." He goes on to characterize "character" as follows:

> Character particularly focuses upon the long-term aspect of our emotional experience. Character is expressed by loyalty and mutual commitment, or through the pursuit of long-term goals, or by the practice of delayed gratification for the sake of a future end. Out of the confusion of sentiments in which we all dwell at any particular moment, we seek to save and sustain some; these sustainable sentiments will serve our characters. Character concerns the personal traits which we value in ourselves and for which we seek to be valued by others.[17]

Ego Identity

In our approach, the basis of the person's sense of continuity of purpose is underscored as a simpler way of understanding the idea that people strive to experience themselves as continuous "entities" embodying their personal and social identities. It is also important to note that our approach emphasizes that this sense of continuity normally involves fluctuations over time and in different contexts, and is not a one-time "achievement" that lasts for the remainder of one's life (see box 3.1 for examples of common misconceptions about scientific approaches to identity formation).

Accordingly, in describing the differing processes by which the sense of purpose undergirds how the sense of ego identity is formed:

- premodern societies tend to require their members to adopt their purpose in life from traditions early in life and not question that purpose later in life;
- early-modern societies have expectations that people will construct their purpose in life as they come of age, based on the opportunities available to them; and
- in late-modern societies people are encouraged to (continually) discover or "find themselves" through an array of available experiences and on this basis establish the sense of purpose on which to predicate their personal and social identities.

This socio-historical framework proposes that growing up and attempting to come of age as an adult in late-modern societies has psychological challenges, whereas doing so in premodern societies had more physical/survival challenges. The ego, in constructing and maintaining its sense of purpose—its identity—can face a lifetime in late-modern societies where maintaining stable, long-term commitments is challenging. A variety of responses to these challenges have been studied for the past half-century, beginning with Erik Erikson in the 1950s, as noted earlier. Our approach characterizes these responses as ranging from passive, inactive ones, through active ones, to proactive ones, responses that can be understood in terms of the **identity strategies** discussed in Chapter 7. Meanwhile, box 2.3 provides a useful way of recalling each level of identity, especially as each is optimally experienced in late-modern societies.

BOX 2.3 EXPRESSIONS OF OPTIMAL IDENTITY FORMATION

A useful way to characterize the three levels of identity is by expressing experiences of them in the first person. And, if we were to question a well-functioning person in (late-modern) society, we would expect the following answers to the "who are you" question:

Social identity: "I am an esteemed member of this/these group(s), but not that/those groups." In this answer, the person locates him/herself in terms of being a valued *member* of one or more groups, and shows the importance of the *integration* aspect of human identity. Suboptimal experiences of social identity would elicit responses of alienation from any group(s) and feelings of not being valued in terms of any memberships in concrete (e.g., peer) or abstract (e.g., student) groups.

Personal identity: "I am someone who looks, speaks, thinks, and believes in this (these) ways." This response provides an expression of *individuality* that is experienced as a more or less stable set of attributes, showing the importance of the *differentiation* facet of human identity. Suboptimal expressions of personal identity would prompt answers of uncertainty and instability about how the person presents him/herself in terms of appearance, speech, and a worldview.

Ego identity: "I feel/sense that I am a (strong) person with a (valued) past, (engaging) future, and (foreseeable) future." In this reply, as in premodern and early-modern societies, the person expresses a sense of *temporal-spatial sameness*, the *continuity* element of human identity. The parenthetical adjectives—strong, valued, engaging—represent agency and resilience of ego identity over time and in a variety of social situations. Suboptimal manifestations would bring expressions of confusion about the person's experiences among the past, present, and future, as well as passivity and resignation about building a sense of purpose that unifies these three temporal points in a variety of contexts. There would also be a narrow sense of *spatial* options, in the sense that the person has not developed a widening radius of social experiences beyond those of childhood and adolescence. Such a person would have narrow **identity horizons** (see Chapter 8).

To summarize, most Western societies have undergone changes over the last several centuries that have created circumstances in which people have been freed from the physical drudgeries and health hazards of premodern society and have been given a relatively high degree of latitude in terms of self-determination. At the same time, however, many people are given little guidance in the enterprise of identity formation, as major institutions have de-structured and decoupled from each other, and cultural norms have evolved from being duty-based to being choice-based. The impact on individual lives has likely become increasingly accentuated with each successive cohort or generation over the course of the 20th century, so that many of those now attempting to formulate an adult identity have little idea regarding how their lives will unfold because their sense of purpose in life is no longer dictated by their society; instead, the onus is now on people to discover their own sense of purpose as they develop and mature into adulthood. Confronted with a longer period of youth and expected to define their own purpose in life, those in current cohorts are experiencing an unprecedented un-coupling of life-course events, as traditional forms of adulthood have progressively de-structured. This precarious situation prevails in most Western countries and appears to be increasingly the case in many non-Western nations as well. In the next section, we turn to an examination of the more serious identity problems this risky situation can foster.

Individualized Societies and Identity Problems

A consensus is growing that identity problems are *the* major "symptoms" of the late-modern era, in the same way that neuroses were *the* major "symptoms" of Victorian society. Neuroses seem to emerge under conditions of emotional repression, while identity problems appear to emerge when there are inadequate norms governing behavior alongside a surfeit of choices, the net results of which are deficits in establishing a stable sense of purpose in life with which to anchor a sense of ego identity. As noted earlier, the life course among those living in secular segments of society in the West has become individualized, marked by a weaken-ing of the person's ties to social collectivities, leaving these people to decide for themselves what values to support, what social roles to adopt, and how their life courses will unfold in terms of commitments to others; in other words, determin-ing a purpose in life is now left largely in individual hands for people affected by the individualization process. To make matters worse for them, when choices do not work out, as in school failure or employment problems, the individual tends to be held accountable, often "blamed" for circumstances, even if there is a structural element involved (e.g., some unemployment is *structural*—there are simply not enough jobs for everyone, even those with high-level qualifications).

Without sufficient structure and guidance, some people can become confused, lose purpose, and get lost in terms of their sense of place in society. And, without sufficient self-management, some people can take longer to become "mature" members of the human species in whatever roles they eventually play. What this suggests is that Westerners are susceptible to identity problems associated with the individualization of the life course that would likely have been uncommon in the past. This contrast is especially evident with premodern societies characterized by collectivism and firm normative structures that minimized individual choice. We next describe three types of these identity problems apparently becoming increasingly common in late-modernity.

Developmental Problems

The developmental approach to identity formation has yielded a wealth of information concerning the trajectories people now take in entering adult communities. As noted, the most popular approaches are derived from Erikson's work, studying differences in how individualized choices are made in forming adult commitments. This research suggests that even in the "normal" population of Westerners, a relatively large percentage encounter emotional difficulties while taking the individualized choice/commitment route to forming an adult identity. For example, a longitudinal study of the identity formation of a group of women, tracking them from college in the early 1970s through middle age in the early 1990s, found that a majority had sought mental health assistance at some point in their adult lives.[18] For others, the difficulties are more severe, involving a variety of adjustment problems.

Eriksonian research has found that **identity diffusion** is relatively widespread during adolescence, and there is some evidence that it is becoming increasingly prevalent even among adults, so in some sense it is now a "normal" problem. The term identity diffusion includes being *inactive* during the transition to adulthood, largely by ignoring or putting off developmental tasks associated with developing the goals associated with a sense of purpose that would provide the basis for an adult identity. Those who put off these tasks exhibit a litany of characteristics associated with lower and more risky levels of functioning. They are at the highest probability of drug abuse, unsafe sexual behavior, eating disorders, and susceptibility to peer influence and academic failure.[19] In terms of adaptability, those who exhibit high levels of identity diffusion have lower levels of self-esteem, greater difficulties adapting to new environments (like university settings), and are more self-focused. Cognitively, they tend to have disorganized thinking, to feel that their lives are externally controlled, and to procrastinate and avoid dealing with daily tasks and personal issues. And, they score lowest on measures of moral reasoning and ego development.[20]

By its nature, inactivity can become a permanent approach to identity formation, although some people can pass through a period of identity diffusion as a temporary respite when they are not up to a particular developmental challenge or are confronted with obstacles that prevent them forming certain commitments. For some people, experiencing identity diffusion can be a temporary response to the identity **moratorium period** of youth and adolescence, a permissible delay of adult commitments that some societies grant young people who need to take more time in the transition to adulthood. University students seem to be particularly prone to this if their professional aspirations are dashed by poor or mediocre academic performances that prevent them from qualifying for their career of first choice. For others, however, it can become a permanent feature of their adult identity—remaining characterologically uncommitted to productive adult roles, as the next set of problems describes.

Characterological Patterns

The empirical literature surveying student populations indicates that about 30 percent of adolescents can be classified as inactive, with diffused identities. This proportion among the young adult population drops to about 20 to 25 percent, and to about 15 percent among adults.[21] By adulthood, those with a long history of inactivity in developing a sense of purpose on which to base stable identities are unlikely to change: it is likely a permanent feature of their personality that either dates back to their childhood or is developed during their adolescence.

As noted earlier, simply living in an individualized society puts some people at risk of adopting identity-related stances through which a sense of purpose based on commitments to future occupational roles is chronically frustrated or avoided. The source of this pattern is not well understood, but one source is likely the person's learning history over a period of time, especially in schools that can be experienced as punitive among those who are not academically inclined or who disengage from learning even if they have the academic abilities. The primary suspects in these cases are the structural obstacles related to social class, ethnicity, gender, and so forth. Negative experiences with these obstacles can diminish young people's sense of themselves as worthy of taking on meaningful roles in society. Other negative experiences in school settings can interfere with young people's "personal individualization projects," by pushing them in the opposite direction toward a form of *learned helplessness*. In these cases, they may be conditioned by experiences that defeat their senses of purpose and continuity, creating avoidance and anxiety in the face of challenges. This conditioning can affect their ability or willingness to *even think about* the future for planning purposes, to deal with the present in terms of meeting expectations, or to develop an understanding of their past. In these cases, personal agency is undermined in academic and occupational spheres.

Trauma/Stress-Based Pathologies

Marlene Steinberg and Maxine Schnall[22] argue that many people experience identity-disruptive symptoms because of a conditioned response to past trauma. This happens because a trauma can trigger a brain response that creates mild, adaptive dissociative responses that prevent people from experiencing intense fear that might otherwise be debilitating. However, those who have experienced prolonged and intense trauma may have this brain response triggered on a regular basis in the absence of a trauma, and therefore regularly experience dissociative symptoms of identity confusion, derealization, depersonalization, and amnesia.

The brain mechanisms involved are in the thalamus, which processes incoming information; the amygdala, which sets off fear responses; and the frontal cortex, where conscious and analytic thought takes place. In the case of dissociative symptoms, the thalamus sends information to the (primitive) amygdala that should have first been sent to the frontal cortex for processing to determine if a fear response is warranted. Because the information is not routed through the portion of brain that would help the person control his or her emotional reactions and response, the person is helpless to control the dissociation. Because of this "short-circuiting," many people can experience episodes of dissociative symptoms on a regular basis. And because they regularly experience one or more of these symptoms, they may consider them normal or something they merely have to live with.

Thus, a possible early origin of a chronically diffuse-inactive identity may be traumata experienced early in life.[23] These childhood experiences may interfere with later developmental aspects of identity formation, thereby locking the person into self-disabling habits that interfere with the developmental processes associated with the transition to adulthood. More research is needed to investigate the extent to which the developmental processes underlying identity formation are disrupted in this way, leaving the person chronically identity confused and therefore unable to explore positive options in life and form commitments to future courses of action.

At the same time, a significant proportion of the population appears to experience psychiatric symptoms that directly interfere with their identity formation. For example, personality disorders apparently took on epidemic proportions in the latter half of the 20th century. These disorders constitute enduring, pervasive, and inflexible patterns of behavior and experience that cause significant distress and impairment for the individual inflicted. The most prevalent personality disorder, borderline personality disorder, whose chief symptom is the lack of a "core" sense of (ego) identity, afflicts an estimated 10 million people in the U.S. (about 3 percent of the population). Its origins have been traced to childhood abuse and neglect.

In addition, Steinberg and Schnall argue that when the array of dissociative symptoms are counted, including those experienced during mild episodes, this disorder periodically troubles an estimated 25 percent of Americans, with a further 1 percent apparently having the full-blown dissociative identity disorder (DID) involving multiple personalities. They submit that dissociative symptoms are often mistaken for major depression and anxiety disorders, so a one-year prevalence estimate of the disorder in all of its manifestations might be closer to 10 percent of the population. They contend that this disorder also originates in childhood trauma, especially resulting from abuse and exploitation, which they estimate are experienced by some 70 million Americans.[24]

If the earlier claims about these two disorders are correct, then a sizable portion of Western populations is experiencing identity-disabling symptoms that could seriously interfere with normal developmental processes associated with the transition to adulthood. These estimates suggest a considerable percentage of the (American) population experiences mild to severe forms dissociation, particularly periodic episodes of identity confusion, derealization, and depersonalization. Given that people without mental challenges can have difficulties with their identity formation in a late-modern society, clearly those who have additional mental problems must face a formidable task. Even if these disorders existed in premodern societies, it is arguable that they would not likely have been as debilitating in terms of identity formation. In late-modern societies, where people are expected to form individualized identities, and be the "architects of their own destiny," the potential problems for self-management are obvious. And, to the extent that schools do not recognize that a sizable proportion of their students have these identity-disabling problems, these young people may find their identity problems compounded by an environment for which they have a poor fit.

Conclusion: Identity Formation and Its Discontents

In this chapter, we explored a variety of themes that provide logics for understanding various micro-macro connections among different manifestations of identity at three levels of analysis. With the aid of a socio-historical perspective, we have seen how changes from premodern to late-modern societies have culminated in the formation of a contemporary social organization that has stimulated qualitative changes in the dominant modes of ego-, personal-, and social-identity formation. In the most recent era, there appears to be a proliferation of identity problems associated with the loss of traditions and weakening of social institutions that once provided ready-made identities and purposes in life for people. To the extent that developing a purpose in life upon which to base a stable adult identity has become an individualized project for a sizable portion of the population, a number of problems seem to have emerged, ranging from the "normal" challenges of accomplishing these developmental tasks as part of an individualized transition to adulthood, especially with minimal guidance, to the special challenges of undertaking identity formation in the face of the three sets of identity problems and related disorders now common in late-modern societies.

3

A SOCIAL PSYCHOLOGY OF IDENTITIES AND THEIR FORMATION

"Neither the life of an individual nor the history of a society can be understood without understanding both."

C. Wright Mills[1]

We first examined the philosophical and conceptual foundations of theories of self and identity (Chapter 1), and then moved on to the socio-historical manifestations of identity, including problems associated with identity formation in the current era (Chapter 2). In the present chapter, we delve deeper into issues of how the various types of identities are formed, in the first instance, and then maintained or modified, in the second instance. In doing so, this chapter aims to provide a well-rounded *social psychological* framework of identity formation that takes us past some of the limitations of more focused, discipline-based theories, as in the cases of psychology concentrating on the *subjective* aspects of identity (i.e., the sense of identity) and sociology focusing on the *objective* aspects (i.e., in the roles people play or the social statuses they occupy). For example, as noted above, the senses of self and identity develop from people's social experiences. Yet, when we examine some sociological theories of identity, we find that they cannot account for how identities are formed because these theories deal only with the objective aspects of identity. It needs to be emphasized, though, that identity formation is a process and not a "thing." Hence, both the subjective and objective aspects of identities are always "works in progress," but some psychological theories focus on only adolescence, and not on other periods in the life course. However, subjective senses of identities may change rapidly in certain contexts and during critical periods in the life course, while in other contexts and periods of life they can be rather static. Many of the disputes in identity studies involve confusions over these points (see box 3.1 for examples). Accordingly, this chapter presents a way of understanding contextual and developmental variations in identities and their formation in both their subjective and objective manifestations.

BOX 3.1   COMMON MISCONCEPTIONS ABOUT IDENTITY FORMATION

As noted in Chapter 1, there are three broad approaches in identity studies: scientific, philosophical, and political. There are many disputes among those taking these different approaches, some of which appear to be due to the limited knowledge of the other approaches. For example, a number of people taking an *identity politics* approach dismiss the scientific approach based on several mistaken assumptions about the Eriksonian approach. By this point in this book, readers can evaluate these types of dismissals for themselves. Here are a few of them:

Misconception #1: That the Eriksonian approach assumes that identities are fixed and remain unchanged, as claimed by a postmodernist who asserts: "Scholars are now suspicious of stasis and fixed traits and determining and unchanging essences, which were so crucial to the past history and etymology of 'identity'."[2]

Misconception #2: That Eriksonians believe people have a core identity—an essential self. For example, other postmodernists claim that Erikson promoted "the idea of a 'core self' that is established relatively early and remains as an essential organizer of the subject's relations with the social world" and "following Erikson, many psychologists construct identity as an inner-core which is the self."[3]

Misconception #3: A common belief among those with little knowledge of identity studies is that people either "have" or "do not have" an "identity." Figures 2.1, 3.1, 3.2, and 3.3 illustrate how uninformed this belief is in relation to the scientific taxonomy. There is no singular "identity" proposed in the scientific literature that people can "achieve" once and for all. Identities exist on several levels of analysis and are better understood as processes, with changing structural arrangements (see figure 1.3).

A variant of this misconception is the notion that the terms identity and individuality are interchangeable. This misconception sometimes includes the idea that people who are "conformists" do not have an identity. As we have discussed above in detail, a certain amount of conformity is desirable, because it is a necessity for the individual and the community—the basic integration component of identity. At the same time, a certain amount of individuality is desirable for the individual and community—the fundamental differentiation component. See box 1.2 for optimal distinctiveness theory and box 3.4 for the importance of feeling like an "individual" during the identity stage, as identities are experimented with.

The following type of situation is repeated daily in doctors' waiting rooms around the world in contemporary societies: Two strangers find themselves in a small room waiting for a doctor's appointment. Both are feeling friendly that day. A conversation begins about the weather, and then moves to a story featured on the cover of a magazine that has been left for patients to read while they wait. The two strangers feel they have something in common associated with the magazine story. Where does the conversation then go?

Before trying to answer that question, let us pause for a moment and reflect. In an attempt to gain a visual image of the story we are telling, many readers may by now be wondering whether the people we are describing are men or women, what their ethnicities are, and how old they are. What is being described in the story, and what readers are experiencing, is the desire to "place" people in terms of their locations in society. This is the first step in *impression formation*—people want to know who other people "are" at this very general level. Similarly, modern societies keep track of their citizens at this social level of "who they are." In fact, we "carry our identities" around with us in our wallets and purses on various ID cards that "locate" us in a society for authorities, should they need to verify who we are and if we are entitled to certain rights and privileges, like driving an automobile or claiming health insurance. Although knowing someone's occupation, marital status, gender, race, age, and so on is not very interesting beyond "placing" them, these aspects of a person's social location—their objective social identities—are important determinants and predictors of their life styles and life chances.

Back to the two people in the waiting room: After they have located each other within the structure of society, and feel that they have enough in common to continue talking, the conversation likely moves to more personal matters. They will have already sized each other up in terms of appearance and demeanors, and these nonverbal cues will trigger curiosity about each other's likes and dislikes, habits, activities, and general beliefs. The odds are that the strangers begin asking each other personal questions, such as what they do for a living, whether they are married, have children, and so forth. The two will have been relatively honest about these things if they felt comfortable with the other, but a certain amount of impression management will have taken place to the extent that they want to create a favorable image with the other. If they had felt uncomfortable to some extent, or felt that there was something more to be gained from this conversation, they may have attempted to create an even more favorable impression. Knowing about someone's personal life adds more to the goal of placing that person, so the situation can quickly become more complex. Throughout the conversation, each person will have presented a set of cues and images with which they want the other person to perceive them. These projected images will reflect the person's self-concepts and reflexive understandings of others' views of them.

This encounter may continue to be a pleasant one if these images and definitions coincide and find mutual affirmation. If not, the encounter may become unpleasant as one or both begin to realize that, although their social identities are compatible, their *personal identities* may not be. This is the case because it is likely that each person will have been displaying a personal identity assuming the other's identity is compatible. For example, if both like sports or the theater, vote Democrat or Republican, and have the same tastes in music, they will likely feel comfortable about the encounter and will continue. But, if it comes out that one hates sports, likes the theater, votes Democrat, and listens only to New Age music, whereas the other does the opposite, the chances are that this encounter will not go any further, and each will attempt to avoid further conversation by, for instance, reading a magazine or looking at their watches to signal that they hope to be called soon for their appointment with the doctor.

A similarly uncomfortable situation can arise when one person attempts to present one self-definition or *definition of the situation*, while the other perceives different definitions. In this case, the personal identity as subjectively experienced by one person is not the same one received by the other as an "objective" identity. For example, suppose one person is dressed sloppily, speaks without sophistication, and fidgets during the conversation, yet attempts to project an image of being cultured and knowledgeable about the arts. The chances are that the other person will define that person in an entirely different manner—as uncouth, unmannered, and a phony.

Note that at this point in the story both people have information only about each other's social identity (their locations in society) and personal identity (their concrete presentations of behavior to others, which include their personal beliefs and attitudes). The level of identity of most interest to developmental psychologists—ego identity—has not entered the picture, except to the extent that ego identity is, by definition, implicated by social and personal involvements (e.g., the level and stability of commitments in these areas, which reflect a sense of purpose in life).

So, let us assume that the two people have inferred each other's social and personal identities are compatible enough to continue speaking with each other, and that the doctor is running late. Once past the formalities of social-identity placement, and the camaraderie of personal-identity engagement, the conversation might become more in-depth (although most people are hesitant to take things further with strangers because the situation needs to move from the *front stage* of impression management—see box 2.2—to the *back stage* of the "real self"—see box 3.2). However, if this happens, they would begin talking about what they think are their "true" feelings and who they "really" are—their subjective experiences of their own lives. For example, they might talk about how fulfilling they feel their career or family lives are, that these experiences have brought great meaning to their lives and given them a sense of purpose for the future. Or, they would perhaps talk about how stressful the workplace now is and how they would really like to start a new career where they are self-employed. They would perhaps talk about how difficult it is to find meaning in many of the things they do, or how they no longer feel they are same person they were a few years ago. Or, they may confide that their feelings for their mate have changed.

BOX 3.2 AUTHENTICITY: IS THERE A REAL SELF . . . AND A ROLE SELF?

As the opening quote for Chapter 2 suggests, in premodern societies not only were people defined by their main societal roles (e.g., woman, mother, farmer), but deviating from these roles for personal reasons was considered deviant, even sinful. As long as people performed their ascribed roles in life well, they were considered respectable people of character. Character was synonymous with dependability and legitimacy, and at the time implicitly linked with the idea of *authenticity*. The perception of the issue of authenticity as a personal problem appears to have been largely a 20th century concern. As the "age of identity anxiety" dawned in the post-Second World War period, and people began questioning some of the fundamental tenets of beliefs system, such as "Is God dead?," the validity of their own existence came under scrutiny. And, whereas in premodern societies there was little choice in the major roles people played in their lives, more choices opened up during the 20th century. Consequently, people began to question the value of committing themselves to conventional societal roles, particularly as a "one of the masses." This *role distancing* from mass conformity to "the system" has taken many forms, which sociologist Erving Goffman found fascinating (box 2.2): the sense of separation from the roles one plays in formal, social spheres, and the sense of who one really is in informal, personal situations and even "deep down inside." Thus, people began reporting a sort of split existence, playing more rigid formal roles during their workdays but "letting their hair down" in their leisure time, doing things that contradicted their more formal presentations of self.

But aren't people the products of their experiences with the roles they play in life, as symbolic interactionists argue? Is there really a discrete distinction between our public and private selves? Is there really something like a "true self" or "real self" that can be distinguished from a "role self"? And, can people have two forms of self, between which they vacillate on a regular basis? Various answers to these questions have been posed from each of the three approaches to identity studies: political, philosophical, and scientific. Scientifically, such a question is very difficult to answer with certainty because of definitional ambiguities.

Several attempts have been made to do so, including distinguishing between the *institutional self* and the *impulsive self*.[4] This research investigated differences between those who are institutionally oriented, attaining a sense of self through normative achievements, and those who are impulsively oriented, "discovering" themselves in part through a rejection of institutional constraints. It is possible that institutionally oriented people place greater emphasis on their *social* identities, while impulsively oriented people are more concerned with their *personal* identities. This possibility finds support in empirical research that dates back to the 1950s, wherein among college students, personal identities (defined in terms of styles of self-presentation) seem to be increasing in importance, and social identities (understood as socially recognized roles) appear to be increasingly *less* important. By the end of the 20th century, 80–90 percent of college students appeared to favor personal identities as their primary source of self-definition, compared to only about 30 percent in the 1950s.[5]

All of the above examples have in common manifestations of people's sense of ego identity—their subjective sense of continuity of being the same person over time and in different situations. If they have a strong sense of ego identity that is nurtured and reinforced in their lives, they should feel a sense of continuity with the past, meaning in the present, and direction for the future. If their sense of ego identity is weak, or has weakened for some reason, they may feel that what was important is no longer as important, or who they felt they once were no longer applies. If they are experiencing severe problems at this level of (ego) identity, they may even question whether they have or ever have had a sense of "core" identity—whether there was ever a stable entity in their consciousness in charge of anything. Conversely, people with a stronger sense of ego identity may sometimes experience these things, but are able to recommit themselves to functioning personal and social identities. The kernel of all of these experiences is the sense of continuity embedded reciprocally in a sense of purpose (i.e., ego identity and sense of purpose are mutually reinforcing).

We provide this story here to help us explain in the remainder of this chapter the concepts derived from the SIFT that help to explain how identities are initially formed, then maintained, and subsequently changed over the life course.

The Triadic Model of Identity Formation

The framework underlying the SIFT stems from an older social psychological tradition in sociology called the *personality and social structure perspective*.[6] James House argued some time ago that as a field of study, social psychology actually has "three faces." Only one of the faces corresponds with most people's conception of "social psychology," namely, the version found in mainstream psychology departments, which he calls psychological social psychology. However, House identifies two social-psychological traditions in sociology that constitute the other faces: Symbolic Interactionism (SI, discussed in Chapter 1) and the Personality and Social Structure Perspective (PSSP).

The PSSP seems most suitable to the task of developing a comprehensive understanding of identity for several reasons, foremost of which is its explicit

recognition of the relevance of three levels of analysis: society, interaction, and personality. In fact, from the PSSP, a comprehensive theory of human behavior *requires* that these three levels of analysis be identified and analyzed in terms of their junctures, which together form an *iterative process model* of human behavior. In our case, we are specifically interested in a simplified, yet comprehensive, theory of human identity formation. The language of this more traditional social-psychological perspective is also useful in sorting out a taxonomy of identity concepts. This is the case because new theories tend to overuse the concepts of identity and self, thereby creating the terminological confusions discussed above (see box 3.3 for examples of some of this more traditional social-psychological terminology).

BOX 3.3   SOME USEFUL SOCIAL-PSYCHOLOGICAL TERMINOLOGY

There has been a tendency for the concepts of "identity" and "self" to be over-used, and consequently each concept has lost some of its meaning and utility (see box 1.3). Previous generations of psychologists and sociologists found that a more diversified terminology adequately accounted for the processes now often (overly) ascribed to "self" and "identity."[7]

For example, all of the formal and informal *roles* people play need *not* be called "identities," as some sociologists do. Developmentally, identities are complex composites of a variety of "elements," some of which come from roles, but others come from configurations that have been synthesized from previous internalizations of social norms, self-concepts that assume salience, functional capacities and personal needs, and identifications with various people and value systems. It is the synthesis of these various elements into a coherent structure that is functional in terms of various social roles that mark the formation of the "adult identity," an umbrella sense of integration/differentiation/continuity that can carry the person into maturity. Roles are but one part of people's adult identities, so the two should not be confused.

Similarly, all of people's experiences do not have to be identified as part of a "self" entity. People are required to be *role players*, who engage in various *role enactments*, some of which involve *role conflicts, role strain*, and *role ambiguities*. Terms such as self-esteem, self-efficacy, self-monitoring, independent self, and interdependent self do not require a belief that there is an "entity" called the self that is akin to the soul or some other fixed, immutable core. These terms all describe aspects of *reflexivity*—the ability to treat oneself as an "object" of scrutiny, in a sort of "fly on the wall" way. In our view, as much as language allows, it is better to use the term "self" in its hyphenated sense (self-) to designate these aspects of reflexivity.

The three levels of analysis of the PSSP form the triad of (1) personality, (2) interaction, and (3) social structure:

- *personality* comprises the mental processes traditionally studied by developmental psychologists and psychoanalysts that form the basis of human agentic capacities. Depending on the school of thought, these capacities have been referred to variously as the ego, the self, cognitive structures, and so forth.
- *interaction* refers to the concrete patterns of behavior that characterize day-to-day contacts among people in families, schools, and so on—the focus of study by symbolic interactionists and other micro-level researchers.
- *social structure* denotes the cultural, political, and economic systems, along with their subsystems, that define the normative structure of a society. This last level of analysis is most commonly referred to as the macro-sociological level of analysis.

Figure 3.1 illustrates these three levels of analysis along with their four junctures, signified with a series of four arrows, which represent the continual iterative flow of influence among the three levels. The influence of social structure on day-to-day interactional processes involves *socialization and social control* processes represented by arrow 1 that provide cultural norms and symbols for people. Arrow 2 signifies how day-to-day interaction with others culminates in the *internalization* of social structural norms and values, as mediated by ego-synthetic abilities, while arrow 3 illustrates ego-executive abilities involved in producing *self-presentations* (recall the discussion of the ego and its abilities in Chapter 1). Finally, the person inevitably engages in various group activities (arrow 4) on the basis of the three previous influences (represented by the first three arrows): (1) cultural norms and symbols become (2) internalized and (3) are used by people to guide their participation in collective activities. Through these iterative processes, social structures

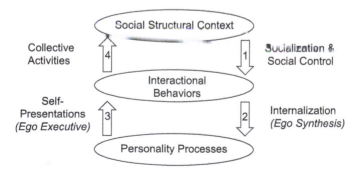

FIGURE 3.1 The personality and social structure perspective (PSSP) model.

are maintained/altered, interactional situations are normalized/disrupted, and individual personalities are formed/transformed.

In general, human behavior can be characterized in this model beginning with the juncture between social structure and interaction (arrow 1). This arrow represents a causal influence of social structure on interaction through the implementation of laws, norms, values, rituals, and so forth that have been previously codified or institutionalized. In other words, while engaged in concrete day-to-day behavior, people generally look to institutionalized norms and conventions to structure their behavior, thereby giving it meaning and justification. With this iterative process, social structures are reproduced, however imperfectly, through *socialization* processes and *social control* mechanisms: socialization generally corresponds with learning through imitation, instruction, and such; social control is accomplished with rewards and punishments associated with conformity and deviance in relation to institutional norms and conventions.

Moving to the next juncture (arrow 2), representing the connection between interaction and personality, we find the subjective processes by which individuals internalize the outcomes of their experiences with ongoing, day-to-day interactions. During this process, people actively define situations for themselves and individually construct their sense of reality. This internalization is subject to basic learning principles and is imperfect to the extent that people employ various cognitive and perceptual filtering schemas that bias their views of the world and their place in it. As noted previously, Erikson refers to the competencies associated with perceiving and filtering information as ego-synthetic abilities (the "knower" or sentient part of the person). However, the general point here is that the content of peoples' internalizations comes from their concrete contacts with others, including their knowledge of, and sentiments toward, social norms and conventions.

When people re-engage in an interaction process, or are continuing an ongoing one (arrow 3), they tend to rely on previous internalizations with which to first define the situation and then present the suitable impressions that they intend others to perceive. Erikson refers to these capacities as ego-executive abilities (the "doer" or dynamic part of the person). The overall point here is that an individual's behavior is in part a product of past internalizations—in part a result of his or her attempt to act appropriately in a given situation and in part a product of abilities to reproduce the behaviors previously experienced as suitable. We can see in the second and third junctures (as represented by arrows 2 and 3) the potential for both agentic and passive responses, depending in part on the strength and appropriateness of the ego-synthetic and ego-executive capacities possessed by a given person—the "knowing" and "doing" capacities developed thus far in his or her life.

Finally, when people are interacting with each other in symbol-based, collective activities, a byproduct of their communication with each other is a social construction of reality. As part of the general tendency to want to avoid interpersonal conflicts and find consensus, people normally seek out compatible definitions of situations with each other. These processes can be seen continually in day-to-day behaviors, especially when situations are novel or relatively unstructured by norms and conventions. In the latter case, humans exhibit a tendency to want to settle definitional disputes, at least with members of in-groups, so that problems do not continually arise. Consequently, over important matters, formally codified agreements tend to be reached and enforced in subsequent interactions (back to arrow 1). For example, in a highly structured society, ongoing discussions over the nature of reality tend to be over concrete, day-to-day, instrumental matters, because general definitions of situations have been previously codified, institutionalized, and enforced through socialization and social control processes (arrow 1). Accordingly, most group discussions normally involve relatively minor matters, such as the "right" way to dress in given situations. Occasionally, however, broad principles underlying norms and conventions may be the subject of discussions, such as the possible exploitation of the workers who make the clothes the people are wearing.

In literate societies, this social construction process culminates in the creation of codified laws. Social constructions in preliterate societies are symbolized differently, being passed on orally, and represented in *mores* and *folkways*. After social constructions have been objectified, there is a tendency for people to internalize them as "real" and "concrete"—to reify them. We can note here, however, how Western societies have been dismantling many of their old cultural norms and conventions on the basis of wider, more democratically institutionalized processes of social reality-construction, aided by modern media technologies. The old norms served best those with power; now that more people can engage in the collective process of social construction, new norms are being constructed that serve wider interests. For example, over the past century and a half, individual rights formally expanded in Western countries, as in the spread of the voting franchise, and certain individual entitlements were put into place, as in the social safety nets that ostensibly keep people from suffering the worst effects of poverty. Of course, the balance of power has been continually contested, more so in some countries than others, with the wealthy attempting to protect and expand their advantages and the less powerful attempting to hold on to their rights and entitlements.[8]

In sum, the model represented in figure 3.1 is a process model that provides a way to explain (1) how culture is reproduced, thereby maintaining structural stability, as well as (2) how both culture and social structure can change. The model is unique in incorporating macro-structural factors and micro-interactional factors with individual, psychological factors, showing them as part of an iterative process that is in continuous motion as people associate in groups and participate in communication processes. This model also provides a useful framework for understanding the multidimensionality of identity formation and maintenance, as illustrated in the next section.

Identity Processes: Forming and Maintaining Self-Definitions

In this section, we illustrate the prototypical processes by which identities are (first) formed and (then) maintained, following the conventions of the PSSP in identifying the analytical importance of social structure, interaction, and personality. Figure 3.2 maps the following concepts onto figure 3.1, thereby laying the basis for the Triadic Model of Identity Formation: (1) *social identity* corresponds with the person's position(s) in a (macro-level) social structure; (2) *personal identity* is found in the individual's concrete behaviors that make up (micro-level) interactions; and (3) *ego identity* refers to the person's sense of continuity which is characteristic of the (subjective-level) personality.

Using the logic of the PSSP, figure 3.2 illustrates several postulates concerning the basic social and psychological processes by which people form identities in the first place and then later maintain them. In so doing, it helps to classify identity terminology into coherent taxonomies, mapping the different facets of human identity, as follows:

At the level of social identity, people are influenced by cultural factors and social roles, pressured in sometimes subtle, and other times forceful, ways to fit into the available objective identities. Social identities include objective *master statuses* associated with race/ethnicity, social class, gender and the like, over which people have minimal control as to membership, as well as roles to which they may have aspired, such as their occupational or educational status.

At the level of personal identity, people find a fit between the requirements and scope of their social identity and the uniqueness and idiosyncrasies of their life history (i.e., their "learning history"). As well, personal agency and biological dispositions (e.g., potentials, desires) can create an identity "style" at this level, producing a form of "individuality" within the bounds allowed by the society and one's place in it (recall *optimal distinctiveness theory* described in box 1.2). Personal identities include informal statuses, such as being a fan of some activity (specific forms of music, sports, social media, and other leisure activities), and informal roles,

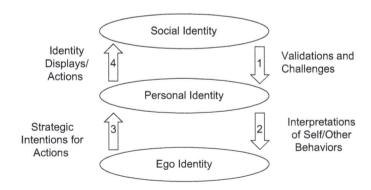

FIGURE 3.2 The triadic model of identity formation.

such as "life of the party," jock, or serious student. Increasingly, people attempt to create a "brand" to represent themselves, including unique names or names with unique spellings, so that these various personal identities are readily associated by significant others to them and their name. Most recently, social media like Facebook have become a new tool for constructing individualized personal identities and a "personal brand."

Finally, at the level of ego identity, in addition to the influences from personal and social identities, people's particular mental processes can influence their sense of continuity (e.g., the factors associated with identity problems discussed in Chapter 2). The sense of ego identity is thus strongly affected by "self-relations" (especially in terms of basic mental health requirements), but is also predicated on primary and secondary "other-relations" for validation and confirmation. The subjective experience of ego identity can only be observed indirectly, through its objective features, namely, behavioral continuity, as evidenced in the stability of people's commitments, goals, and beliefs—in other words, through manifestations of their overall sense of purpose.

The beginning point for describing the identity process cycle illustrated in figure 3.2 is arbitrary, but if we begin with arrow 1 (the juncture between social identity and personal identity), we can note how a person's location in a social structure provides the possibilities and limits for his or her personal identity. That is, only a certain range of possibilities will occur because of social customs and conventions and prior socialization specific to role locations and master statuses. In other words, certain social identities limit the types of personal identities that will be validated by others (to use an extreme example, a 70-year-old man is unlikely to find validation if he tries to dress and act like a 17-year-old woman).

As the story at the beginning of this chapter illustrates, potential validations and challenges to projected identities are foremost in people's minds when they attempt to relate to each other. In daily interactions people execute "real" components of their identities that they feel are appropriate to the social context, namely, personal identity displays presented to specific others (e.g., clothing, demeanors, and speech). Behavior is objective in this sense, and once displayed, cannot be taken back in a temporal sense. This principle can be remembered in terms of the old adage that people only have one chance to make a first impression. Similarly, social identity is "real," with objective impacts on a person's life, to the extent that societies provide different opportunities and limitations for different status groups of people, defined by their social-identity designations (male–female, black–white, old–young, etc.). In social contexts where identities assume an objective quality, however, identity negotiations can occur by which people attempt to manage aspects of their identities, sometimes defending them and other times trying to modify them.

The arrow (2) between personal identity and ego identity represents people's perception and ego syntheses of their own personal identity displays, along with what they think are others' appraisals of these self-presentations. The mental activities involved culminate in internalizations of people's validated social and personal identities. These internalizations are in turn used as a basis for strategies about how to behave in subsequent interactions in ways that either confirm the internalizations or seek ways to modify them. It is at the juncture between ego identity and personal identity that agency is exercised. Arrow 3 represents the influence of the ego-executive processes made possible by ego-synthetic abilities to produce personal identity displays during group activities (arrow 4), which are related to social identity in several ways: (a) they can validate a social identity when they conform to expectations about what is appropriate for a particular "type" of person, thereby maintaining an individual's status in a group or society (e.g., students meeting deadlines in course assignments); (b) they can be fashioned to increase an individual's standing in a society, exceeding expectations for what is considered by others to be appropriate for upward mobility (e.g., as ambitious students do when interacting with professors in ways intended to impress them); or (c) they can undermine and disavow a person's social and/or personal identity, as when expectations for proper decorum are violated (e.g., when students are caught secretly texting in classes or otherwise violating classroom rules).

Through these three levels of identity and four identity processes, identities are formed, maintained, and changed, depending on the circumstances outlined above. This is a continual process that affects everyone in a society. Differences emerge depending on the type of society in which a person lives (e.g., socio-historical period, as in the preceding chapter), the material and mental resources that a person has at his or her disposal, and external events that affect this process over a person's lifetime. For example, negative events can damage a person's sense of ego identity, as in the case of repeated trauma, and personal identity can be marred by stigmatization, as in the case of being the target of bullying.

A key feature of this model is the contention that personality and social structure *indirectly* affect each other—societies require people to interact with each other in order for societal norms, values, and the like to be actualized, and people only encounter that society when interacting with other people from it. More importantly, though, by designating the subjective and objective components of personal and social identity, we can identify a key focal point for identity problems. That is, when there is a discrepancy between people's self-definition versus other's definition of their personal or social identities, identity problems can emerge.

This aspect of the model is most easily illustrated in the case of the adolescent attempting to make the transition out of childhood. Others may still define the adolescent as a child, ascribing a child's social identity to the adolescent, and/or the adolescent's behavioral displays may be interpreted as childish. When this happens, the adolescent's sense of ego identity can be disrupted, as can his or her personal identity displays. Such events can precipitate the type of identity crisis whereby the adolescent struggles to establish an acceptable social identity via personal identity displays. This situation can rapidly become very complex, particularly in societies that do not allow much latitude for the social identities of adolescents. For example, in late-modern societies, younger adolescents are legally "nonpersons," and have a limited number of social identities available, leaving only student, delinquent, athlete, and the like. This helps explain why teenagers often form their own subcultures or create peer groups in which validated social identities can be assumed, however parochial or negative. This also helps explain why teens can become so preoccupied with their personal identity displays—because social identities with a significant positive value are out of their reach for years to come (until they achieve some recognition of adult status), so they are using their primary resources at hand—their bodies and behaviors. Box 3.4 presents excerpts from two newspaper articles in which teens express these identity-based ideas with surprising clarity.

BOX 3.4   WHAT'S IN A UNIFORM? THERE ARE DRESS CODES . . . AND THEN THERE ARE DRESS CODES

For a variety of identity-related reasons, people of all ages in late-modern societies are quite attentive to how they dress, making choices that follow various context-specific norms. In many school districts, for instance, especially more affluent ones, school uniforms are required. The reasons for these dress codes vary, but what is interesting from an identity studies viewpoint is how students react to them.

In one instance, there was talk in a part of Canada about requiring all students in public high schools to wear uniforms. The outcry was strongest among students. A reporter interviewed one student who presented himself with spikey blond hair, loose baggy jeans set low on his hips, and hiking boots. This 13-year-old student protested that "your clothes show your style—what you wear, the music you listen to. . . . My outfit says I'm a skateboarder, snowboarder and that I like hip-hop music." His identical twin brother, dressed in the same manner, similarly protested, "If we had to wear a uniform we would all look the same. It'd be pretty scary. . . . They don't know about kids. They should just let us do what we want."[9]

The irony of these teens feeling they need to look a certain *uniform way* for each other, but objecting to uniforms selected by someone else, seems to be lost on them. However, they do seem to sense that it is important for them to express elements of their *personal identities* for each other and in opposition to others (especially adults). For instance, another student said, "I couldn't express my inner self," and yet another opined, "everyone would lack individuality if they were forced into standardized dress." They are correct in a way, although the feelings that "uniforms will turn all students into soldiers" overstates the fact that schools requiring uniform dress impose the *student role* on them, which is part of a social identity. At their stage in identity development, displays of personal identity are important for their sense of themselves as non-conforming "individuals," even if they are conforming to fairly rigid youth-culture norms. In either case they are conforming to context-specific norms. It is unlikely that they will feel the same way in 10 years, although they may then rely on other popular-culture norms as a way of securing a sense of personal and/or social identity.

And, as norms and tolerance levels change, some 15 years later, still in Canada, a 17-year-old high-school student who self-identifies as *androgynous* challenged in the national media his "school's dress code, arguing that banning [him] from wearing [his] lycra bodysuit to class is more a human rights issue connected to [his] gender identity than a matter of appropriate fashion."[10] The school officials sent him home after he attended wearing a multicolored, David Bowie-like, tight-fitting tailor-made body suit, replete with a revealing crotch bulge. The student told the press that he "recently came out as androgynous—which means [he] doesn't identify as strictly male or female but rather gender-neutral." Eventually, a compromise was made with the student and he returned to school, telling the press, "As terrible as an experience as this has been, it has sort of helped me really accept who I am." This student's experiences provide an illustration of the possible consequences of discrepancies between the subjective and objective aspects of identity.

Figure 3.3 takes these analyses further by illustrating identity formation patterns specific to late-modern society. As noted in the preceding chapter and illustrated in figure 2.1, in late-modern societies, social identities often comprise multiple societal roles that need to be continually managed to varying degrees. This is the case because the social contexts of late-modern societies often involve interactions with strangers who have little or no knowledge of one's past. Consequently, it becomes necessary for people to manage the perceptions of others with respect to those identities that they themselves value. Without a detailed knowledge of each other's biographies, it becomes necessary for people to try to ensure that strangers have the "proper" information to validate an identity they consider being salient and positive. In contrast with the past, then, this information tends to be superficial and more easily contrived (cf. box 2.2).

The following provides a contrasting example of the need to continually manage identities for legitimacy. In early-modern societies, professors could expect that their status would speak for itself and they would be respected in most social interactions, because they had respected academic credentials and accomplishments. This was in part because of narrow norms concerning professors' personal deportment and in part because of a high level of respect for expertise and authority in the society at large. In late-modern societies, this is hardly the case

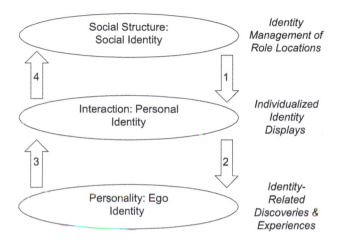

FIGURE 3.3 Identity formation patterns specific to late-modern society.

for a variety of reasons, including loose norms for professorial deportment (e.g., casual clothing) and a decline in respect for authority, especially among students. In these contexts, professors often find themselves defending the legitimacy of their social identity both individually (e.g., with students, colleagues, and administrators) and collectively (e.g., with governments and the corporate community).

Moving to the level of personal identity, presentations of self are based increasingly on contrived image-projections. Many people in late-modern society engage in strategic projections of images aimed at fitting in or gaining advantage somewhere. In instances where the people involved have little or no knowledge of each other's biographies, they can create images of themselves, including fabricated biographies that suit the requirements of a given situation. If these *individualized identity displays* are successful, people can gain membership or validation with a group, along with certain rewards, for being simply "who one is thought to be."

Finally, at the level of ego identity, these late-modern trends can affect people's senses of continuity and purpose in a variety of ways. On the one hand, current opportunities open up myriad forms of identity-related experiences, through which people can "discover" and actualize their potentials that give them a sense of purpose, and in so doing lay the basis for a rewarding adult-identity configuration. This is the proactive type of identity formation discussed in Chapter 6 and described as **developmental individualization**.

On the other hand, certain societal influences (e.g., consumer culture) can turn people into passive acceptors of whatever they find in their day-to-day worlds. These influences provide a sense of purpose that is superficial, fragile, and easily manipulated. For example, those caught up in popular culture influences may remain open to each new trend, malleable in their worldview, and anxious to please others (both significant and generalized others). In essence, they can become afraid not to conform, buckling under the pressure to continuously present pleasing and situationally appropriate impressions to others. This inactive type of identity formation is examined in Chapter 6 in terms of **default individualization**.

Those who are passive in the individualization of their life course can become identity diffused, with no real sense of inner continuity and purpose based on their own ego-synthetic and ego-executive abilities. Instead, they look to others to synthesize information about the world for them and tell them how to behave—they are inactive rather than proactive. Accordingly, identity formation processes can involve a process of "discovery," but not of anything from "within" the person in terms of their potentials and "real self" (see box 3.2). Instead, the identity contents come entirely from outside the person, leading these people to enact mainly a "role self." This external, *other-directed* form of discovery is of new experiences, pleasures, and trends with, and through, other people in temporarily contrived contexts (as the venues for many hedonistic pursuits are). The drawback is, however, that agentic-ego capacities can become weakened by these experiences. Analogous to muscles, the ego needs to be "exercised" to grow and remain strong, but when people go without this exercise, their ego can become weak. Hence, because late-modern societies have fewer traditional forms of identity validation, the sense of ego identity can become weak when people become dependent on concrete day-to-day validation and direction from others, rather than maintaining an internal frame of reference for themselves.

The multidimensional model underlying the identity process cycle has further implications for the social psychological research that has focused on identity formation. For example, as highlighted in box 3.2, according to research using the Twenty Statements Test,[11] Western young people are forming their identities more elaborately at the level of personal identity than social identity, whereas in the past the reverse was apparently true—social identities were more important than personal identities.

This research helps explain a number of current trends in youth development. One trend is that young adults are becoming less oriented to mainstream adult society—feeling less connection with mainstream institutions and authority structures. This transformation may not be too surprising, but it suggests that an increasing number of young adults are also less willing or likely to engage themselves in institutional processes, including those of political and community governance. Those young adults who are not forming and making commitments to viable social identities in these institutional spheres will be more likely to remain in a period of extended youth. Moreover, while elaborate personal identities may be personally "empowering" with one's peers and immediate associates, they may do little for one's ultimate life chances and economic prospects, especially if they are based on the current hedonistic ethos of popular culture. For some young adults this "empowerment" may actually involve a retreat to, or self-absorption in, a sort of personal identity that makes them easier to control politically and to exploit economically. If young people are more concerned with how they look and feel than in larger issues of meaning in their lives and the direction their communities are going, it is easy for others to set their own political and economic agendas, while at the same time profiting from sales of items that feed the personal identities of those absorbed with nurturing such limited aspects of their identities.[12]

Conclusion: Cars, Engines, and Traffic Congestion

A lesson about the need for multidimensional models of human identity can be gained with a comparison that helps us appreciate why there are inherent differences between psychology and sociology. These differences are rooted quite literally in the different perspectives they take toward human behavior, and hence the different levels of analysis they use in explaining behavior. From the following concrete analogy, we can see why abstract social structural explanations are not reducible to individual actions, and vice versa, and why both sociological and psychological approaches should be used.

By merit of their disciplinary mandates, psychologists are more interested in what happens "inside" individuals, and sociologists are more interested in what happens "inside" societies. Neither is wrong in doing this; rather each simply focuses on a different level of analysis by merit of its own "character." While the two levels are related in certain ways, they are not reducible to one another, as the following comparison of different forms of knowledge about the "behavior" of the automobile shows.

Internal combustion engines power most automobiles. A few people (mechanics and engineers) have an extensive knowledge of these engines, and they can tell us how they are built (structure) and how they run (process). But the engine-expert mechanics rarely know more than the average person about traffic patterns. A mechanic does not normally possess advanced knowledge about the complex patterns that traffic can take (structure) or how they can change (process). Nor can a mechanic usually explain any better than the average person why certain types of accidents take place with predictable frequency, why traffic jams occur at certain times and not others, or why gridlock is a problem in some cities and not others.

However, there are a few people who are experts in the field of traffic and safety, and they do have explanations for these non-mechanical phenomena.[13] They likely do not have an extensive knowledge of auto mechanics, however; in fact, such knowledge would play little role in their explanations of traffic flow. The common denominator in this example is the car and how it "behaves," but we are talking about two different levels of analysis, even though there are areas of interrelation (e.g., engine capacity, mechanical failures, pollution produced, and car/truck size). Put another way, an extensive knowledge of auto mechanics does little to explain traffic patterns, and an extensive knowledge of traffic patterns does little to explain the workings of the internal combustion engine.

To return to our disciplinary discussion, psychologists study mental processes and related individual actions, while sociologists study social structures and related individual actions. Their common interest is in how people behave (individual actions), but this does not mean that social structures can be reduced to (i.e., fully explained by) mental processes, or that mental processes can be reduced to social structures. Although there are areas of interrelation that constitute the focus of social-psychological explanations, these mental processes and social structures exist at two different levels of analysis. To confuse these issues is to commit an error of *reductionism*, sometimes called *psychologism* and *sociologism*, depending on the form the reductionism takes. One purpose in writing this book is to show how to avoid both errors in identity studies. We believe that the social psychological theory of identity formation illustrates how to do so.[14]

PART II

Late Modernity

CONTEXTUAL ADAPTATIONS TO INDIVIDUALIZATION PROCESSES

4

MORAL REASONING

A Relational Basis of Individualized Identities

"You must be the change you wish to see in the world."

Mahatma Gandhi[1]

In Part I, the Triadic Model of Identity illustrates how the formation and main-tenance of identity are multidimensional, cyclical processes involving iterations among social, interpersonal, and intrapsychic levels. Like a fish in water, humans "breathe" through their relationships with others and "survive" because they live in cooperative societies based on certain forms of trust and reciprocal obligations. It is also true that cultures vary in terms of how much these relational, or collective, pro-cesses are recognized in shared belief systems and emphasized in daily activities. And, at the same time, people vary with respect to how much they feel their identities are their own doing or the product of their relationships with others, and how much obligation they feel for others and a collective good. Buddhist cultures have empha-sized relational aspects of human experience for some 2,500 years. Judeo-Christian cultures did as well in certain respects, although their collectivist aspects have been de-emphasized in the modern era as capitalism gained dominance in dictating how Western societies were structured (see box 4.1 for an analysis of the transformation of "normal" character traits associated with this massive economic change).

**BOX 4.1 FROM THE SEVEN DEADLY SINS
TO THE SEVEN CARDINAL VIRTUES**

A variety of changes took place in the transition from premodernity to moder-nity, without which it is unlikely that the current form of consumer-corporate capitalism would have been possible. Key to these changes was a revolution in the moral basis of acceptable identities, whereby degrees of selfishness became more acceptable as Western societies moved from being collectivistic to individualistic. In one analysis from the 1940s, a historian argued that the seven deadly sins—pride, greed, lust, envy, anger, sloth, gluttony—which in the medieval period were equated with social decay because they impeded individual spiritual development, gave way to the "seven cardinal virtues" of capitalist consumption. This historian encapsulated the impact of capitalism on Western Civilization in the following way:

> The whole moral change that took place under capitalism can be summed up in the fact that human purposes, human needs, and human limits no longer exercised a directive and restraining influence upon industry: people worked, not to maintain life, but to increase money and power and to minister to the ego that found satisfaction in vast accumulation of money and power. . . . [Before] the emergence of capitalism, economic life had a strong moral foundation. It was rooted in the notion that every act of life was under the Judgment of God: the trade of market stall no less than the judgments of the market court. Hence the conception of the just price: a price determined by the intrinsic value of the commodity and its actual cost of production, divorced from the accidents of individual preference or material scarcity. The guilds set themselves to establish standards of workmanship and to maintain price levels: an active war went on against those who debased commodities, who tried to corner them, or who sought to avoid selling them in the open market at the standard price, first come, first served. Against the Roman legal motto, Let the buyer beware, the medieval economist held rather, Let buyer and seller both fear God. Medieval production, down to the sixteenth century, centered on security, regularity, equity: social justice was more important than private advantage.[2]

The seven character traits that were once admonished slowly became normalized in Western societies over the past few centuries as successive generations adapted to new forms of selfishness—the behaviors that provide the basis for consumer-capitalist societies—and which we now call self-esteem and vanity (pride), materialism (greed), competitiveness and drive (anger), sex appeal (lust), initiative (envy), leisure (sloth), and "the good life" (gluttony). See box 1.1 for more about the Seven Deadly Sins in relation to other modes of conduct in different times and places.

Setting aside issues associated with historical changes in identity formation, such as how benign or dreadful premodern societies might have been, the distinguishing feature of late-modern societies, for good or bad, is that the onus is increasingly on people is to be the "agents of their own development." This feature of late modernity is the result of the life course becoming more individualized as traditional institutions such as religion declined in their influence on people's lives. For instance, without religious guidance, or with less of it than in the past, people increasingly have had to decide for themselves what moral codes to follow: how to differentiate right from wrong in each of their varying degrees, as well as how they as individuals are obligated to a "greater good," especially in terms of situations where competing "rights and wrongs" and "good vs. evil" are at issue.

As we see, an important consequence of this secularization trend is that identity formation and moral development have become inextricably linked with each other in terms of the agentic capacities of the person: non-agentic forms of identity formation are correlated with non-agentic forms of moral development; conversely, optimal types of identity formation are associated with optimal levels of moral development. In these respects, we can speak of "moral identities" or "ethical identities" in the sense that "who we are" is intimately linked with the respect we have for those people with whom we interact and share various roles in the broader society.

This chapter outlines the developmental bases of moral reasoning as it is related to identity formation and self-development. As we see, these three forms of human development share the following qualities in late-modern contexts:

They each entail a broadening of people's awareness of themselves in relation to their world. Optimally, people learn how to reflect upon, and regulate, their thoughts and behaviors in order to reach personal goals while maintaining interpersonal commitments and social responsibilities.

People who are proactive in their own development of these forms of awareness tend to have more positive and optimal outcomes in adulthood. In many ways, the formation and maintenance of interpersonal commitments and social responsibilities is crucial to social integration and thus the effective transition to adulthood; in the ideal, the more ethically principled the bases are of adult identities, the more reliable and stable the person's social roles will be.

The Cognitive-Development Approach

Jean Piaget was the pioneer in the cognitive-developmental field, positing four stages of cognitive development spanning childhood through adolescence, culminating in "formal operations"—also known as abstract thought. Formal operational thought is propositional thinking and abstract reasoning about actual and possible states of the natural and social world. When assimilated with *perspective-taking* capacities, people acquire the ability to conduct "thought experiments" involving the self and others in hypothetical situations. Developing the capacity for formal operational thought requires that people first pass through several more elementary stages of qualitatively different structures of cognitive reasoning. As they grow to understand the world in more complex and abstract ways, they come to appreciate the rights and perspectives of others, and thus they become less egocentric about their own place in the world. However, the rate at which people pass through these early developmental stages varies greatly, and many people do not make it to, or complete, the formal operations stage.

For the developmental transformation of cognitive stages to take place, people normally need to experience something that causes them to doubt their previous conceptions of reality. Such experiences are known as experiences of *cognitive dissonance*. Dissonance involves becoming aware of two conflicting thoughts that create disequilibrium in thought processes, which create a sense of confusion and contradiction in thinking that can only be resolved by a reconfiguration of existing cognitive structures. The concept of personal agency is thus "built in" to the cognitive-developmental approach because people are "forced" to actively and reflexively modify their cognitions when they experience cognitive dissonance. This dissonance sets into motion the processes of *assimilation* and *accommodation* that can result in the acquisition of more inclusive and organized levels or stages of cognitive functioning. Thus, children, adolescents, and young adults become active in their own mental development to the extent that they endeavor to address cognitive dissonance by reestablishing a cognitive equilibrium at more complex levels of understanding.

After observing children and young adolescents (ages 11 to 13) playing games, and after asking them to respond to dilemmas about justice, punishment, and responsibility, Piaget reported that moral reasoning developed through two major stages of increasing cognitive complexity. The first and most elementary stage he called *moral realism*, a stage most common for children, based on reasoning that rules coming from the authorities with whom they are familiar are unquestionably right, and that what is right or wrong behavior is determined by whether or not the actions in question are in conformity with the rules. In addition to concerns with conformity, young children also focus on the physical consequences of behaviors when assessing the extent to which they are considered wrong behaviors. What children do not do is consider the relevance of a person's intentions when making judgments of right and wrong. This stage of reasoning is thus fundamentally egocentric.

After passing through a phase of moral relativism, a transition induced by disagreements with peers about how to play organized games, older children begin to understand the need for cooperation and, for Piaget, it is this peer group experience that stimulates mutual perspective taking and enables young adolescents to begin to consolidate a second, more socio-centric stage of moral judgment that he called the stage of *moral autonomy*. At this stage, moral judgments of right and wrong weigh the importance of the intentions of actors. In addition, the perspectives of relevant others are considered in order to negotiate and compromise when formulating rules of conduct that all consider appropriate. The authority of rules now stems from the realization that they were mutually formulated and conformity to the rules is sensed as "freely given."

Lawrence Kohlberg modified Piaget's theory by studying moral development longitudinally into the adult years, with a focus on describing the underlying cognitive processes required to engage in moral reasoning. His work identifies three levels of moral reasoning: the pre-conventional, the conventional, and the post-conventional, with each of these levels containing two stages of moral development, yielding a six-stage model. Development from stages one through six can, in the most general sense, be understood as growth from (a) *egocentrism* (stages 1 and 2) through (b) *socio-centric perspective taking* (stages 3 and 4) to (c) principled moral reasoning (stages 5 and 6).[3]

Childhood is characterized by the two pre-conventional stages. At stage 1, children's reasoning emphasizes fear of punishment from the failure to obey law, while at stage 2 their moral reasoning begins to emphasize concerns with self-interest as relevant to making moral decisions.

When people's points of reference expand to include social convention and social order, they move into the level of conventional reasoning. Stage 3 reasoning sees right solutions to dilemmas being those that conform to social expectations of appropriate interpersonal behavior and that therefore assure social approval (the "good boy/girl–bad boy/girl" stage). At stage 4, there is an acceptance that deeds that are moral are done out of a sense of duty and obligation, respecting societal norms and values (the "law and order" stage).

At Kohlberg's post-conventional stages, moral reasoning can be described as autonomous in that it expresses a commitment to self-chosen moral-ethical principles that represent cognitive strategies for making moral judgments. Moral judgments at stages 5 and 6 express a "prior to society" perspective, emphasizing a belief that people should act on the basis of conscience concerning such ideals as the requirement to respect human rights, the responsibility to construct better societies, and a hierarchy of values reasoned to be valid for all people (e.g., life is more important than property). Thus, such principles express concerns that transcend the immediate and concrete, that "go beyond" the cultural norms and values of any particular society.

Post-conventional thinking—or principled morality—emerges when the person questions laws and social conventions previously accepted as truths, and sees them as contextual or historically specific. A doubt that begins with suspicions that conventional "truths" are alterable can lead to attempts to develop new "truths" that are held to be valid cross-culturally and historically. At stage 5, moral judgments can claim that orderly social change is possible if people "integrate their varying perspectives by formal mechanisms of agreement, contract, objective impartiality, and due process."[4] For example, the person can see how discriminatory laws and prejudicial practices associated with problems such as racism and homophobia can and ought to be collectively addressed and altered. Those who reach this stage can also see how they themselves are part of the process of the creation of a more just society, and thus feel obligated to personally involve themselves in that process. At stage 6, moral reasoning responds to dilemmas with the particular principle that can be called "respect for persons," a principle focused on moral judgments being valid if they achieve fairness by successfully balancing the requirements of justice with those of care (ideally through dialogue with relevant others).[5]

Research results indicate that only a very small minority of people operate at the post-conventional level, even in adulthood, so reasoning at this level is rare. These findings do not invalidate Kohlberg's theory, though, but merely indicate that adolescence and early adulthood are not unique developmental periods for the emergence of principled morality.[6] Moreover, stage-4 law-and-order reasoning is highly functional in most societal contexts, so the theory does not portray the average person's reasoning as morally inadequate. Stage 5 reasoning remains a "potential" for many people that under certain circumstances can be positive for both individual growth and societal development when large numbers of people use this level of reasoning.

The Developmental Bases of Moral Reasoning

The social-scientific study of moral reasoning gained impetus after the atrocities of the Second World War, stimulated by a sense of urgency to better understand how humans can rise above pressures to obey the immoral demands of authorities. This concern with conformity and obedience was particularly focused on why apparently normal people could take human life on a mass scale either by their own hands or by participating in internecine conflicts.[7] It was believed that understanding how people reason their way through moral issues involving human life and dignity could provide insights into ways of educating people to advance to levels where they become immune to, or inoculated from, societal pressures toward blind conformity, when that conformity clearly does harm to others.

Because of these roots, moral development research following Kohlberg combines the scientific study of how people do reason about "oughts" with a developmental view of how they ideally ought to reason. In other words, this scientific enterprise is not simply descriptive but is also to some extent prescriptive—implying what people *ought to do*. The field is also deeply rooted in Western philosophy, with its tendency to try to understand how people can act as individuals, opposing social convention when opposition is judged to be necessary for moral reasons.

There is considerable consensus in this field that empathy (and its cognitive organization as sympathy) and perspective taking are essential for the development of people's ability to reason about issues of right and wrong. It is widely accepted that the emotional capacity for empathy is to some extent innate, and that it strengthens during childhood and adolescence in response to socialization experiences. In addition, the adequacy of perspective-taking ability has been empirically demonstrated to develop through a series of increasingly complex stages. Finally, there is general consensus that the capacity for empathy needs to be cognitively coordinated with the capacity for perspective taking for the more complex forms of moral reasoning to develop, and to steer the person away from antisocial activities during adolescence and adulthood.[8]

Empathy and Perspective-Taking Capacities

Kohlberg's research indicates that empathy and perspective taking are necessary but not sufficient capacities for moral reasoning. In order to reason about moral issues at Kohlberg's stage 2 and beyond, people need to develop the "socialized" capacities for socio-centrism. Socio-centric awareness stems from both empathy and perspective taking; while these capacities are required for moral development beyond stage 1, they are not, in and of themselves, moral or prescriptive capacities. It is when a person, apprehending a dilemma and sensing the need to respond to it, coordinates these capacities with what Kohlberg calls the "justice operations" of *equality, equity*, and *reciprocity* that empathy and perspective taking become required for the construction of a prescriptive moral judgment. In other words, people can be empathetic and can perspective-take in many social situations; it is only when they sense a moral dilemma that their thought processes become prescriptive, leading them to feel they *ought to* perspective-take and empathize with others in order to make what they believe is an adequate moral judgment in that case.

Empathic capacities that can be coordinated with perspective taking may to some extent be hardwired in humans, as research with infants has shown in reference to their sensitivity to distress in other infants. Parents and peers can then reinforce this capacity as well as the capacity for perspective taking. Both provide a basis for rudimentary pro-social behaviors, such as sharing and expressing sympathy.[9]

A five-stage theory has been proposed, and empirically verified, in the development of the perspective-taking abilities that underlie moral reasoning.[10] Children tend to have a difficult time separating their perspective from others' perspectives, or understanding that others may have a different perspective in a given situation or on a specific issue. In adolescence, the person can come to understand that other people may hold different perspectives and that those people appreciate different perspectives themselves (this is called *mutual perspective taking*). By late adolescence, people can come to understand how these mutual perspectives are in turn influenced by people's social roles and their understanding of their social worlds more generally. It must be stressed, though, that while this developmental progression has been empirically supported, it is not tightly linked with age. For example, while many teens are capable of mutual perspective taking, it is not uncommon to find young adults and even those well into adulthood who are not capable of it.[11] What seems to help young people most to become better perspective takers are peer socialization processes, like making new friends and becoming accepted among these friends.[12]

Although empirical research has shown that this developmental progression in perspective taking is correlated with the capacity for higher levels of moral reasoning, perspective taking on its own will not contribute to the development of higher levels of moral reasoning without its coordination with the emotional capacity for empathy. Without an empathic connection, a person can take advantage of others with the knowledge gained from their perspective-taking abilities, especially if that person is reasoning at a pre-conventional level. This is the type of developmental hiatus underlying interpersonal manipulation and sociopathic behaviors. More generally, research results indicate that those with an arrested capacity for empathy along with poor perspective-taking abilities do not progress far in terms of the stages in moral reasoning, and have been found to be more prone to antisocial activities and delinquency.[13]

Stages of Moral Reasoning

Over 1,000 studies have been conducted using Kohlberg's measure of moral reasoning, examining differences over the lifespan, among cultures, and between the genders. In addition, various correlated psychological variables have been identified and numerous social contextual influences have been investigated.[14]

This body of research has confirmed that there is a steady normative progression through Kohlberg's first four stages from childhood through to early adulthood.[15] A series of longitudinal studies of samples have been undertaken, confirming an age-based relationship with Kohlberg's moral stage development that is curvilinear:[16]

- The minimum age at which children enter stage 2 is six years old and the minimum age for stage 3 is eight.
- At 10 years of age, most children are at stage 2 or making the transition from stage 1.
- By age 13, most adolescents are making the transition to stage 3.
- By age 18 some young people have begun reasoning at stage 4, although about half of late adolescents are stage 3.
- During the early 20s, the prevalence of stage 4 reasoning steadily grows, with about one fifth at stage 4, although most are still in stage 3 or in transition to stage 4.
- By the late 20s, the percentage in stage 4 or in transition to stage 5 grows to over 30 percent, and by the mid-30s the percentage in stage 4 reasoning is over 50 percent.
- However, even as adults, few people progress in their reasoning beyond stage 4 and those that do demonstrate some stage 5 reasoning are at least in their mid-20s.[17]

The research literature also generally supports Kohlberg's prediction that the stages are sequential and invariant: people move from one stage to the next and do not skip any.[18] And, as one would expect, those who reason at more advanced stages are also more pro-social (including engaging in volunteer activities) and socially competent (e.g., greater social problem-solving abilities and greater degrees of social adjustment).[19] These are important attributes for identity formation because they support the young person in developing an increasingly wider radius of social involvements with age. Research supports this proposition, reporting that those who are more proactive in their identity formation score higher on moral reasoning abilities and are more likely to be capable of principled reasoning than those who are inactive, or merely active (the latter basing their identities on their parents' commitments).[20] In addition, while intelligence scores are correlated with the development of moral reasoning, this finding may be confounded with the effects of education and socio-economic status, variables that are also positively associated with moral development.[21]

In terms of non-development, a consistent finding over decades of research, involving dozens of studies, is that juvenile delinquents exercise a level of moral reasoning that is significantly below their non-delinquent peers. At the same time, adolescents scoring at low levels of moral reasoning are also more aggressive and more accepting of inappropriate acts of violence, including fighting in sports.[22]

The Developmental Contextualism of Moral Reasoning

The capacity to engage cognitively in increasingly complex and adequate reasoning about moral issues of justice and care apparently does not naturally unfold across the life span. Rather, it is stimulated by contextual experiences that challenge people to consciously reason through conflicting moral-ethical issues, and in so doing advance developmentally.[23] In other words, influences that stimulate people to be proactive in their own self/identity development can also have a beneficial effect on moral reasoning abilities and vice versa. However, in contrast to self/identity development, moral-reasoning capacity is not expected to be associated with certain "contexts" related to a person's phenotype, like ethnicity, or their special needs, such as physical disabilities or family-origin issues (like adoption), so no studies have been reported on these topics.

A major controversy in this area is whether Kohlberg's post-conventional stages of reasoning express universally valid principles of justice reasoning or whether they are forms of reasoning peculiar to Western cultures that have no greater validity as moral points of view than do other moral logics and values that have been documented in non-Western cultures.[24] Kohlberg's critics in this respect can be considered relativists who argue that the validity of moral values and logics peculiar to a specific culture must be judged within the context of that culture.[25] Other critics argue that there is a secular bias in Kohlberg's theory and that the reliance on abstract principles makes it insensitive to people's moral sensibilities in everyday life.[26]

An adequate analysis of the universal/relativism debate in reference to Kohlberg's claims is beyond the scope of the present book, since a fair treatment of it would require a careful analysis of his very intricate and detailed technique for scoring moral reasoning as well as an exposition of the structural/cognitive components of what he claimed was a "stage" of moral reasoning. Suffice it to say that Kohlberg did designate the highest stages as *post*-conventional, namely "beyond" the status quo moral expectations of a given society and what follows from his theory is that the stronger the conformity pressures are in a given society, the less common post-conventional reasoning will be. Recalling the origins of this research in the wake of the genocides of the Second World War, one point of his research was to determine how capable humans are of transcending their particular cultural imperatives when those imperatives endanger human life and dignity. The value of the theory thus lies in learning how to help the human species develop the capacity for more complex forms of moral reasoning so that it might evolve cultures to the point where humans can resist pressures to harm others simply because there is something in it for them, or because they are ordered to do so, or because everyone else they know is doing it.

In spite of criticisms of limited cross-cultural validity, Kohlberg's predictions regarding stage progression up to stage 4 moral reasoning have been replicated in 23 Western and non-Western countries,[27] as well as among cultural groupings within the U.S.[28] And, perhaps not surprisingly, evidence indicates that post-conventional reasoning is not common in Western countries and is even less so in non-Western societies.

It is important to understand that Kohlberg's work was an attempt to empirically demonstrate that individual moral reasoning develops through increasingly complex stages of cognitive operations that involve the use of perspective-taking skills in order to understand and evaluate social relationships. In addition, his concern was with the opportunities that cultures provide for people to reach higher levels of reasoning;[29] this concern extended to his own recommendations for moral education, discussed in box 4.2.

BOX 4.2   CAN MORAL REASONING BE TAUGHT?

Kohlberg experimented extensively with teaching moral reasoning in school contexts, finding considerable success in doing so. These techniques are based on the cognitive-developmental assumption that reasoning abilities are not passively acquired through socialization experiences, but rather require that the person actively engage in reasoning through conflicting alternatives. The approach is to teach students in small-group discussions how to take steps in sorting out the issues in moral dilemmas. These discussions must be appropriate for the students' level of development in terms of reasoning capacities and challenge them by presenting arguments about dilemmas slightly above their reasoning level. This technique thus stimulates active problem-solving strategies, providing "mental work-outs" rather than the passive absorption of information.[30]

Empirical evaluations of these techniques have found that about one half of students can be advanced by one stage and 10 percent advanced by two stages, and that these become permanent changes in the students' reasoning abilities. These techniques have also been found to be effective in improving the reasoning capacities of juvenile delinquents, helping them develop beyond pre-conventional reasoning to conventional reasoning.[31]

In reference to more micro-developmental-contextual concerns, some research suggests that family social class is related to the development of moral-reasoning capacities, with adolescents from middle-class families scoring higher on moral reasoning than those from working-class families, but it is difficult to separate this relationship from the effects of education.[32] Indeed, educational level has been found to be associated with the stage of moral reasoning, especially at the post-secondary level where post-conventional reasoning is more likely to be promoted.[33] In addition, while it is the case that children and adolescents develop increasingly complex moral-reasoning capacities with age, it is questionable whether this development can be attributed to the influence of schooling at the primary and secondary levels. Kohlberg was very critical of the moral reasoning that is modeled by most schools, which is a contradictory combination of stage 1 (fear of punishment) and stage 4 (law and order).[34] Too often, teaching style and school management is authoritarian rather than *authoritative*—a consensus approach in which issues are openly discussed and jointly reasoned—and many primary and secondary schools do not do this. In contrast, school management techniques and teaching styles at the college/university level are more likely to be democratic and consensus-based, and the curricula are more likely to encourage critical thinking. These factors can combine to encourage university students to confront moral conflicts, and thus help them move toward the consolidation of the more principled post-conventional level—to apply universal moral principles rather than use reasoning dictated by social conventions and societal authority.[35]

Principled reasoning has been found to increase among university student populations between their first and fourth years, especially for those enrolled in small liberal arts schools. While this finding does not appear to be related to students' "major" field of study, it does appear to be a function of involvement with diversity-related curricula that expose students to various contentious moral concerns involving, for example, racism, gender discrimination, social class bias, and homophobia. Finally, students who work off campus and/or are disengaged from their collegiate experience are less likely to make these gains as a result of university attendance.[36]

Lastly, moral development is influenced by both family factors and peer relationships. As in the case of self and identity development, parents can directly influence their children's moral development, either by example or through their involvement in their children's lives. Parenting styles, discussed in detail in Chapter 8, have been found to be correlated with the development of moral reasoning: the *authoritative* parenting style promotes it, by encouraging discussion about issues between parent and child/adolescent,[37] while the *authoritarian* style inhibits it, because of the recourse to fear of punishment and the demand for obedience.[38] Adolescents will tend to replicate their parents' stage of moral reasoning; as adults, some 20–30 percent will surpass their parents' stage.[39]

Peer interactions can also stimulate the development of higher forms of moral reasoning to the extent that adolescents and young adults engage in challenging conversations about relevant issues where conflicting views are raised and disagreements are resolved. In fact, in theory, peers can be more influential than parents because peer relationships tend to be more egalitarian, and peers negotiate issues at more comparable status levels than do parents, thereby facilitating more perspective taking.[40] Socio-metric and group status factors also appear to be relevant: those with more friends and/or higher peer group status tend to have higher levels of moral reasoning.[41]

Synthesizing the Self/Identity and Moral Reasoning Literatures

Figure 4.1 shows a way of synthesizing the main developmental findings in these three literatures. In the upper cells, the normatively interrelated trajectories of self and identity development are depicted, beginning with the formation of self-concepts and identifications in childhood, through to their integration into identities in adolescence, and to their eventual synthesis into an overall coherent identity in early adulthood. No age-specific or institutionally based milestones have been identified for self/identity development because of the wide variability in these forms of development. In contrast, the development of moral reasoning ability has been identified as more age-predictable, as noted in the earlier section, such that normatively, the two forms of pre-conventional reasoning are exercised in childhood ("don't hurt me," and "what's in it for me"), and the two forms of conventional reasoning are typically accomplished in adolescence ("do you like me now," and "society needs me to conform"). In early adulthood, conventional social-order reasoning prevails, and for some people, post-conventional reasoning emerges ("what is the greatest good when all circumstances are considered").

In individualistic Western societies, where most of the research has been carried out, the normative—or most typical—trajectory is for concrete self-concepts and identifications to be formed into hierarchies in childhood, and then to be integrated during adolescence into more abstract trans-contextually stable identities. In early adulthood, these identities can then become consolidated into more coherent adult identities, optimally based on commitments to a productive role in society and shared belief systems.

	Childhood (Ages 7–12)	Adolescence (Ages 13–18)	Early Adulthood (Ages 19–25)
Self/Identity Trajectories	**Self → Self-Concepts**	**Identifications → Identities**	**Domain Exploration → Identity Coherence/ Synthesis**
Normative Paths	Hierarchies of concrete self-concepts and identifications	Integration of self-concepts and identifications into abstract identities	Active and proactive formation of domains of commitment (e.g., occupation, religion, worldviews) into a coherent synthesis of various domains of identity
Problematic Paths	Fragmentary self-concepts and identifications	Non-integration of self-concepts and identifications; avoidance of identity issues	Avoidance of commitments and goal setting with the result that the various domains are undeveloped and unsynthesized into a coherent identity
Moral Development	**Pre-Conventional Morality**	**Conventional Morality**	**Conventional/Post-Conventional Morality**
Socio-Centric Paths (Pro-Social)	Obedience to authority → Instrumental morality	Approval-seeking morality→ Social order morality	Social order morality → Principled morality
Egocentric Paths (Arrested)	Poor empathy development	Poor perspective taking	Instrumental relativism

FIGURE 4.1 The developmental trajectories and milestones of self/identity and moral reasoning.

At the same time, moral reasoning and social perspective taking develop through a hierarchy of increasingly complex stages, moving from egocentrism in childhood to socio-centrism in adolescence and early adulthood; for some, these forms of development continue on to principled moral reasoning in early and mature adulthood.

Personal agency stimulates all of these developmental trajectories. those who are more agentic tend to have the highest self-esteem, the most effectively consolidated self-concepts, to be most self-efficacious, to be most proactive in their identity formation, and to reach the more advanced stages of moral reasoning.

Problematic trajectories undermining social adaptation can stem from difficulties encountered during childhood in the formation of coherent hierarchies of self-concepts and identifications. The effects of these problems can compound during adolescence and result in identity diffusion (inactivity in relation to identity issues), such that the young adult either avoids making commitments in various identity domains and/or refrains from setting life-course goals. In either case, the subsequent formation of "incoherent identities" in adolescence can result in an arrest in adult identity formation. These incoherent identities may involve over-identifications with popular culture-based self-concepts and identities, and under-identifications with adult roles.[42]

At the same time, if empathy and perspective taking do not develop, the young person has little emotional and cognitive motivation to engage in conventional, let alone post-conventional moral reasoning and is likely to remain egocentrically committed to a form of instrumental relativism (stage 2), where his or her reasoning is based on calculations of self-interest, with little regard to the interests of, or consequences for, others.

Low levels of personal agency are associated with developmental arrest: those who are most inactive in their identity formation also tend to have the lowest self-esteem, the least effectively consolidated self-concepts, fewer positive beliefs about their self-efficacy, and to reason at the lowest levels of moral reasoning.

The Eriksonian Approach: The Developmental Basis of Ethical Identities

Based on his familiarity with Kohlberg's stage model of moral development, Erik Erikson theorized that people potentially pass through three stages of "value orientation" that reflect the relationship between their senses of identity and sense of obligation to others and that parallel Kohlberg's three levels of moral development. He labeled these value orientation stages the *moral stage*, the *ideological stage*, and the *ethical stage*. These stages represent the ethical components of identity development.[43]

With this stage model, Erikson proposed an interesting approach to the fundamental "identity question" raised in Chapter 1, arguing that social and personal identities have been evolving from being based on "difference" to being based on "similarity." That is, he argued that the identity-formation potentials of the human species have been evolving in ways that have broken down the limited scope of parochial in-group identifications and have broadened them to include more members of the species. As societies have become more inclusive, people living in them have included more and larger groups into their sense of an "in-group." Erikson's proposition is consistent with the classic scientific postulate about the relations between the evolution of the species (*phylogenesis*) and the lifetime development of the individual (*ontogenesis*).

In reference to individual development, Erikson associated the moral stage with childhood, the ideological stage with adolescence, and the ethical stage with adulthood. According to Erikson, these stages reflect varying levels of reasoning ability about the source and nature of individual responsibility in complying with authority:

- The moral stage reflects the reasoning capacity of the child and is characterized by a categorical belief in absolute authority.

- The ideological stage involves an attempt on the part of the individual to reason in relation to multiple authority sources in an expanding social environment. Thus the individual at this stage must decide which "truth" will guide her or his sense of justice and way of life.
- This ideological awareness may be implicit, an intuitive faith that "society" is benign and "knows" what it is doing; or it may be explicit, mediated with an elaborate framework constructed by individuals to explain to themselves and others why things are the way they are, or to indicate what things ought to be like.
- Lastly, Erikson contended that during adulthood people who have experienced these first two stages (both of which in different ways are egocentric) may develop beyond them and acquire an ethical awareness. An ethical awareness involves the recognition that all people are ultimately responsible in some sense for their actions and that all have a responsibility to some degree for the entire species, not just to their "in-group," however narrowly or widely that group is defined.

Erikson believed that the possible existence of these stages provides considerable insight and reason for optimism for the future of the species. Most of the history of Western civilization has been characterized by a moral orientation involving a blind obedience to one absolute authority. Deviations from moral proscriptions, whether in the form of deliberate action or merely as a result of group membership, were often met with swift and unrelenting censure. Over the past few centuries, movement has been into the ideological stage, with many people in Western societies attempting to confront various political and social conditions of life, but with an orientation that still has an "us-them" mentality. However, Erikson saw signs of an emerging awareness of the limitations of the ideological orientation and of the promise of the ethical orientation. Currently, though, because of the hegemony of the ideological mode of awareness, most people find it difficult to develop and to sustain even an "intuitive" ethical awareness. Full movement into the ethical stage is likely still quite rare (see box. 4.3).

BOX 4.3   HOW COMMON IS THE ETHICAL AWARENESS?

Several studies have operationalized Erikson's value orientations, with some interesting results, including confirming that those who are more proactive move closer to both an explicit ideological and an ethical awareness of identities. In one study, about half of 149 undergraduate and graduate university students (up to age 35) were found to have some sense of ethics that went beyond moralism and ideology.[44] However, only one person was "firmly" in the ethical stage, and this student appeared to be experiencing considerable stress and a severe identity crisis due to a relative absence of social support for her highly developed reasoning capacity.

In another study, the correlation between Kohlberg's moral stages and Erikson's ethical stages was confirmed.[45] This study found that Erikson's moral stage corresponds with the Kohlbergian pre-conventional stage, the implicit ideological stage with the lower half of the conventional stage (especially, the "good boy/girl–bad boy/girl" stage), and the explicit ideological stage with the upper half of the conventional stage (the "law and order" stage). This second study was also longitudinal, following a group of Israeli adolescents living on a kibbutz at three points in time. Over half of the subjects had made advances through the value orientations stages each time they were retested (between ages 13 and 20), and most were in the explicit ideological stage by the third testing. Similar to the other study, no subjects were found in the ethical stage (which would roughly correspond with Kohlberg's stage 5, and the transitional phase to that stage), although about 20 percent were in a transitional phase to Erikson's ethical stage by their later adolescence (i.e., they could be said to be striving for an ethical awareness).

Thus there is reason for guarded optimism that the human species will become sensible enough to stop trying to destroy itself, one group at a time. If Erikson was right about the value orientation stages and their relationship to the other dimensions of human development, we should be witnessing a continuing movement away from parochial ideologies toward universalistic ethics. Erikson believed that both a universalistic set of ethics and universalistic identities will emerge out of the various forms of *humanism* that are now understood by many at only a parochial ideological level. Suffice it to say that, for Erikson, identity and morality are inextricably linked, and the empirical evidence supports this idea.

Figure 4.2 illustrates the three levels of increasing complexity in the eventual ethical grounding of identity formation with which people experience themselves in relation to others, ranging from the parochial binary self-definition to the universalistic conception where group boundaries have dissolved in people's thinking as their social radius has expanded to include the human species.

At the moral stage, which would correspond to the most primitive level of ethical identity, people possess a dichotomous "me vs. you" and "us vs. them" view of themselves in relation to others. At this primitive level, there is a clear in-group and a clear out-group. An essential part of people's self-definition is "what they are not," namely, members of one or more out-groups, which are perceived as threatening or antagonistic in some way. People whose self-definition is at this basic binary level are very much tied to *place*, and have difficulty moving through social *space*, given the rigid in-group/out-group distinctions they perceive and endorse.

Value Orientation Stage: Group Identity Sense	Fundamental Group Identity Experience	Implicit Validating Metaphor
Moral Stage: Binary in/out-group boundaries	Me vs. you → Us vs. them →	I am what I am not. **We** (in my group) are what we are not (i.e., not similar to inferior out-groups).
Ideological Stage: Multiple group allegiances and boundaries	Me vs. you and them → Us vs. their kind →	I am an individual who needs to feel different from others in some ways. **We** are different and need to show it and be recognized for it.
Ethical Stage: Universalistic, no in-group boundaries	Me and us, including you and everyone else →	**Me and you** are members of the same species, and therefore have responsibilities to all others of our species.

FIGURE 4.2 The ethical components of identity formation.

As Western civilization has evolved, and as people's radii of social involvements have expanded, the basis of self-definition has become more complex, moving to an ideological level. At this level there still exists a strong sense of identity based on in-group membership, but the conception of out-groups has become more differentiated into a typology of "acceptable others" as the person has more group memberships corresponding with a larger array of enacted roles. A person is now more able to see "the other" in larger, more neutral contexts, as one of many other groups of possibly threatening and non-threatening "others." This form of self-definition corresponds to the ideological stage that Erikson believed corresponds to the "adolescence" of civilization, as well as to the adolescence of the individual life course.

Erikson believed that many people can, and do, continually push back the boundaries of their sense of in-group membership—expand their social radius—to include more and more out-groups as part of their self-definition. As this happens, people increasingly experience their personal and social identities as including the sense of being a member of the human species, rather than as being simply a member of a specific, "exceptional" group. This is the ethical stage that Erikson attributed to advanced forms of civilization and to individual maturity. A person who reaches this advanced stage of value orientation has a more inclusive and universalistic identity. Out-groups are not viewed as threats so much as constituting people who define themselves differently but with whom communication ought to be sought and cooperation solicited. All humans are understood as having particular identity needs, along with material needs, and as being minor actors in larger systems. Moreover, it is realized that all humans have ultimate responsibility for their actions, and neither identity needs nor material needs justify the exclusion or persecution of others, regardless of their group membership.

Conclusion: Ethical Identities

When we combine the Kohlbergian model of moral reasoning with the Eriksonian formulations of ethical awareness and identity formation, it becomes apparent why more proactive identity formation is associated with the movement through these moral reasoning and ethical stages. This is especially the case to the extent that people exercise proactivity in an ever-widening variety of contexts, expanding their social radii and therefore interacting with an assortment of hitherto out-group people. Stated in this way, we can assert claims regarding the intricate interrelationships between ethical awareness and optimal identity formation, a topic to which we return in the concluding chapter.

5

PROACTIVITY

Agency in Identity Formation

"A clever person solves a problem. A wise person avoids it."

Albert Einstein[1]

A perennial debate in the social sciences involves the extent to which human behavior is the result of external, social, political, and economic forces on the one hand, or internal, individual, willful intentions on the other. This controversy is referred to as the *structure–agency debate*. In sociology, there is an emphasis on the primacy of macro-level social-structural causes over the willful actions of individuals, a position that has been debated by generations of sociologists. In psychology, there is not so much a debate as a disciplinary consensus that human behavior is the result of micro-level and psychological factors, and that macro, social-structural factors are remote or distal causes.

Unfortunately, arguments about whether the sociological or the psychological level of analysis is the "right" one to employ often derail productive enquiries about the relative importance of structure and agency. The social-psychological analysis of identity underpinning the SIFT provides a way around this problem by showing that both forms of analysis are useful, as opposed to being simply right or wrong, depending on what is being analyzed and in which contexts. In the SIFT, as we saw in Chapter 3, the various types of identity are functions of both external (social structural) and internal (agentic) factors; these functions are often context-dependent; and both the sociological and psychological perspectives are essential for a comprehensive understanding of the complexities of human self-definition (see the conclusion of Chapter 3 for an analogy of this disciplinary problem and a proposed solution).

Objections to the Concept of Structure

A primary reason for the persistence of this debate in sociology may be that many sociologists have been trained to focus on the normative structure of societies as explanations for behavior patterns. This training dates back to Émile Durkheim (1858–1917), who, in his attempt to distinguish sociology from psychology, argued that the "proper" purview of sociologists lies with the study of *social facts* (persistent manifestations of normed patterns of thinking and behaving, as found in stable, population-level rates of complex phenomena like suicide), and that exclusively psychological explanations are misleading.[2] For a good portion of the 20th century, then, sociologists shied away from explanations that implicate internal thought processes and self-directed behavior. With the exception of some minor dissent, the "structural" paradigm associated with Durkheim's work has dominated sociology.[3]

Perhaps because of Durkheim's influence, the sociological community has not been able to consistently define the concept of agency, and sociologists tend to be reluctant to propose concepts that represent psychological processes and structures. However, without these concepts, the "individual" is under-conceptualized, and consequently so is the relationship between person and structure. The individual is left as a "black box."

Unfortunately, a resolution to this debate is not to be found in psychology either, because psychologists have tended to see social structures as simply products of human needs and traits rather than as having a level of existence in their own right, as sociologists do. One developmental psychologist contrasts his approach with that of sociologists, arguing that sociologists

> tend to place structural factors at the center of their interpretive frameworks—in contrast to developmental psychologists like me, who tend to view structural factors as one influence among many, with other important factors including personality, intelligence, and relationships with family and peers, among others. Developmental psychologists usually view the developing person as an active agent in the environment, whereas sociologists are more likely to view people as unwittingly subject to structural factors over which they have no control. . . . structural factors are seen more in terms of environmental influences and constraints in the way of life goals rather than as shaping, in a fundamental way, roles and identities to match modern conditions.[4]

Regrettably, problems emerge with this sort of agency-emphasizing approach when they are insensitive to the structure–agency *interactions* (i.e., mutual influences between structural and agentic causes). Other psychologists have accounted for these interactions with the model of *developmental contextualism*, which we explore in more detail throughout the remainder of this book.

Our response to this sort of criticism of the sociological approach by psychologists is implicit in the social-psychological approach illustrated in Chapter 3. The SIFT addresses the structure–agency debate at the contextual levels associated with identity formation, and thus focuses on interactions between identity-based agency and *identity-conferring* social structures. As we further see below, the SIFT can take us beyond this either–or impasse by specifically postulating the contents of this black box as well as specific elements of the nature of the relationship between the contents of the black box and its social context. Identity-based agency is theorized and operationalized in terms of proactive approaches to identity formation that produce individualized syntheses of various identity elements in various domains (e.g., occupation, religion, worldview, and personal beliefs). In late-modern societies, people who approach identity formation with higher levels of agency should experience forms of developmental individualization that result from the planful and purposeful integration into the context of an adult community. People who find a niche in that community in this proactive manner are more likely to fulfill two of the three basic identity processes—integration and differentiation. Identity-based agency thus involves self-directed personal growth and the forging of some sort of life project within available societal contexts. In contrast, inactive approaches to identity formation characterize default individualization—following paths of least resistance and effort, where people "allow" decisions to be made for them as a result of their inaction in certain contexts. These low-agency approaches can lead to a deferred or passive formation of an adult identity and thus to weak forms of integration and differentiation in an adult community. Following developmental contextualism, the relevance of a continuum of agency from high to low is context-specific, as we discuss throughout the remainder of this book. In other words, people may be more agentic in some contexts than in others.

The Importance of Locating Agency in Structure

Although many sociologists seem to have been on the right track in trying to demonstrate the interpenetration of agency and structure, they have failed to distinguish agency as an analytical category in its own right, with distinctive dimensions and manifestations. Consequently, some concepts of agency offered in sociology have been defined in terms that tie it too closely to social structure. Of the resolutions to this problem that have been suggested, one recent one stands out.[5] In this formulation, agency is defined as

> the temporally constructed engagement by actors of different structural environments—the temporal-relational contexts of action—which, through the interplay of habit, imagination, and judgment, both reproduces and transforms those structures in interactive response to the problem posed by changing historical situations.[6]

In other words, people are always functioning is social contexts, so it is erroneous to conceive of individuals as separate from structures. At the same time, certain contexts support specific agentic orientations, which in turn constitute different structuring relationships of people toward their environments. It is the organization of such orientations within particular structural contexts that gives form to effort and allows actors to assume greater degrees of transformative leverage in relation to the structuring contexts of action or inhibits them from doing so. School contexts provide a ready example of this to the extent that they are enabling for some students, who thrive in specific school contexts, and disabling for other students, who flounder in those contexts.

In sum, the potential for agency in a given individual depends both upon the specific qualities of that individual and the specific qualities of the context in which the individual is acting. Actors, by definition, function in contexts; as such, they are never free from structure, but they vary in terms of their ability to utilize and transform that structure. The challenge for social scientists, therefore, is to empirically document relationships among different types of agentic processes in interaction with specific social contexts. This position corresponds with a fundamental postulate of the SIFT and is also compatible with developmental contextualism. As noted, developmental contextualism emerged out of psychology to account for agency in relation to structure, and is used by some psychologists to develop more complex models of human behavior.[7] We can see here a common ground between cutting-edge research in both psychology and sociology in locating potentialities for agency within social structures.

Objections to the Concept of Agency

Thus far in this chapter, we noted some sociologist's objections to the concept of agency as well as some psychologist's objections to the concept of structure. Before proceeding with our elaboration of contextual identity-based agency, it is helpful to backtrack and review some earlier objections to the concept of agency in favor of structural influences, including (meta)physical, political, economic, and cultural ones. As we see, from a number of quarters there have been objections to the various theories of agency offered over time. After reviewing each objection, we provide our response based on the SIFT.

Philosophers have tended to emphasize the problem of associating agency with free will, objecting to the idea that humans can act independently of the causal chain of events that have driven the physics of the universe for time immemorial. These concerns have been echoed in psychology, especially among behaviorists (with their stimulus–response theory) and neuropsychologists (with their study of neural structures). We would argue, however, that the possibility that physics-based causal chains of action determine human behaviors does not preclude the possibility that people differ in their levels of agency. In fact, the possibility that people's varying agentic capacities are determined by prior causal factors (conditioned by prior stimuli or made possible in the first place by certain neural pathways) does not mean that we will not find that people vary in their degrees of proactivity or that people cannot learn to be more proactive in certain contexts.

Thus, we are not contesting these basic philosophical arguments about free will vs. determinism. Furthermore, delving into these arguments would divert our attention from our primary task. Instead, we are interested in differences in people's observed abilities to direct their behaviors in planful and purposeful ways in certain contexts, regardless of the causal source of this ability. For example, as noted in Chapter 1, the basic assumption in the self-efficacy literature is that people's *beliefs* about their abilities to influence future events affects whether they will actually attempt to do so. Still, there are other objections to the idea that people can act independently of social-structural and other influences, so we will briefly discuss these in turn.

Political Objections

Objections about formulations of human agency can be found in the identity-politics approaches and more general political economy approaches. In the identity-politics approach, the emphasis is on social identities, oppression, and privilege. At the individual level, some people must cope with multiple forms of oppression as certain identities "intersect" (e.g., poor, Black, female) and others must manage hybrid identities (e.g., Asian American). Although this is an interesting and useful area of study, the focus is on social-identity management and not the development of the three levels of identity necessary to understand the complexities and nuances of identity formation. At the same time, there is hostility in this approach to anything that smacks of "essentialism," including theories of self-development and identity formation, rendering this approach of little use for present purposes.[8] In other words, our response to this approach is that it is excessively structural because the importance of psychological processes is dismissed, reintroducing the black box problem.

Turning to a second political approach, many sociologists have argued throughout the history of the discipline that political power relations and poor economic opportunities can make the exercise of personal agency difficult, if not impossible, especially for people from lower socio-economic and otherwise disadvantaged backgrounds. More recently, this position has been updated with arguments that theories of agency can naïvely serve the more ruthless economic consequences of *neoliberalism* by implicitly encouraging young people to conform to alienating conditions.[9] The concern is that if people are believed to be capable of unconstrained agency they can then be "blamed" for their poor economic prospects, which may be beyond their control. For instance, in capitalist societies a certain amount of unemployment is "structural" (i.e., government policies can keep unemployment rates at higher levels intended to keep wages low). In addition, some sociologists have also argued that playing up the importance of agency is a morally reprehensible thing to do, since it can encourage people to mindlessly seek employment that is exploitive and alienating.

Our response to these objections is that although both of these problems—victim blaming and oppression—are serious, the evidence against an extreme structuralist position in many developmental contexts is mounting, and more nuanced and contextually specific evidence is emerging, especially in accounting for outcomes that do not specifically involve social-class relations (e.g., why there are different life-course outcomes among young people from the same social class backgrounds). This evidence points to a more complex structure–agency position that helps us to understand the range of identity formation processes and outcomes in the variety of late-modern social contexts among the entire socioeconomic spectrum. This evidence goes beyond a simplistic opposition between "society makes them fail" (i.e., the belief that causation is all structural) and "it's all their fault if they don't succeed" (i.e., the conviction that causation is all agency), as this dichotomy is sometimes commonly expressed.

The more nuanced approaches to the structure–agency dichotomy point to the importance of context-specific resources in societies where many social roles and statuses are no longer strictly ascribed and where opportunities for various lifestyle choices and life-course outcomes exist (see Chapters 2 and 3). The decline in identity ascription by its very nature requires many people to structure their own lives in certain ways, and the resulting individualization of the life course requires forms of identity-based agency. For example, in late-modern societies most occupations are less likely to be passed from one generation to the next, so each generation must take up its own planning process. In some cases, this planning can result in forms of upward social mobility that were not possible in the past. Box 5.1 presents an example of differences in educational opportunity structures in two countries that highlights the potential role of agency in upward mobility.

BOX 5.1 DIFFERENCES IN EDUCATIONAL OPPORTUNITIES AND THE ROLE OF AGENCY

Structural barriers to upward social mobility clearly differ from country to country, with more opportunities in some countries than others. This appears to be the case in Canada in comparison with its mother country, the UK, with respect to social class differences in educational attainment. The educational prospects of Canadians from the least affluent segment of society have clearly improved over the past several decades, as they have in some other countries.[10] Consequently, the gap between the rich and poor in educational attainment has narrowed: although about half (46 percent) of children from families in the highest income quartile attend universities, a quarter (25 percent) of those from the lowest quartile do so as well.

In contrast, in the UK, only 9 percent of those from the lowest income quartile attend university compared to 46 percent of those from the highest quartile. In comparing cohorts born in the late 1970s with those born in 1958, the wealthiest quartile increased its university completion rate from 20 percent to 46 percent, while the poorest quartile increased its completion rate from 6 percent to only 9 percent over the same period.[11] Comparing the British figures with the Canadian ones, those in the poorest quartile in Canada are about three times more likely to attend university than their counterparts in England. Based on these figures, social class advantage appears to have been more completely preserved intergenerationally in one country than the other.

Moreover, what appears to be a clear "class issue" in Britain is not necessarily one in Canada. The 21 percent gap in university attendance is still a concern in Canada, but research reveals that it is not necessarily a class issue so much as a matter of the intangible "educational capital" that parents transfer to their children. That is, an examination of the family background influences of those who attend Canadian universities finds that parental income largely "washes out" when these influences are taken into account. For instance, one study reports that in comparing the university participation rates of those from the lowest income quartile with those from the highest income quartile backgrounds, noneconomic factors explain 84 percent of the gap (reading abilities, school grades, parental influences, and high school quality).[12] Financial constraints (such as tuition costs) account for only 12 percent of this gap (while parents' educational level accounts for twice as much). Other Canadian research confirms that parental education level—and not income—is the strongest predictor of university attendance, with each year of parental university education increasing the likelihood by about five percentage points that a child will attend university.[13] According to this research, holding income constant, if their parents have just a high school education, in the early 2000s the likelihood of young men attending university was 29 percent, while for young women it was 37 percent. However, this probability jumped to 53 percent and 65 percent, respectively, if at least one parent had some university education.

An explanation for these findings is that parents with higher educations can give more appropriate advice and information and act as intellectual and emotional role models. Thus, children with more educated parents are more likely to grow up seeing higher education as part of who they are—their identity—and to not feel that the university environment is a foreign or hostile one to them. In other words, university-educated parents have more identity-based agentic resources to pass onto their children that are relevant to the university context, so their children are more likely to have broader identity horizons (discussed further in Chapter 8).

Passing through or penetrating a given structural barrier requires that the person doing so understands the social-identity dynamics by which people are judged based on "who they are." For example, it has been long established in sociology that each social class or status group has its own symbolic codes in terms of language, attitudes, and habits.[14] Learning and managing new codes requires an ability to properly manage identities and appropriately present oneself in those new contexts. Additionally, it is crucial for the person to have a working knowledge of the contents of identities in differing situations for various audiences; that is, an understanding of role expectations and how to meet them.

Current prospects for upward social-class mobility in some societies provide an example of this last point. Changes in the educational requirements for entry into the labor force in various countries mean that for some young people the education-to-work transition is also a social-class transition of upward mobility. A particularly difficult form of mobility is from the working class to the middle class (e.g., from blue collar work prospects as a child to white collar roles as an adult). Adjusting to the middle class can pose difficulties in terms of the need to manage deeply ingrained behavior and language patterns, especially in the face of middle-class prejudices based on negative stereotypes about "working class" behaviors.[15] Those who change social classes must learn many things as adults that are taken for granted by those whose primary socialization prepared them for their adult lives. Those who begin new lives in different social contexts are acutely aware of many things that are taken for granted by those who have only known that one way of living. Indeed, late-modern societies are producing more people who have experienced *contradictory class-locations*[16] and bi-cultural dislocations.[17] As these have become mass phenomena, sociologists have attempted to understand these new experiences. At the same time, those who are unable or unwilling to undertake status or class transitions need to be better understood, especially when they appear to be "self-handicapping" or when their significant others hold them back by threatening to stigmatize or ostracize them. We can understand these latter cases in terms of identity horizons, or their equivalent, namely, how broadly or narrowly the person conceptualizes his or her future prospects in terms of a social radius.

The developmental contextual model helps us to understand these circumstances. In late modernity, although societies continue to present barriers associated with social class and other forms of disadvantage, in some societies educational institutions can be open enough in certain respects for some people to overcome those barriers by adapting their agentic efforts to compatible contexts. In other words, countries vary in terms of the role played by education in intergeneration inequalities.[18] Nevertheless, certain contexts can adversely affect the well-being of some people, as in the case of the forms of mentally disabling stress experienced among university students who are mismatched with that learning environment.[19] Even so, research shows that those with more personal resources fare much better even in these contexts.

In clarifying which agentic capacities are most useful in context-transition and contradictory-location management, this line of research has the potential to help young people improve their life chances, including the economically and socially disadvantaged. In particular, this knowledge should be useful to those who do not have the benefit of an affluent background, and/or have parents who do not know how to pass on more intangible resources, such as effective impression management in higher-educational contexts. In advocating the exercise of agency, therefore, the intention behind this research is not to increase existing social-class advantage, or advocate some sort of *neoliberal* or Machiavellian agenda, but rather to help all young people better negotiate the confusing transitions in late-modern societies, including those young people who are without birthright or other socio-economic advantages. For those sociologists who are skeptical of the use of agency or other psychological concepts involving personal strengths, we remind them that those from disadvantaged backgrounds need to learn how to identify and mobilize their internal potentials if they are to improve their life chances, regardless of the type of society in which they live (e.g., capitalist or socialist). Structural changes that simply place people in positions for which they are ill equipped are not viable solutions.

Nonetheless, it is also the case that in many regions and countries, even where there are opportunities for upward mobility, the non-ascriptive opportunity structures have not adequately replaced the ascriptive structures, leaving many people from less advantaged backgrounds floundering in the face of diminished material and emotional life chances. The diminished normative and opportunity structures in these societies are a concern because they can make identity formation far more complex and precarious, sequestering young people from mainstream society—socially excluding them—for longer periods than is desired by many of those young people. Still, in some countries the job opportunity structures are so poor in general that the viability of any attempts to exercise agency is extremely limited.[20]

While certain structural changes should still be our goal if we are to improve the life chances of the disadvantaged, and we must continue to identify structures that discriminate against people in harmful ways, structures are slow to change. In the meantime, for the sake of those facing current circumstances, especially late-modern ones, we need to learn how to help people now, so they can successfully "penetrate" structures that might otherwise constitute barriers for them. Our position resonates with conceptualizations of agency as "bounded" by a person's specific circumstances and opportunities rather than with the idea that choices are merely structured.[21]

We have developed a way of estimating the extent of these structural disadvantages in conjunction with the extent of agentic disadvantages. With these estimates, we can gain a better sense of the scope of the problems different types of people face in penetrating structural barriers. It is a tenet of the SIFT that young people need a repertoire of psychological and sociological resources to manage various transitions and diverse contexts in late-modern societies, and that those without these resources face the risk of social and economic exclusion. To illustrate this tenet, two sets of resources—structural and agentic—are cross-tabulated in figure 5.1, providing an algorithm for estimating these risks. Structural resources include parental affluence, ethnic group, and social capital networks, while agentic resources include mental health, IQ and the various ego/self capacities discussed thus far in this book.

This typology is useful in evaluating various risks and benefits in both the general and disadvantaged populations. To illustrate the algorithm in a general application, in many Western countries about 20 percent of the population lives below the poverty level—a structural disadvantage associated with various risks (leaving 80% above the poverty line). Additionally, in many countries, at any one time some 20 percent of the population struggles with some sort of psychiatric problem or disorder, rendering them low in agency (leaving 80% higher in agency). Entering these probabilities into the respective cells in figure 5.1, at any given time only about two thirds of the population would be estimated to have "sufficient" structural and agentic resources for "risk-free" functioning (.80 [above the poverty line] x .80 [with higher levels of agency] = .64, or 64%, for the +/+ cell). The remaining one third of the population lacks one or both of these crucial resources (the two low/high cells have 16% probabilities [.80 x .20], and the low/low cell has a 4% probability [.20 x .20]).

To show how this typology would work for a disadvantaged community, such as an impoverished inner city area, the proportion of the population inadequately resourced can be similarly identified. For example, if the poverty rate is 40 percent for the area and the poor mental health rate is 40 percent (e.g., as a result of a local culture of heavy drug use), the estimate would be that only about one third of the population is adequately resourced (.6 x .6 = .36, or 36%). Young people growing up in such areas would thus be at compounded risks of low structure and poor mental health. In addition to providing a means of estimating population risks, this typology reminds us that young people are not homogeneous in their resource needs and that theories and policies need to take this into account.

In sum, faced with the challenges endemic to late-modern societies, young people more than ever need a repertoire of personal, social, and economic resources

		Agentic Resources	
		High/Present	Low/Absent
Structural Resources	High/Present	++	−/+
	Low/Absent	+/−	−/−

FIGURE 5.1 A model of structural and agentic resources and an algorithm of their risks/benefits.

to manage various transitions and diverse contexts. It is well established that those without adequate structural resources face greater risks for social and economic exclusion. But those without agentic resources are also at increased risk, even if they have structural advantages, including the risk of diminished wellbeing, so an exclusive focus on structural solutions does little for these people *now, in the present*.

Feminist Objections

As in other areas of the social sciences, the self and identity literature is replete with a variety of claims that existing theories are male-biased and only apply to contemporary Western societies. In the present section, we deal with the claim that identity formation theories emphasizing agency are androcentric; in the next section, we respond to the charge that they are Eurocentric.

Some academic feminists claim that the processes governing women's identity formation are different than those governing men's, and that such processes have not been adequately researched. Hence, claims are made regarding differences "in kind," not "in degree," between men and women; specifically, that entirely different processes are involved in male and female identity formation rather than different degrees of the same processes.

Popular among some feminist scholars is the so-called "relational model."[22] Based on this model, Judith Jordan criticizes the work done in the psychology of self in the following passage:

> In traditional Western psychological theories of development, the "self" has long been viewed as the primary reality and unit of study. Typically, the self has been seen as separated from its context, a bounded, contained entity that has both object and subject qualities. Clinical and developmental theories generally have emphasized the growth of an autonomous, individuated self. Increasing self-control, a sense of self as origin of action and intentions, an increasing capacity to use abstract logic, and a movement toward self-sufficiency characterize the maturation of the ideal Western self.[23]

Jordan believes that the above describes a "male" model of development that does not apply very well to women. She believes that the idea of a "relational self" better characterizes the psychology of women. Jordan argues that this *feminist relational model* emphasizes the connections that women have with others, which she believes are uniquely different from the connections men make with others. Men, she believes, construct boundaries that protect and define themselves. In contrast, she claims that women are more contextual and intersubjective in their relations with others, creating more flexible and fluid interpersonal boundaries. Thus, she sees women as more embedded in context, more concerned with those in their immediate presence, and more able to establish dynamically mutual relationships. Relational theorists believe, therefore, that women are more concerned with care-taking and the empowerment of others, whereas men are more concerned with exercising such agentic capacities as engaging in power-based dominance patterns, thinking about abstract and universal principles, and exercising self-empowerment.

However, other researchers warn that we must be careful in postulating differences "in kind" in this area of research. For example, one group of researchers analyzed this problem and concluded that:

> Amid the eagerness to understand and measure identity development, researchers may be culpable of underestimating the complexity of the identity process. On the surface there do appear to be gender-specific patterns of identity development. However, in reality, these differences may be most accurately described in terms of nuances rather than exaggerated terms of dichotomous gender differences.[24]

Thus, although the feminist relational model seems to have some merit, versions such as Jordan's commit the error of dichotomizing and stereotyping male and female patterns of identity development. At the same time, many "pop" psychologists promote dichotomous conceptions of gender differences. However, when these ideas are scrutinized from a social scientific point of view, the limitations of such notions become clearer.[25] When reading this literature we are asked to take seriously the proposition that, in general, women are more *other-oriented*, whereas, in general, men are more *self-oriented* and more likely to be interpersonal opportunists. And after reading and rereading such claims, the caveat "in general" gets read as "all," and the stereotype emerges. Consequently, there is little conceptual room left for understanding women who have supposedly agentic, masculine tendencies and for men who have supposedly relational, feminine tendencies. But, surely there are merits in both "connection" and "autonomy." Indeed, as we noted in Chapter 1, the first two principles of identity formation—integration and differentiation— emphasize both of these qualities as well as their interrelationships.

Additionally, a highly idealized state of being, such as "connection," may not always be very functional in the "real world" or be very representative of the population. For example, overly flexible self/ego boundaries can leave a person disorganized and open to manipulation in late-modern contexts. To the extent that this happens and contributes to the formation of an unformulated sense of identity, people may simply drift along through life, not attending very well to their own needs for security and survival, let alone the needs of others.

As we have been at pains to express, the key to functional identity formation appears to be a *balance* between concerns with self and concerns with others, a point also made by others, as with optimal distinctiveness theory (see box 1.2). Both women and men with a well-developed relational side, but not a well-developed agentic side, are likely to be open to exploitation by others. At the same time, women and men with a well-developed agentic side, but without a relational side are likely prone to a variety of narcissistic excesses and exploitive tendencies, as discussed in the preceding chapter on moral reasoning.

Finally, when the claims of the relational model have been put to empirical tests by social-scientific standards, there is little evidence for stark differences between the identity formation of men and women in late-modern societies, as we see in Chapter 8 where we examine contextual differences. In the meantime, it is worth pointing to one longitudinal study of women's identity formation that explicitly addressed the feminist relational model, which concluded:[26]

> Identity resides at the intersection of competence and connection: this is where people feel most fully themselves—and are most recognized by others as being who they are. Adult crises in identity among these women have most often involved the struggle to keep experience of competence and connection in balance. . . . All women want a sense of competence and a sense of connection. . . . How to go about achieving them is often the enigma. Choice is a slippery process, as is self-knowledge. To "know what one wants for oneself" is not an easy matter and is often a lifelong quest. Freedom is liberating, but it can also be terrifying.[27]

Objections Based on Cross-Cultural Research

The feminist perspective on the "relational self" has parallels in other dichotomous conceptions, including those that contrast Western and Eastern (or Asian) cultures. In this case, a distinction has been drawn between the *independent self*, proposed to be characteristic of Western societies, and the *interdependent self*, claimed to characterize Eastern societies.[28]

Unlike the feminist binary claims regarding gender differences in the self and identity, the originators of these concepts, Hazel Markus and Shinobu Kitayama, argue that cultural differences in the nature of the self are a "matter of degree" and not a "difference in kind." Accordingly, the two types of "self" represent possible ways that people reflexively *construe* themselves in relation to others. In other words, this is a theory of *self-construals* that form the *self-schema* of interpersonal relationships.

This cultural model proposes that the independent self-schema involves a sense of autonomy and separateness from others, and the right to choose the duties and obligations that will form the basis of allegiances with others. The self is perceived as maintaining a unitary core and as being, more or less, constant.

The interdependent self-schema, in contrast, is more likely to be found in the more duty-bound cultures of Asia, in premodern Western societies, and to some extent in more family-oriented modern Western cultures.[29] Here the self is defined as more context-specific, relationship bound, and part of a complex set of duties and obligations. While an interdependent self may hold personal beliefs, values, and desires, those personal preferences are subordinate to these complex duties and obligations. In other words, the person believes that these personal preferences must be controlled and often inhibited if the self is to maintain connection.[30]

Markus and Kitayama review a substantial amount of literature documenting the cognitive, emotional, and motivational consequences of the above two self-construals. As one would expect, those using an interdependent-self construal are more likely to process self-relevant information in a situationally specific manner and be attentive to the expectations and needs of others. For example, in a situation requiring decisions about the distribution of property, interdependent self-construals consider obligations not to exclude the other in the distribution. Conversely, independent self-construals focus on the acquisition rights of the individual over the collective. It follows that the interdependent self is more likely to experience and utilize "other-focused" emotions and cognitive operations, such as empathy, sympathy, and shame, and to identify these feelings as properties of context and relationship with the other. Finally, those with the interdependent-self construal understand their own motives and goals (i.e., their sense of *agency*) in the context of accommodating to or at least cooperating with others, with the assumption that others understand their own motives and desires in a similar fashion. In contrast, the independent self perceives others and contexts as phenomena to be avoided, manipulated, or controlled if the self is to be fulfilled—duties and obligations are seen as optional matters of individual choice.

In conceptualizing the above two dimensions of self-construal as ideal types and in noting how they function in processing self-salient information, the work of Markus and Kitayama is an important contribution to the self and identity literature. At the same time, other researchers warn us not to over-extend these concepts or reduce them to cultural stereotypes.[31] The importance of this warning has been borne out by empirical research. For example, the empirical measurement of the general concepts individualism–collectivism has not been very successful, and the independent–interdependent self-construals is a subset of these concepts. In addition, a large-scale, multi-method study of an array of empirical measures concluded that numerous problems exist with these concepts in terms of cross-cultural validity.[32]

At the same time, and consistent with developmental contextualism, the manifestations of self-construals vary within cultures and within individuals in those cultures. That is, there are differences within Eastern cultures just as there are in Western cultures (e.g., between southern and northern European cultures), and people within each culture can be found to represent the range from interdependent to independent. Moreover, individual differences appear to be based on developmental factors in some contexts. For example, in contemporary Japanese society, research has found that interdependent self-schemas are passively acquired in late childhood, actively internalized in adolescence, and then rearranged into more independent self-schemas in adulthood (presumably as part of the formation of proactive adult identities that are now functional in contemporary Japanese society).[33]

Other research in Japan reports that in addition to the traditional collectivist orientation of self-development and identity formation, there is an emerging form of *individualistic collectivism*, where people value both individualism and collectivism.[34] Kazumi Sugimura and Shinichi Mizokami are researching the possibility that "adolescents following this pattern project their own needs and interests onto society (i.e., "inside-out dynamics") rather than adapting to the society's expectations (i.e., "outside-in dynamics"), an adaptation that once was highly valued in Japan."[35] Sugimura and Mizokami also report that the Eriksonian model has been generally validated in research on Japanese young people over the past three decades. Thus, the benefits of proactivity in identity formation have been replicated, as have the drawbacks of inactivity. Overall, however, identity explorations appear to be less extensive among Japanese youth, with about half exercising *passive autonomy*—"weak or vague identity exploration, refraining from strong self-expression and avoiding differentiating self from others, in addition to narrow exploration."[36] But, this type of identity formation is not necessarily inactive; instead, it "fits with the demands of a cultural context emphasizing emotional bonds between self and others, such as attuning to other people's expectations and maintaining harmonious relationships with others."[37]

Thus, the integration–differentiation balance in Japan is complex as a developmental task, and seems to be a new *identity domain* for Japanese youth. Indeed, the primary cross-cultural differences in identity formation appear to involve the importance, or salience, of various domains. In this case, among Japanese youth, the domains of politics and religion have lower salience as areas of exploration and commitment, perhaps because of the strong Buddhist influence there. That is, Buddhism differs from many other religions in that it provides a ready-made philosophy in which questioning reality is an essential part of spirituality. Accordingly, when young people are socialized into this way of thinking, following its principles does not require proactivity on their part. At the same time, resolving self–other, individual–group issues receives more attention in Japan as a result of its particular "historical moment"[38] in which traditional collectivist norms are being merged with modern individualist ones (see box 5.2 for more about the changes in Japanese society that are affecting identity formation there). Many of those forming their identities in this context are seeking new ways to balance their relationships with their accomplishments, exercising agency in both aspects of their lives, a situation that is complicated in a culture where self-criticism has traditionally been more valued than self-esteem (see box 5.3 for more about the cultural relativity of the value placed on self-esteem). It is also possible that there is a greater distinction experienced among Japanese youth between their public and private selves, just as differences are postulated to exist between the role self and real self among Westerners (see box 3.2). If this is the case, Japanese youth may be more attuned to public performances that conform to traditional collectivist norms, whereas their private lives and subjective experiences are more influenced by their personal constructions of the self.[39] Following this logic, and what we know about trends in the West, it may be the case that the discrepancy between the role self and real self is increasing in countries like Japan, but is decreasing in Western countries, with the latter more concerned about a form of authenticity where there is less discrepancy between the role self and real self.

BOX 5.2 RECENT CHANGES IN JAPANESE SOCIETY AFFECTING IDENTITY FORMATION

Two Japanese researchers, Kazumi Sugimura and Shinichi Mizokami, recently provided a review of the research on identity formation in Japan, evaluating the extent to which the Eriksonian model fits there.[40] In general, it does fit, although some of the content areas or domains appear to differ in importance. As noted in the text, the tradition of collectivism in Japan still influences the importance people place on interpersonal relations for their sense of identity, even among those who are seeking more individualistic identity-formation resolutions.

A number of economic developments have undermined Japanese collectivism, however. As recently as the 1980s, employment prospects were far less individualized than is the case today. Following a severe recession in the early 1990s, work opportunities have been relatively poor in Japan, especially for young people. For all workers, there has been a decline in the tradition of life-long employment with one company or organization. Part-time employment is now common and employee's performance is more closely monitored. The reduced demand for youth labor has led to greatly increased enrollments in universities. In the past, competition to enter the best universities was fierce, as it still is, but the prestige of the university attended was more important than what was learned once admitted. Corporations would recruit from universities, reducing the amount of identity exploration necessary to find suitable employment. However, at the less prestigious universities, many students are poorly motivated academically, while at the same time these universities are being pressured by governments to provide more instrumental job preparation.

For previous generations, then, the formation of occupational identities did not require as much individual effort because the education-to-work transition was highly normed. However, in the past 25 years, Japanese education systems have changed along with the education-to-work transition and subsequent employment conditions.

This situation has led Japanese researchers to examine the formation of occupational identities more carefully. It appears that this identity domain becomes salient earlier in life for many Japanese than in the past and is more individualized. One line of research treats *educational identity* as a domain, and operationalizes the range of inactive to proactive stances that can be taken. This research finds that many Japanese students have a difficult time developing an individualized identity in the areas of education and occupation in a society that traditionally highly structured people's transitions, and which rendered "choice" as the outcome of early educational competitions to get into the right schools. Some young people find this poorly normed, individualized situation so intolerable that they go through a period of extreme social withdrawal, often never leaving their parents' house. They are referred to as *hikikomori*.[41]

BOX 5.3   IS THE VALUE PLACED ON SELF-ESTEEM PART OF AN AMERICAN OBSESSION?

The self-development literature is vulnerable to the criticism of ethnocentrism. Most of the research on self-development, and especially self-esteem, has been conducted on adolescents in the U.S., largely on White, middle-class adolescents. One potential bias in this literature has had some serious repercussions. The initial research raised great academic concerns and public anxieties that adolescent females have self-esteem problems. However, more recent research suggests these findings apply mainly to White females. One possible reason is that this segment of the American population is particularly prone to modeling its behaviors on advertisements portraying unrealistic standards of beauty and sexuality.

More recent research examined various American ethnic groups, finding that Black adolescents have higher self-esteem than their White counterparts. In turn, both of these groups have been found to have higher self-esteem than Latinos, Asian Americans, and Native Americans. Of particular note, given the early anxieties about female adolescents, are the findings that Black females are far more satisfied with their body image than are White females—a 70 percent vs. 10 percent satisfaction rate. This is in part because being "overweight" is more acceptable among African Americans.[42]

So, is the anxiety about nurturing self-esteem among young people part of a more general American obsession about *the individual* (see box 2.1)? Certainly we can see this concern in American schools, where it has been assumed that the more young people value themselves, the better they will do academically and socially. Not only has this assumption about the *inoculation effects* of self-esteem not been borne out (see Chapter 8), but also the research shows that the U.S. does stand out from other Western countries with this concern about self-esteem—perhaps because of its high level of individualism—and that there is a gap between the U.S. and other Western countries in terms of the value placed on adolescent self-esteem. This gap is even greater in comparison with non-Western countries, such as Japan, where self-criticism is valued over self-esteem as a sign of character.[43]

We return to the issue of cultural differences in proactivity in the next chapter, where we consider adaptations to late-modernity as it affected the West, and as we have seen, increasingly the East. We also examine cultural differences in identity formation below in Chapter 8.

Conclusion: Agentic Identities

Approaches to understanding human agency have varied dramatically. Often the conclusions reached reflect the disciplinary assumptions of the researcher, with philosophers arriving at one set of conclusions regarding free will, psychologists arriving at another concerning agency, and sociologists reaching yet another conclusion in terms of the effects of social structure on individual opportunities. At the same time, debates have emerged within these disciplines regarding the nature and role of "agency" following the assumptions of various theorists with respect to politics, feminism, and culture. This situation is changing as more scholars are recognizing the limitations of single-cause explanations and the need for nuanced, contextually based formulations of structure, agency, and the relationship between the two where various structure–agency interactions take place. These interactions include those studied by developmental contextualists (e.g., the *goodness of fit*; discussed in Part III) and those examined by sociologists in terms of how people with certain resources can penetrate social structures, as in social class mobility. The more general concept of domain-specific proactivity proposed by the SIFT appears to be a more apt approach for understanding the role of agency in identity formation; additionally, it is not as burdened with a history of varying definitions and disciplinary assumptions.

6

IDENTITY CAPITAL

Strategic Adaptions to Late-Modern Societies

"The human being is in the most literal sense a political animal, not merely a gregarious animal, but an animal which can individuate itself only in the midst of society."

Karl Marx[1]

The Identity Capital Model (ICM) provides a perspective with which social scientists can study the ways in which people can strategically manage the various elements of their ego-, personal-, and social- identities. Strategic management of these identities involves developing, managing, and executing a "portfolio" of resources suitable to various institutional contexts, such as the labor force—and more generally, adulthood—in a given society. The basic premise of the ICM is that certain context-specific resources are particularly important in societies where many roles and statuses are no longer strictly ascribed (e.g., where occupations are less likely to be passed from one generation to the next), and there is little normative structure to replace the ascriptive processes. As described earlier, late-modern societies are of this type. There is reason for concern with respect to these societies, because their weak normative structures can make identity formation more complex and the passage to a functional adulthood more precarious, even unwelcoming.

To address these conditions found in late-modern societies, the ICM adopts an integrated and interdisciplinary social-psychological framework based on the following bodies of work that date back to the early social sciences: symbolic interactionist models of identity management techniques in the presentation of self (Chapter 1), sociological conceptions of late-modernity (Chapter 2), and developmental psychology approaches to identity formation (especially Erikson's work, throughout the preceding chapters):

From symbolic interactionism, the ICM embraces the pragmatist assumption (dating back to William James) that people are meaning seeking, problem solving, and goal oriented. People can use these capacities to adapt to their environments in practical ways that overcome obstacles and take advantage of opportunities.[2]

Following late-modernist theory, the ICM adopts the assumption that traditional normative structures have diminished (cf. Durkheim's concept of *anomie*), requiring people to individualize their identities in the face of certain risks and opportunities.

The Eriksonian influence is evident in the assumption that people seek to resolve conflicts in their lives in growth-producing ways that are meaningful to them as they make their way through the periods of life (stages) that are associated with specific, role-based societal demands. In adulthood, these demands include assuming responsible and productive roles, developing intimate relationships, and making contributions to a community, local or otherwise.

Origins of the Identity Capital Model

The ICM owes its origins in part to Côté's[3] own lived experiences of moving among various cultural contexts and through certain social structural barriers, especially the experience of moving from the working class (as a factory worker) in a small town to the middle class (as a professional academic) in a large city. As discussed in the preceding chapter, making the transition from one social class context to another often requires "penetrating" structural barriers, and in this case requires that the person doing so understands the social dynamics by which people from out-groups are judged on the basis of language, attitudes, and habits, or what some sociologists call *cultural capital*. Learning and exhibiting new forms of cultural capital requires certain cognitive and impression management skills, including the ego-synthetic and ego-executive skills that Erikson argued are an important basis of agency. As discussed in the following, cultural capital can be considered a part of identity capital when it is combined with other forms of capital (or resources) to negotiate passage through various "identity markets."

In addition to the perspectives noted in the preceding section, the ICM is also influenced by developmental contextualism.[4] In an early version of the ICM, the Integrated Paradigm of Student Development was developed and empirically tested.[5] This model of student development proposes that students' own personal efforts can help them to transcend or overcome structural barriers through specific forms of active educational involvements. In late modernity, although societies continue to present barriers associated with social class and other forms of disadvantage, institutions like universities can be open enough in certain respects for some people to overcome those barriers by adapting their developmental efforts to compatible contexts.

As box 5.1 illustrates, significant changes have taken place over the past few decades in countries like Canada with respect to the permeability of some structural barriers. Research in Canada consistently finds that parental educational level—and not income—is the strongest predictor of university attendance. Furthermore, tracked over time, there has been a significant increase in university attendance among first-generation university students (i.e., students who are the first in their family line to attend). For example, between 1986 and 2009, the percentage of Canadian-born first-generation university graduates aged 25 to 39 increased from 12 percent to 23 percent, compared with increases from 44.7 percent to 55.8 percent for those with at least one parent who had a university degree.[6]

In spite of these improvements in access, however, the contemporary university setting in many countries still constitutes a "middle-class experience."[7] Most students have parents whose occupations range from the lower-middle-class service occupations through to the upper-middle class professional ones, and most professors have middle-class or higher backgrounds. This relative homogeneity raises several questions of interest for those who want to learn how to better help those from disadvantaged backgrounds:

1. Why do students of similar family origins have different educational and occupational outcomes (i.e., outcomes are apparently not totally determined by family-based social-structural opportunities, so what else explains these outcomes)?
2. What would we recommend to *our own children* when counseling them on strategies to maximize their life chances via educational routes to adulthood?
3. What can we learn from those who are most successful in capitalizing on their educational opportunities?

The first question raises the issue of individual differences, a concept that is very familiar to psychologists but somewhat foreign to sociologists. Because social class differences are minimized in the university context, thereby constraining the influence of structural factors, the study of university students allows us to better examine *individual variations* in the influence of psychological factors like agency. Based on the assumption that the "educational-status competitions" among the social classes are largely undertaken at the primary and secondary levels, even in societies where class barriers are not obvious, middle-class students are in effect in competition with each other at the university level, so it is important to examine other variables relevant to this intra-class competition.

The second question brings the issue of educational outcomes down to earth for academics who might otherwise be content to deal with other people's lives as abstractions. For example, we personally know some educational specialists who are policy advocates of de-streaming in secondary schools—a policy in which students of all backgrounds and ability levels are put in the same classrooms—to actually send *their own children* to private schools so they get a "better" education and thus get ahead in the status competition associated with the education-to-work transition.

Accordingly, one intention with the ICM is to bring the issues of "dis/advantage" to a more pragmatic level where the concern is for the ultimate welfare of *all* individual students, not categories of students defined by background. In this way, the ICM should be helpful to parents with offspring to advise, as well as to academics who are asked by young people facing the university–work transition what is best for them to do. Both parents and social scientists need to be able to say something to young people more specific and definite than offering a critique of late-modern educational systems or pointing out the complexities of the structure–agency debate.

Finally, the third question leads to the program of research undertaken to develop and test the ICM. After learning what gives different types of people currently involved in the status-competition context of education-to-work transitions advantages or disadvantages, we should be in a position to recommend to others what works and what does not work. Importantly, this status competition is not necessarily a *zero-sum game*, with the exception of those who are aiming to gain access to specific occupations, such as medicine, where few people receive training in relation to the numbers seeking them. Rather, the intention is to understand how people can best mobilize their own personal resources so that they find their most suitable person-context fits. In many cases, these best fits are not with the high-status professional occupations and knowing this information can be a valuable piece of information for people who might otherwise spend considerable time and effort pursuing a goal that is unsuitable for them, even if their parents hold some sort of professional status. Indeed, some people are better off taking themselves out of these status competitions because their best-fit occupation may be found elsewhere (e.g., the trades, fine arts, or crafts). We thus stress that the ICM does not advocate that people mindlessly pursue materialist goals, or fit themselves into careers that are alienating and/or exploitative.

Fundamental Assumptions of the Identity Capital Model

As noted earlier, the ICM approach to life-course transitions and functioning integrates (developmental) psychological and (late-modernist) sociological understandings of identity. Sociologically, it is based on the assumption that, as a result of global economic and political changes—most recently *neoliberal capitalist* ones—that have eroded traditional normative and community structures, the life course in late-modern (contemporary Western) societies has become more individualized. As noted in Chapter 2, the individualization process is a function of normative de-structuring processes: as a society undergoes reorganization, old norms become obsolete, often leaving many people to their own devices in making major life decisions, including finding communities within which to establish integrative bonds. Individualized life courses can involve lifestyles and values based on personal preferences and choices.[8] Accordingly, an emerging normative course of maturation in late-modern societies compels people to develop themselves as self-determining, independent "individuals," especially in terms of negotiating their own life courses (setting and achieving goals).

According to the ICM, the stances that can be taken toward an individualized life course can range from default individualization through developmental individualization. As noted in Chapter 5, default individualization involves following paths of least resistance and effort, where people "allow" decisions to be made for them as a result of their inaction; in turn, this lack of effort can lead to a deferred or passive formation of an adult identity and adult-community commitments. In contrast, developmental individualization refers to proactive and strategic approaches to personal growth and a life project, which can lead to finding a well-suited niche in an adult community. Conceptualizing variations in the default-developmental individualization continuum are useful in understanding both the range of agentic potentials and the variations in how active people can be in taking advantage of the potential benefits of "open" developmental contexts that facilitate the agentic penetration of structures, such as universities.

By explicitly taking into account agency—taking it out of the black box discussed in the preceding chapter—the ICM adopts a more nuanced view of structural barriers than do sociological approaches that emphasize structure without taking into account either the capacity for agency or person-context interactions that can occur in those structures. For example, with respect to potential person–context effects in higher educational settings, the ICM is sensitive to the possibility that these contexts can vary by institutional ethos, teaching philosophy, and so forth, and that within each setting there can be a variety of opportunities for self-exploration and self-development. A developmental-contextual prediction is that, regardless of social class origin or prior ability level, growth can take place if an individual finds an educational setting that is well suited to his or her characteristics. More specifically, individuals should be able to acquire identity capital if they find a university context developmentally appropriate to them, despite disadvantages associated with a less privileged background.

Additionally, the ICM recognizes that although the requirement to individualize their identities clearly presents potential benefits to young people, it also presents them with potential risks. While late-modern societies provide more freedom from traditional normative constraints (such as restrictive norms concerning sexual orientation), they often do little to help people overcome the obstacles associated with social class and other "older" structural barriers.

Thus, to ensure that the ICM is not misunderstood, it must be stressed that it is based on the late-modernist assumption that individualization involves *freedoms from* normative constraints and some identities that were in the past ascribed or stigmatized, not *freedoms to* pursue activities independent of systemic barriers such as social class disadvantage or racial and gender discrimination, even if some of these barriers are under assault in some countries (e.g., in Canada, same-sex marriages have been legal since 2004, a trend which is slowly spreading to other jurisdictions).

Moreover, the freedom to individualize has emerged because of *a relative lack of structure*, which can create serious challenges for some people, whereas persisting social barriers along class, race, and gender lines present *too much unwanted structure* for those placed at a disadvantage because of those barriers. Some specific deficits in normative structures include:

• diminished norms and ideologies (e.g., norms concerning what it means to be male or female [gender], conventions for establishing intimate relationships [marriage], and guidance for dealing with one's sexuality);
• disjunctive links among institutions (e.g., ambiguities and dead ends in the education-to-work transition); and
• de-structured social markers (e.g., community recognition of events like leaving home, securing employment, and establishing a family during the transition to adulthood).

What is vital in the late-modern context, then, are the resources that the individual can muster to deal with both the lack of normative structure *and* the residual burdens of older structural barriers. In opening up the "black box of agency" in its relation to structure, the ICM proposes that the personal resources acquired developmentally become important in late-modern contexts, particularly those psychological resources that can facilitate the agentic movement through, and negotiation with, various social contexts. In this sense, certain internal resources acquired at one point of development are postulated to enable subsequent agentic mastery of later tasks as required by specifically linked late-modern contexts. To cite a couple of examples, higher levels of ego strength associated with early task mastery can help the person undertake more challenging tasks that can lead to future benefits; a greater sense of purpose in life associated with task mastery can facilitate long-term planning, increasing the likelihood of accomplishing later higher-order personal and occupational goals. Box 6.1 provides an illustration of this growth-enhancing effect by applying the *Matthew effect* to identity formation.

BOX 6.1   THE MATTHEW EFFECT AND DELAYED ADULTHOOD

The developmental assumptions of the Identity Capital Model correspond with the Matthew effect.[9] Reflecting the wisdom of the ages, this term is taken from the New Testament (Matthew 25:29): "For to all those who have, more will be given, and they will have an abundance; but from those who have nothing, even what they have will be taken away." In essence, this passage is reflected in the adage "the rich get richer and the poor get poorer."

Applied to identity formation in a prolonged transition to adulthood, the Matthew effect predicts that those who are able to proactively resolve identity formation issues during their teens or early 20s may be able to move more deliberately into adulthood and reap more benefits from their adult identity. Conversely, those who do not have a strong beginning in their agency-based identity formation in their teens and early 20s may struggle throughout their adulthood with these issues and then miss out on the potential benefits derived from resolving them in a timely manner. Of course, a key factor is the extent to which adult roles are available to them and/or whether they have to forge them for themselves.

Still, the results from a variety of studies suggest that potential "late bloomers"—those who do not make sufficient progress with the identity issues by the time they are in their thirties—may suffer the most in terms of their emotional health and integration in the occupational system and social structure of their society.[10] As we see in Chapters 8 and 9, those who delay taking on adult roles in order to experience supposed benefits of "emerging adulthood" may encounter serious problems that require counseling—assuming they are affluent enough to afford it.[11]

Identity Capital Resources

As noted earlier, identity capital resources can be broadly categorized as both sociological and psychological. Sociological resources tend to be more tangible and psychological resources more intangible.

Tangible resources include: ascribed or conferred statuses derived from parents' social class/wealth/networks; the person's gender and ethnicity as related to specific *social capital* networks; and achieved or attained statuses such as the person's earned credentials, peer/professional networks, and other reputational markers. Tangible resources can also include the material possessions that constitute status symbols[12] and the demonstrable behavior patterns of the person that Erikson associated with ego-executive abilities, including impression management skills and social skills. For instance, charismatic people are especially advantaged in this respect, as are those who are good actors and role players. Box 6.2 illustrates how status-based identity displays have changed over time as the options available for doing so have changed.

BOX 6.2 IDENTITY DISPLAYS OVER TIME: THE DEMOCRATIZATION OF PERSONAL DISPLAYS

Several observers have commented upon the exercise of impression management as an identity capital skill that is useful for moving among diverse and sometime contradictory audiences. One researcher used the concept of identity capital to explain how material-culture objects can be used for impression management in projecting cultural and social status images. In traditional societies, only the wealthy had/have the material means for carefully constructed identity displays. In late-modernity, however, people can manipulate tangible resources such as clothes, jewelry, and automobiles to project the images appropriate to certain contexts, thereby using these resources as "passports into desired social, cultural, and institutional spheres."[13]

Similarly, the author of a blog wrote that the idea of identity capital is useful in understanding identity management on the Internet. She noted that

> The lack of hierarchical structure on the Internet minimizes the importance of how you [were] socialized (which ties into social, cultural, and human capital), [so that] the power of your thoughts, and your knowledge, and how it is presented, becomes more important than the amount of degrees you have hanging in your office, or the kind of car you drive, or the number of "clubs" you belong to.[14]

Intangible resources include capacities such as ego strengths, an internal locus of control, self-esteem, a sense of purpose in life, critical thinking abilities, cognitive reasoning abilities, social-perspective taking, and moral reasoning abilities, all of which can constitute context-specific elements of agency,[15] or what Erikson associated with ego-synthetic abilities. The common feature of intangible attributes is that they can afford the person the cognitive capacities with which to understand and negotiate the various obstacles and opportunities commonly encountered throughout the late-modern life course, with its decoupled and multifaceted transitions. Perspective-taking and moral-reasoning skills become relevant to identity formation in the ICM to the extent that they can facilitate integration into a wider social radius, which requires mutual perspective taking, and access to the benefits that this provides. In turn, these ego-synthetic capacities buttress the ego-executive abilities identified earlier as the tangible resources supporting strategic forms of identity maintenance.

The ICM also proposes that, optimally, people will combine their tangible and intangible resources to take advantage of, or compensate for, the institutional deficits of late modernity by making "identity investments" as they individualize. Such investments can involve a strategic development of "who one is" on the basis of "exchangeable" resources such as money, abilities, appearance, and interactional skills. Identity exchanges involve the mutual validation of actors in specific situations, as when for example, professors acknowledge the accomplishments and potential of a student in assigning good grades and writing letters of reference; that student in return might validate the professor's authority and competence through supportive and complimentary gestures.

Tangible resources can include parents' social class (in contexts where that is advantageous) and parents' financial assistance in role transitions and other opportunities.[16] Resources that can be strategically exchanged can also include gender, ethnicity, and other existing group memberships as well as agentic attributes, prior identity capital acquisitions, and levels of emotional and cognitive development. As argued in the following section, when all of these resources are viewed as a portfolio, they can be used to gain access to various "identity markets," including the transition to adulthood itself. A partial list of identity capital acquisitions that have been empirically found to result from these strategic exchanges during early adulthood includes adult-identity resolution, societal-identity resolution, salary and job satisfaction, desired personal development, and progress in one's life project.[17] Box 6.3 gives an example of what an identity capital portfolio might look like for "auditing" purposes.

BOX 6.3 THE IDENTITY CAPITAL PORTFOLIO AUDIT SHEET

Goals:

Occupation/Career
Marriage/Family
Societies/Organizations
Lifestyle/Other
Goal attainment to date in these areas

Resources

Tangible:	Intangible/Functional Capital:
Human Capital:	*Impression Management Skills:*
Degrees	Verbal abilities; dialect/accent
Certificates	Languages spoken
Awards	Public speaking (experience/ability)
Personal talents/abilities	Intelligence (cognitive/emotional)
Workplace skills	
Social Capital:	*Moral-Ethical Reasoning Abilities:*
Parent's education	Empathy
Parent's wealth	Perspective-taking
Relationship with parents conducive to intergenerational transfer	Broad social radius of experience
Peer networks	
Contextual (+/–):	*Agentic Capacities:*
Age	Self-esteem/self-efficacy
Appearance	Purpose in life
Race/ethnicity	Ego strength (self/impulse control)
Gender	Internal locus of control
Sexuality	Broad identity horizons/low levels of identity anxiety
	Contextual (+/–):
	Personality/character traits
	(Flexible) hybrid identities (e.g., ethnic; social class)

Finally, an optimal strategy for the acquisition of identity capital involves the utilization of existing resources to gain more resources—that is, to compound one's identity capital. Note, though, that the person does not have to be consciously aware that these strategies are being used, because strategic behavior can result from imitation and forms of cultural conditioning.[18] However, the more reflexive people are about their own thoughts and behavior, the more conscious these strategies will be. Over time, the gains made through these efforts can become resources for further exchange.[19]

In understanding how these intangible resources are developed and employed, it is important to first note that they can be developmental in terms of cognitive-structural/moral-ethical (Piaget/Kohlberg) and psychosocial (Freud/Erikson) capacities. Thus, it should be emphasized that the development and use of such resources needs to be understood in terms of how social environments influence them. Environments that expand people's social radii, such as the university and college, can contribute to, rather than inhibit, the growth and utilization of such intangible resources. Moreover, we believe that these resources have an inoculation quality in the sense that they can enable people to reflexively resist and/or push back on the social forces impinging upon them. In this way, individuals should be more likely to develop a sense of authorship over their own biographies, of taking responsibility for their life choices, and of creating for themselves a meaningful and satisfying life. Note that these tasks are central to the individualization process. Thus the notion of identity capital provides a way of theorizing agency for people confronted with the task of individualization, and it does so with the explicit use of established theoretical concepts that have empirical referents. Moreover, the intangible resources are tied to well-developed ego-synthetic and ego-executive abilities that are fundamental to Erikson's formal theory of psychosocial health and development. When these abilities are coupled with advanced forms of moral-ethical reasoning, the person's reflexive capacities can be more appropriate for a widening array of experiences with people in circumstances that might otherwise have been previously part of that person's out-groups. In these cases, individual identity capital acquisition also benefits other people, adding to the cultural evolution toward ethical identities that Erikson foresaw.

A couple of examples can illustrate what we mean by identity capital and its situational relevance. First, take the instance of a young woman entering her first year of college or university. Depending on the academic program, being female may be either a potential asset or deficit. For example, in programs where there is a "chilly climate,"[20] being a woman will likely be a situational deficit that can inhibit identity negotiation processes. Being an attractive woman, however, may neutralize this deficit and turn being female into an asset in some ways.[21] The more articulate this female student is, net of the other characteristics just described, the more likely it is that her professors will take her seriously and engage her in conversations that will lead them to more favorably evaluate her, either in terms of the grades assigned for essays and presentations, or in terms of letters of reference which potentially open a variety of doors for the student.

However, in this case, tangible resources such as attractiveness and articulateness may not be invested at all, or invested wisely. The student may take the wrong courses, may not engage in a sufficient amount of interaction with her professors, may not apply herself sufficiently in learning the basics in each course, may not seek to acquire a felicitous combination of skills, and so forth. Such poor planning and weak self-application may be a result of being aimless, having low self-regard, or being shy and anxious. Whatever the cause, the outcome will be basically the same: the student may not have wisely or sufficiently invested her efforts and time in this particular context in order to negotiate and exchange the resources she had upon entering it, and is therefore unlikely to accrue further assets as a result of her involvement there. The student may not finish her schooling, and if she does, she may have poor grades and poorly developed *human capital* skills such as self-management and self-motivation.[22] In relation to other graduates, her balance of identity capital assets may be far below average, which puts her at a competitive disadvantage in making the transition from the educational system to the work world. Moreover, it is likely that she would not have acquired additional nonacademic identity capital resources with which to successfully negotiate this increasingly difficult transition.

The preceding example should resonate with student readers, while the next example will have personal relevance for faculty readers and students aspiring to professional positions. In this second example, we are using the prototypical situation of a fresh Ph.D. applying for a faculty position. In this case, Doctor Y has all of the credentials explicitly required in an advertisement for a faculty position at university Z, but of course so do dozens of other people with doctorates. From the perspective of the ICM, the interest lies in what differentiates the person hired from the dozens who were not hired. Typically, recruitment committees look for candidates who will best "fit in" to the department and university. Therefore, being hired depends on "who one is" in some key respects in the eyes of the recruiters. Recruiters will initially see only the candidate's C.V., which explicitly lists the most obvious tangible assets (implicitly revealing race and gender, but explicitly showing degrees held from specific schools, publications, conference papers delivered, and special skills with computers or statistics). Only if the candidate is called for an interview will there be an opportunity to display other tangible assets, such as personal deportment, articulateness, contacts in the profession and department, and so forth. Moreover, it is only the short-listed candidate who has the opportunity to display his or her intangible assets, including personality attributes (e.g., charisma, charm, confidence), short-term and long-term strategies in terms of goal setting and career objectives, and ability to cultivate rapport with department gatekeepers. However, existing *social capital* networks often get the person short-listed in the first place, and these networks will have been established through previous activities with key faculty members during the person's student career, while at conferences, and elsewhere (e.g., through journal submissions and email communications).

To advance this illustration, let us assume that Dr. Y gets hired and becomes Professor Y. He or she then faces the sometimes grueling task of getting tenure and promotion, and movement through the academy. At this career stage, there will be more of the identity displays previously discussed, but Professor Y will now have to demonstrate the ability to follow through on his or her career strategies concerning research and publishing, and maintain a current written portfolio (C.V.) to show that investment strategies have worked out. If they do not work out, the person may have to lower goals (say, by being a part-time instructor) or change goals (say, by going into a research position for a private business). During the early career phase, the self-presentation strategy regarding "who one is" likely involves identity displays as someone with promise, commitment, and an appropriate intellect for the discipline. Implicitly, the self-presentation strategy should also involve "who one is not," namely, someone who is not a trouble maker, flaky, or "all talk."

Because the academic career involves considerable investments in identity capital, it is particularly useful in illustrating the ICM. As anyone who has attempted this career will know, it is fraught with difficulties, ambiguities, and stresses best dealt with through a series of long-term strategies about how to invest one's time (e.g., on which committees should one sit?) and effort (e.g., on which research projects should one work?) most wisely. In any event, the ICM should apply both specifically and generally (qualitatively and quantitatively) in the variety of contexts in which identities are negotiated rather than ascribed.

In sum, in deploying identity capital resources, a person would ask what is "exchangeable" to invest in "who I am" in relation to an ideal group, goal, value, skill, and so forth. Proactive people engaging in developmental individualization, for example, would be reflexive about what is "exchangeable" in terms of "who they are" in relation to a social status (e.g., adulthood), a goal (e.g., financial independence), or a career (e.g., professor). Inactive or passive people following the default individualization route would not be reflexive about such strategies or resource accumulations. Instead, they would simply and mindlessly follow reinforcement patterns derived from experiences in their family and schools, and from peers and popular culture. In the next section, we further illustrate this exchange process.

The Late-Modern Identity Capital Workplace Portfolio

In this section, we provide illustrations of the ICM "in action" by specifying the portfolio of resources that we propose are necessary for successful integration into the "identity markets" of late-modern workplaces. In the following set of figures, the components of the **identity capital portfolio** are illustrated. Three figures show the place and importance of the various skill-sets identified by the ICM, and how they can play a role in entry into the labor market, which by all accounts is increasingly identity-based, especially in terms of the acquisition of status-conferring credentials. However, although credentials can represent the acquisition of "hard skills" previously thought to be sufficient for occupational attainment, it is increasingly evident that in the highly competitive labor markets of late-modernity, people need additional skills to gain entry into, and maintain good standing in, certain occupational categories.

Figure 6.1 shows the three general sets of skills postulated to be required in the late-modern workplace.[23] The apex of the triangle refers to "soft," agentic (intangible) skills identified by the ICM.[24] At the base of the triangle, "hard skills" and "people skills" are represented. Hard skills are the types of cognitive and motor capacities necessary to engage in many workplace roles. People skills are the social and interpersonal abilities required to get along in workplace settings. There is good reason to believe that all three sets of skills are necessary for successful integration into the late-modern workplace. In the past, hard skills may have been sufficient in many cases, especially in manufacturing jobs and the trades where people were oriented to concrete, repetitive tasks. Additionally, a majority

Soft Skills: Agentic*

SKILLS

Hard Skills:
Cognitive/
Motor

People Skills:
Social/Inter-
personal

* Self-efficacy/esteem; self/impulse control; purpose & planning = functional
resources (in late-modernity)

FIGURE 6.1 Three sets of skills in the late-modern workplace.

of contemporary workplaces are service-oriented, requiring teamwork and nego-tiation skills along with certain impression management skills, especially among those in management or dealing with customers. Most important for current con-cerns, the personal agency represented by these soft skills (e.g., self-efficacy and purpose) is postulated to be necessary to put the other forms of capital into action.

Figure 6.2 expands the core triangle of figure 6.1 by linking each of the three skill types with distinct forms of capital, or more simply resources. Hard skills are more technically referred to as part of *human capital*; people skills are recognizable as an essential component of *social capital*. These two types of capital are repre-sented at the bottom, and "functional capital" is at the apex. Functional capital comprises the intangible resources identified by the ICM that we propose are often necessary for integrating into the late-modern workplace. These resources are functional in the sense that they facilitate integration into workplace set-tings. Functional capital is what is necessary to put the other forms of capital into action, to bring them to fruition in the identity markets of late-modernity in terms of securing a validated social status that integrates the person within a functioning community (social inclusion) and the job market. In the context of the late-modern labor market, this triad of capitals constitutes *workplace* identity capital. Thus, identity capital is considered the overarching resource that subsumes human capital and social capital, as well as functional capital.

Figure 6.3 fleshes out the first two figures by specifying the components of the three forms of capital comprising workplace identity capital. Functional capi-tal thus is shown to comprise several of the agentic resources identified by the ICM: self-efficacy and self-esteem, self-regulation, and a sense of purpose. It is postulated that, with these agentic abilities, workplace skills and formal creden-tials (human capital) as well as memberships and networks (social capital) are

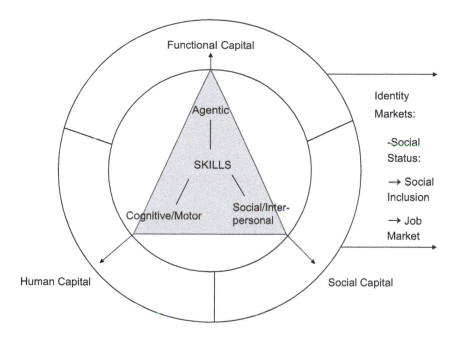

FIGURE 6.2 The triad of capitals appropriate to the late–modern labor market.

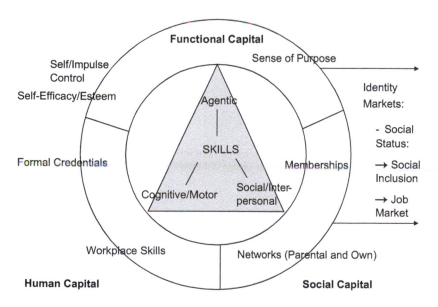

FIGURE 6.3 The late–modern workplace identity capital portfolio.

negotiated and exchanged in late-modern identity markets, generally in terms of "social inclusion" and specifically with respect to the job market. At the same time, this model gives us clues as to why "qualified" and otherwise skilled people cannot find work, net of structural factors, and even why some social networks do not always help in gaining employment.[25]

One way to more concretely frame this model is to place it within the language of policy debates by considering intangible resources more generically as soft skills and tangible skills as hard skills.[26] In the past, it appears that the mere possession of hard skills was sufficient for social inclusion, but it increasingly appears to be the case that soft skills are necessary for people to strategically mobilize their hard skills and combine them with soft skills if they are to gain access to the job market in any but the most rudimentary occupations. For example, while educational credentials are tangible assets that can represent the acquisition of hard skills traditionally thought to be sufficient for success, it is increasingly evident that in the labour markets of late-modernity, people need additional skills to gain entry into, and maintain good standing in, certain occupational categories.

The intention in providing this formulation of a portfolio of skill-sets is not to "blame the (unemployed) victim" or excuse neo-liberalism for the oppression associated with structural unemployment, but rather to help those who find themselves socially excluded or un/under-employed, or who are headed for social exclusion, find ways to overcome it. This intention goes back to the origins of the ICM as a way of learning from those who successfully exchange resources and passing this knowledge onto those who have trouble doing so. The overall developmental implications of the ICM portfolio of skill-sets are based on the assumption that people's acceptability in these "markets" requires that they earn a certain legitimacy that affords them "social inclusion," particularly entry into the job market and the potential to move up their career ladders and/or gain more skill certifications.

Conclusion: The Ripple Effects of Strategic Identities

The Identity Capital Model provides a way of understanding life-course transitions in late-modern societies where old normative structures, and to some extent social barriers associated with class, gender, and race, have broken down. In many cases, these transitions require people to exert personal agency in certain contexts in order to reach self-chosen goals. For those who are able to do so, life chances can increase proportionately; for those who are unable to do so, life chances can be diminished accordingly. The ICM promises to help us understand how people successfully navigate new passages through late-modern life courses; based on this knowledge, the ICM should help us to make recommendations to those who encounter difficulties navigating their life courses, particularly those from disadvantaged backgrounds. The model thus provides a potential framework for recommending policies and for structuring interventions that ameliorate the impact of the disjunctures between institutional contexts as well as fragmentations within these contexts. The ICM is already in use in counseling applications and school settings, as we see in Chapter 9.

We would also like to emphasize that although this chapter did not make reference to the theories of moral–ethical development discussed in Chapter 4, identity capital acquisition does not have to be seen simply as a "selfish" endeavor. In fact, as we see in the next chapter, those who are more proactive in their identity formation also tend to be more capable of higher forms of moral reasoning and of reaching higher levels of ethical awareness. Although we do not have the specific evidence to support the implications of these findings, it is worth speculating about their broad ramifications. Thus, the common thread between proactive identity formation and moral-ethical development may be advanced perspective-taking capacities. If this is the case, those who accumulate more identity capital by undertaking developmental individualization during the transition to adulthood may not only benefit themselves but also those in their lives and the communities to which they contribute. In other words, the strengths and advantages that accrue to people who have proactively acquired identity capital resources as part of their developmental trajectory should be likely to benefit those around them to the extent that they employ their moral-ethical reasoning in their activities. Consequently, the more people there are in a given community with higher levels of identity capital acquired developmentally, the more likely it is that the community will prosper in a variety of senses (e.g., economically and psychosocially) with their cumulative contributions creating a "tide that raises all boats" rather than only their own boats or those of a few privileged people. Empirical tests of these speculations could be undertaken at the individual level through conventional developmental research but also at the macro level by comparing communities and whole nations in terms of the extent to which community/national wealth, health, and well-being are the byproduct of the collective endeavors of critical masses of people who have excelled in terms of the psychosocial development and who are willing to share their good fortune by contributing to the "commonwealth" through productive roles coupled with humanitarian efforts.[27]

PART III

The Transition to Adulthood

DEVELOPMENTAL CONTEXTUALISM APPLIED TO LATE MODERNITY

7

CURRENT SCIENTIFIC APPROACHES TO SELF-DEVELOPMENT AND IDENTITY FORMATION

"Eighty percent of success is showing up."

Woody Allen[1]

Erik Erikson's influence on the scientific study of identity formation is widely recognized. This influence includes the axiom that the major psychosocial task linking childhood with adulthood involves developing a viable adult identity. By focusing on psychosocial development, Erikson recognized the psychological as well as social and personal dimensions of identity, thereby planting the seeds for the comprehensive, multidimensional theory of identity formation that we have developed into the SIFT. Erikson also imbedded a stage of identity formation within a life-cycle stage framework, thereby introducing other psychosocial dimensions related to identity formation. These dimensions include trust, autonomy, initiative, and industry, derived from childhood development, along with intimacy, generativity, and integrity, derived from adult development. The *life-cycle approach* emphasizes the obligations each generation has to those generations that preceded it as well as to those that will follow it.[2] These obligations introduce the importance of phenomena that are "larger" than the individual (e.g., the welfare of the human species), precisely those things that can constitute the basis of an ethical identity.

As noted in Chapter 1, in the context of psychosocial functioning, we can extract three interrelated levels of analysis from Erikson's work on identity formation that have generated scientific investigations: (1) the subjective/psychological element, or ego identity, representing a sense of temporal-spatial continuity and its concomitants; (2) the individual aspect, or personal identity, manifested in the behavioral and character repertoires that differentiate individuals; and (3) the collective facet, or social identity, defined by recognized roles within a local community and wider society. For Erikson, these three components need to coalesce during the identity stage, and during the time(s) when they do not, an identity crisis is evident. Such an identity crisis is, in respect to the three social psychological levels of identity formation, characterized by: (1) a subjective sense of identity confusion, (2) behavioral and characterological disarrays, and (3) a lack of commitment to recognized roles in a local community or the wider society. Accordingly, resolution of the identity stage is facilitated when the three components dovetail: when (1) a relatively firm sense of ego identity is developed, (2) behavior and character become stabilized, and (3) community-sanctioned roles are acquired.

It is important to note that Erikson originally conceived of ego identity when treating identity loss among war-trauma victims during the Second World War. At the time, war trauma was called "shell shock." It is now referred to as post-traumatic stress disorder (PTSD). An epiphany was triggered for him while treating those patients who experienced forms of amnesia, and who in their memory loss had effectively lost their sense of who they were (see Box 7.1 for an example of how traumas affect people's levels of awareness of themselves in time and place). After that war, Erikson noticed the trend toward more problematic identities among the general population of Americans, and he subsequently wrote extensively about the "identity crisis" that he saw as a rising epidemic in modern societies. He later drew a parallel between identity disturbances and the experiences of "severely conflicted young people whose sense of confusion is due to a war within themselves."[3] He also wrote about the identity problems of adulthood that he saw to be "normal" responses to the vicissitudes and alienation associated with modern, technological societies.

BOX 7.1 EMERGENCY PROCEDURES FOR ASSESSING THE AWARENESS OF ACCIDENT VICTIMS

The medical approach to temporal-spatial continuity sheds an interesting light on how people experience themselves in the world on a day-to-day basis. When we peel away layers of consciousness, as do first-responders to accidents, especially those involving head trauma, we see how important it is for people to be able to "locate" themselves in time and space.[4]

If the patient is awake, and knows (1) what happened, (2) what time it is, (3) where s/he is, and (4) who s/he is, the responder can ask the patient a set number of questions about these facts and report "alert and oriented times 4." This patient is apparently in good shape for the time being. However, if the person does not know what happened, but is otherwise self-aware, the report is "alert and oriented times 3." If the situation is worse, the person may not know what time it is and what happened, so he or she would be classed as "times 2." The person who does not know the preceding and does not know where s/he is would be reported as "times 1." In the most serious case where the person does not know any of these facts, or their name, the person is described as "alert and oriented times 0."

This procedure tells the medical team that will take over how severe the trauma is. For our purposes, it reveals the importance of time and place for the sense of self and identity. The amnesia or severe dissociation associated with "times 0" can signal a very serious medical situation—the person subjectively does not "have an identity," and this is precisely the type of condition that alerted Erik Erikson to the wider "problem of identity" at the beginning of his research (as noted earlier).

Thus, in such situations, the first sense to be lost is the victim's recollection of recent events (i.e., what just happened), the second is a sense of time (i.e., what time it is), the third is a sense of place (i.e., where s/he is), and last to be lost is a person's sense of who they are (i.e. his/her name).

Some theorists who follow the political and philosophical approaches to identity studies claim that there is no such thing as a "core" to the personality (with various ideas about what the word "core" means), especially in contemporary Western societies (often they prefer to call these societies "postmodern"). But surely it defies common sense that living in such a society would produce continual and widespread symptoms equivalent to those associated with a severe blow on the head. If so, people would be walking around unaware of recent events, and not know what time it is, where they are, and for that matter, who they are.

Our reading of how Erikson's psychosocial formulations apply to all cultures suggests that for him the crux of identity stability in any culture lies in the interplay between the social and the psychological. That is, a person requires a viable social identity of some sort, and when the person develops a workable social identity based on commitments integrating that person into a particular culture, the psychological sense of temporal-spatial continuity—ego identity—is nurtured. Once a sense of ego identity is established, people are more buffered and protected from the vicissitudes of social conflicts and tensions. We believe that this position describes identity formation in all cultures, not just those that are individualistic and choice-oriented like the U.S. According to Erikson, people of all cultures can develop a sense of ego identity based on role validation and community integration (i.e., sustained commitments).

Another way to express Erikson's views in this context is to speak of three forms of continuity that are developmentally sensitive to contexts: a sense of sameness of the ego with itself; interrelationships between the ego and "the other"; and functional integrations among others in general. The first type of continuity is what Erikson had in mind when he coined the term ego identity (i.e., a sense of self-sameness over time). The second type of continuity pertains to a person's relationships with others that maintain the stability of personal and social identities. Discontinuities in this realm threaten the stability of those identities, although a strong sense of ego identity coupled with competent moral reasoning skills can help people through periods of instability in their relations with others.

The third type of continuity represents the stability of relations among the members of a particular community or group. This is sometimes referred to as *social organization*, with deficits treated as social dysfunctions often associated with *anomie*, a relative characteristic of late modernity. These social factors are external to the person, residing in the interrelationships in general among people in a given community. When these community relations are stable and continuous, people's personal and social identities within the community are safeguarded. However, when these relations are unstable, dysfunctional, or anomic, people's personal and social identities come under pressure and may undergo revision. What is particularly important to note, however, is that problematic community relations (problems in "other–other" continuity) can create developmental difficulties for those experiencing the transition to adulthood. This is especially an issue for those younger members of society who do not have a strong sense of "ego-self" continuity (ego identity) and who experience seriously unstable "ego-other" relations.[5] Box 7.2 provides an illustration of these principles applied to the study of suicide rates among Native Canadian youth.

BOX 7.2 THE PROTECTIVE NATURE OF WELL-FUNCTIONING COMMUNITIES: THE CASE OF SUICIDE

The suicide rate among Aboriginals is high in many countries. However, researchers consistently find that those countries where Aboriginals do not feel as culturally disenfranchised have *lower* suicide rates than countries where they feel more disenfranchised.[6] Research that is more regional finds that those who observe traditional customs or who live in a tribal community with good employment and education opportunities have significantly lower suicide rates.[7] It thus appears that marginalized groups can preserve the basis for their young people to develop a viable sense of identity if these groups are organized socially and economically.

This protective factor has been studied in British Columbia among Native Canadian youth, identifying very strong links between a sense of ego identity (in this case, the sense of self–self continuity, measured using a narrative method) and the extent to which tribal communities maintain their own "cultural identity" in the form of coherent institutional structure (other–other continuity). This research concludes that suicide among First Nations youth is an inverse function of factors that represent community-based efforts to reconstitute a form of cultural continuity and integrity. This research links six protective factors with reduced youth suicide. In every Native community in which all six of these protective factors were in place, no youth suicides were reported during the five years in which they were studied. In contrast, communities that lacked these protective factors showed suicide rates up to 100 times that of the national average. The protective factors identified in this research concern whether communities (a) secure aboriginal title to traditional lands, (b) achieve a measure of self-government, (c) control their educational facilities, (d) control their health services, (e) run their own police and fire protection services, and (f) set up facilities to preserve and enrich their indigenous culture.

It appears that identity discontinuity is now experienced as problematic for a sizable portion of adults in Western societies. Unstable and poorly structured communities and societies make identity formation and maintenance problematic for the individual. In our view, herein lies one of the greatest challenges to late-modern societies.

Some Typical Identity Formation Strategies in Late Modernity

How are people adjusting to the identity-destabilizing influences of late-modernity described in the preceding sections? One way to understand these adjustments is in terms of a range of "strategies" that reflect degrees of identity capital possessed by the individual. An important component of identity capital is the wherewithal to be proactive, even under adverse conditions. Following this understanding, a set of strategies is proposed and encapsulated in this section based on our synthesis of the empirical identity formation literature. Based on our intention to provide a simplified theory of identity formation (i.e., SIFT), we use nontechnical terms to represent "clusters" of people who share certain response tendencies. We have found that the following working typology of five identity strategies captures the range of approaches people take to their identity formation and maintenance in late-modern societies. For heuristic purposes, we have named these strategies as follows: Refusers, Drifters, Searchers, Guardians, and Resolvers.

We offer this typology here to illustrate the following: (1) historically speaking, there are now a greater number of ways in which adult identities are formed;

(2) adult identity formation can be rather chaotic; and (3) for virtually everyone this process now involves an individualized "strategy" that may be carefully and consciously planned or may be part of a continual struggle with people's inner conflicts and resources, or lack thereof.

Refusers typically develop a series of defenses with which to "refuse" entry into adulthood. These defenses include a series of self-defeating cognitive schema that lock them into immature behavior patterns characterized by a dependency, for example, on someone else or on some institutional safety net. Those adopting this strategy may remain with their parents well into their 30s (or for their lives); they may refuse to acquire occupational skills, and thus remain dependent on government benefits, the proceeds of crime, or an underground economy; or they may find a mate or a group of friends that *enable* them to stay perpetually in a pre-adult status. In terms of their character formation, Refusers were likely given little structure and encouragement as children regarding engagements with their social environments, and as adolescents they were likely given little guidance regarding ways in which they could develop themselves intellectually, emotionally, or vocationally.[8] Thus, Refusers have few personal resources with which to actively engage a community of adults. In what should be their early adult years (their 20s and 30s), they engage in a number of behaviors that sabotage their standing in any adult community. For example, they may engage in heavy drug or alcohol use, they may not maintain steady employment even when there may be no barriers to this, and they may periodically act out in immature ways (e.g., temper tantrums). Of course, Refusers could likely have been found in communities throughout Western history,[9] but our contention is that this way of handling the demands of adult identity formation is increasing in late modernity. This type of person seems most likely to take refuge in one of the many youth street gangs now proliferating in urban centers, or in a drug-oriented youth culture, rather than confronting the task of taking on adulthood responsibilities and/or attempting to overcome socioeconomic obstacles through legitimate means.

While Drifters are similar to Refusers in their lack of integration into an adult community, they do have more personal resources at their disposal. These resources could include higher levels of intelligence, family wealth, or occupational skills, yet the Drifter seems unable or uninterested in applying these resources in a consistent and continuous manner. The Drifter may feel that conforming may be a "cop out," or "selling out"; or the Drifter may simply feel that he or she is "too good" to "toe the line." Whatever the reason, the effect is more or less the same: a chronic pre-adult behavior pattern characterized by poor impulse control, shallow interpersonal relationships, and little in the way of commitments to an adult community. This way of handling the demands of adult identity formation also seems to be increasing in late modernity.[10]

The Searcher, in contrast to the first two strategies, has not given up on finding a validating adult community; instead, the Searcher cannot seem to find a community that satisfies his or her often unrealistically high criteria of functioning.[11] The Searcher is habitually driven by a sense of dissatisfaction with him/herself and this dissatisfaction can be projected onto others. Unable to find perfection in themselves, and unable to find perfection in a community, Searchers are locked into a perpetual journey for which there can be no end. They may have sought out role models who have claimed perfection, but when these models are found to be imperfect, the Searcher may grow tired of them. Or, the Searcher's own imperfections—in contrast to those of the role model—may create a sense of despair that drives the Searcher to look elsewhere.[12]

The Guardian, in contrast to the previous three strategies, has likely experienced a well-structured childhood in which the values of the parent and/or community have been thoroughly internalized. This structure gives the Guardian a set of personal resources with which to actively engage the adolescent environment and move fairly quickly into adulthood. However, this internalized structure can be impervious to influence and change if the person is resistant to identity explorations, leaving the person vulnerable in several ways. First, the person can neglect to undergo certain developmental experiences that would help him or her to grow emotionally and intellectually. Second, the person can over-identify with a parent, making it difficult for him or her to individuate during the transition to adulthood.[13] And, third, as an adult, the person may be unduly rigid in terms of his or her own continuing identity formation. In late modernity, change is a fact of life, and a large variety of lifestyles and opinions will be encountered; to deal with these in a rigid manner can lead to all sorts of hardship for oneself and for others.[14] Traditional, premodern societies generally prescribe this identity strategy among their members for the sake of cultural continuity, whereas the prior three strategies discussed earlier can be seen as anomic consequences of the disjunctive socialization process that are becoming increasingly common in late-modern societies.

Finally, the Resolver proactively engages himself or herself in the process of forming an adult identity, taking advantage of the opportunities in late-modern societies *in spite of* the anomic character of these types of societies and potentially in the face of structural obstacles that others might perceive as insurmountable. This strategy involves proactively developing one's intellect, emotional maturity, and vocational skills rooted in one's general competencies and interests. It also involves learning about the world and going out in the world to actualize one's budding abilities. Of course, many people have the potential to be Resolvers but find themselves held back for one reason or another (e.g., various commitments, like having a child, or having parents who are unable to invest in their education). However, even within these constraints, a certain amount of proactive engagement is usually possible; in fact, unless one is pulled by the processes that are felt by, say, Refusers or Guardians, attempting this strategy in some way may be unavoidable in late-modern society, which actively stimulates this type of identity formation in certain ways (e.g., educational systems in which large proportions of populations participate well into the tertiary levels). Whatever the circumstances, those who are disposed to this identity strategy will find themselves yearning to grow in certain ways and will likely do so with whatever means are at their disposal. The impetus for this strategy is likely rooted in an internalized childhood structure and made possible during the transition to adulthood by a conducive, motivational mindset associated with a desire to reach one's potential.[15]

Sociological factors like social class, gender, and ethnicity are not necessarily relevant to our understanding of the nature of these identity strategies, although empirical analyses may show different proportions of them in different demographic categories. For example, a Drifter can come from a wealthy background, be a woman, and a minority group member. Similarly, a Resolver could be a minority woman from a working-class background. Our point is that identity formation in late modernity is not as restricted by social ascription as it was in premodern societies. Those of any social class background who undertake default individualization strategies, such as Drifting and Refusing, would be less likely to maintain their social class of origin, unless it is the lowest already.

Indeed, proactive identity formation strategies such as those of the Resolver seem to be key if a person is to either overcome socioeconomic obstacles to become upwardly mobile, or to maintain the high social status of his or her parents. Resolvers and Guardians are more likely to take developmental individualization trajectories, and thus should benefit from these in terms of social mobility or maintaining a social status or class origin. In other words, simply having wealthy parents or being from an upper class no longer guarantees that one's adulthood status reproduces that of one's parents. However, we suggest that Refusers, Drifters, and Searchers are most likely to experience downward mobility, while Resolvers and Guardians are most likely to experience upward mobility and/or to replicate the social status of their parents.

Based on these considerations, regardless of the identity strategy undertaken, the citizen of late-modern societies will likely encounter continual challenges in the formation of an adult social identity and in the maintenance of that identity once it is formed. Moreover, social identities are becoming increasingly transitory and unstable in late-modern societies. Even those social identities that are maintained throughout adulthood will require a certain amount of management in order to sustain validation for them from others. For example, the person will have to ensure that proper images are created and recreated in interaction with significant others. This form of identity management seems to apply to roles as common as parenthood (e.g., being "fit" or being "good" in terms of shifting standards of child care, including child-discipline practices) and as specific as one's occupational specialization (e.g., being "marketable," "selling oneself," and being "nonredundant"). Under increasingly anomic social conditions and diminishing consensus regarding traditional and contemporary norms, the formation and maintenance of adult identities can be challenging for all citizens of late-modern societies. Indeed, we argue that there is ample reason to believe that this situation is worsening for many people.[16]

In the next chapter, we examine some of the important social contexts that can facilitate or hinder the various identity strategies.

Developmental Trajectories

In light of this typology of the identity strategies, the question arises as to what leads people to adopt one over another, especially given that the strategies can vary dramatically in terms of the benefits people can yield from them in their lives. After all, why would someone undertake a strategy that is essentially self-handicapping, such as avoiding setting goals and not taking on challenges in life when this can lead to a life of unhappiness and poor economic prospects, even if the person is from an affluent background? In this section, we examine the precursors to these strategies in terms of various social contexts, some of which present people with opportunities and others with obstacles. This examination requires first going back to basic theory, extending the material covered in Chapter 1.

Self and Identity

The empirical literature on the forms of self-development and identity formation based on the theories discussed in Chapter 1 is synthesized in this section in a way that helps us understand what leads people to adopt one or the other of the identity strategies described in the previous section. Self-development is discussed first because its growth trajectory takes place largely in childhood and adolescence, providing a basis for later identity formation, with the greatest potential developmental changes taking place during late adolescence and early adulthood. In other words, the self literature is best applied to childhood and early adolescence, the age period when the self forms, and the foundations for self-concept, self-esteem, and self-efficacy are laid; and the identity literature is best applied mainly to late adolescence and early adulthood, the age periods during which most adult-identity consolidations take place.[17]

Developmentally, self-concepts constitute the building blocks of the various identity elements that young people synthesize into an adult identity. In this sense, self-concepts are not "identities" because of their specificity and concreteness; identities are more general, involving a consolidation of concrete elements like self-concepts, social roles, and identifications, along with more abstract beliefs and values. Thus, self-concepts can become consolidated during early to mid-adolescence, providing the foundation for identity formation where these are synthesized with more abstract and general social commitments. Self-concept consolidations are part of what the identity researchers have studied as the early foundations of the content of adult identities.

The Development of Self-Concepts in Childhood and Adolescence

As discussed in Chapter 1, the sense of self forms during childhood, and is then potentially strengthened, consolidated, and differentiated during adolescence. This differentiation during adolescence involves a greater focus on more abstract traits than is the case among children, culminating in the formation of *self-schemas*—cognitive structures that arrange self-concepts and filter information about the self. While this ability to abstract one's sense of self has growth-enhancing potentials, difficulties in developing this ability can lead to self-esteem and self-efficacy problems.

The empirical literature stemming from symbolic interactionism has focused on assessing levels and changes in self-esteem[18] and self-concept,[19] and how these are related to other personality traits. These studies confirm that self-concept becomes more differentiated and abstract during adolescence, and self-esteem strengthens overall. Nevertheless, it is important to clearly differentiate self-concept from self-esteem, as was done in Chapter 1. Self-concept is a qualitative category (e.g., "I am a student"), while self-esteem is a variable assessment of that category (e.g., "I am an outstanding/good/average/poor student").[20]

In spite of the appeal of the concept of self-esteem, there are reasons to question whether *global* measures of self-esteem give accurate assessments of adolescents' senses of competence in the various domains of functioning that produce self-concepts (e.g., student, athlete, appearance). Indeed, there is evidence that adolescents who have not actively engaged the identity formation process do not summarize their self-esteem across these self-concept domains. Moreover, separate self-concept domains are of differing importance for each person, and this importance can shift from day to day and situation to situation. Thus, while self-esteem can be measured in (less accurate) global terms, as well as in (more accurate) specific terms, certain empirical studies of self-esteem cannot be taken at face value because this measurement issue is often not acknowledged.

Still, according to the empirical literature, it appears that self-esteem increases with age, such that when averaged across the life course, high school samples have below-average scores, college/university students and adults present average scores, and the elderly score above average.[21] Self-concepts also generally become clearer and more differentiated with age, although the clarity appears to waver during early- to mid-adolescence. This wavering may be due to early adolescents having more contradictory self-concepts than do late adolescents.[22] With positive experiences, though, the adolescent can learn that different contexts can evoke a range of subjective reactions and require different forms of impression management. Adolescents can thus come to intuit that there can be differences between a "real self" and a "role self"[23] (see box 3.2).

There is evidence that declines in self-esteem during early adolescence are limited to a sub-population of adolescents, with most young adolescents maintaining a consistent level of self-esteem or increasing in self-esteem.[24] For example, in relation to the "on-time" onset of puberty, early maturing females can experience a decline in self-esteem, while early maturing males can experience an increase.[25] These fluctuations are worrisome because low self-esteem has been identified as an important predictor of suicidal ideation and suicide attempts among adolescents.[26]

It appears that the self-esteem of adolescents fluctuates more than that of children and adults, being more determined by the characteristics of the situations encountered and the nature of relationships with people in those situations.[27] It is thus useful to distinguish between "baseline self-esteem" and "barometric self-esteem," the former referring to the level at which people maintain a stable, global view of themselves, and the latter characterizing a sense of self-esteem that is situation-dependent.

Finally, it is prudent to recognize the limitation of this self-development literature. As with the identity research, most of this research is based primarily on White, middle-class American samples. Consequently, the findings regarding situational sensitivity of self-esteem pose a problem in generalizing even to other Western samples. Evidence of this variation among Western samples, and the contextual implications of self-esteem development, are examined in the next chapter. It also appears that research on self-development has been somewhat misled by early beliefs in the importance of self-esteem. More recent research suggests that higher levels of self-esteem can actually have some negative effects, as when the basis of a person's high self-esteem is unrealistic or based on false feedback. That is, these negative effects are found when the person's self-esteem is not based on realistic self-appraisals with respect to things like personal and performance competencies, especially educational and occupational ones.[28] In these cases, as noted in Chapter 1, it is more important to target self-efficacy instead of simply self-esteem in attempts to help young people developmentally.

The Transformation of Self-Concepts Into Identities in Adolescence and Early Adulthood

The Eriksonian approach to identity formation postulates that the transformation of self-concepts (and identifications) into identities in adolescence can be viewed in terms of a bipolar continuum representing identity diffusion/confusion vs. identity consolidation/synthesis. This consolidation optimally involves the formation of a relatively resilient sense of ego identity that provides a psychological basis for a coherent adult (social) identity. Indeed, the empirical research confirms that those with a more resilient ego identity are higher in self-esteem, have more consistency in their self-concepts,[29] and experience a greater sense of self-efficacy.[30] Thus, in reference to the identity strategies discussed previously, Resolvers and Guardians have the most propitious self-development, while Drifters, Refusers, and Searchers experience more difficulties.

Children tend to rely on identifications with role models that over time can become organized into a set of goals and commitments. Identifications are relational by nature, linking the child's own self-concepts with his or her social world of significant and generalized others. In adolescence, these identifications can expand the conception of generalized others as the radius of involvement expands. However, for most people this is a slow process occurring over the adolescent period, and for some lasts into early adulthood. The more proactive the person is, though, the more quickly this consolidation of self-concepts can take place in a wider array of settings.

Thus, most people begin adolescence with a relatively nonintegrated set of self-concepts and identifications. Their identity is diffused (as incipient or temporary Drifters or Refusers). Others have a sense of themselves based on strong identifications with their parents' identity (as incipient or temporary Guardians). During adolescence, most people experience a strengthening in their sense of identity as they reconfigure self-concepts and identifications to formulate goals and commitments based on the adoption of certain values and belief systems. At the same time, this process of realigning self-concepts and identifications and adopting new ones can unbalance the person, precipitating the identity crisis to which Erikson referred. This crisis optimally culminates in the adoption of a Resolvers strategy, although for some it never quite ends if they adopt a Searcher strategy.

For most people, this reconfiguration of self-concepts into identities is a relatively unproblematic process, differing in terms of how inactive or proactive they are in the process. For a minority, it is a major and precipitous life event that can lead to long-term changeability and instability. Erikson described this as a severe and aggravated identity crisis, an event that became generically referred to as adolescent storm and stress.[31] This severe crisis can be resolved during adolescence, often with good developmental benefits, or it can drag on, derailing the person's subsequent development and leading to the adoption of one or more of the less functional identity strategies (i.e., Drifter, Refuser, and to some extent Searcher).

The empirical research indicates that only a minority of adolescents experiences the type of identity crisis associated with the Searcher strategy (some 10–20 percent),[32] and that most people make their way through this process of identity formation in ways that allow them to function effectively as adults. Even so, it appears that the adult-identity formation process is now taking longer than it did in the past. Instead of being largely an "adolescent" phenomenon for most people (with notable exceptions highlighted by Erikson[33]), certain forms of identity formation are now prolonged into (legal) adulthood for an increasing number of people, possibly resulting in greater proportions of Drifters and Refusers in early adulthood.[34]

Although one might think that young people begin adolescence without any prior identity formation activity, this does not appear to be the case. Most appear to have been active to some extent in childhood, at least in terms of building self-concepts into more coherent identities. As noted in Chapter 2, only about 30 percent of adolescents are classified as inactive, "drifting" through their teen years, and this proportion drops to about 25 percent in late adolescence/early adulthood, and to about 15 percent in adulthood. When inactivity becomes a long-term pattern, it can be considered the Refuser identity strategy. In the adult population, then, about one in six people would be Drifters or Refusers with respect to their identities, and are unlikely to experience significant identity formation thereafter.[35]

In contrast, the majority appears to have managed some form of identity synthesis into a coherent adult identity, either based on a continued (active) identification with their parents as Guardians (about 20 percent) or as Resolvers as a result of their own proactive experimentation with values, beliefs, roles, and commitments (about 20 percent of those in their late teens, 30 percent in their 20s, and 50 percent in their 30s). When these latter two types of commitment-based identity syntheses are considered together, the literature thus provides an estimate that about 50 percent of the young adults and 70 percent of the adult-aged population in Western countries have synthesized a coherent, adult identity as either Guardians or Resolvers.[36]

The Synthesis of Identities in Adolescence and Early Adulthood

The underlying assumption of the empirical identity literature based on Erikson's theory is that adolescents differ in terms of how actively they engage themselves in the identity stage, working to formulate an adult identity. Rather than using the nonintuitive technical language of this literature, the following terms can be used to describe the ways in which the adolescent and young adult can approach the task of identity formation:[37]

- proactive approaches (Resolvers): involve a willingness to think ahead in life in a planning and purposive manner, thereby exploring and experimenting with future possible selves and identities;
- active approaches (Guardians): entail a willingness to commit to courses of action, but do not involve exploration and experimentation;
- reactive approaches (Searchers): include exploration and experimentation without necessarily thinking ahead in life; and
- inactive approaches (Drifters and Refusers): characterize a reticence to think ahead, experiment and explore, or to commit.[38]

The empirical literature identifies important personal and social differences among these four approaches to identity formation, although the four approaches should not be seen as developmentally hierarchical (i.e., people do not necessarily develop from inactivity to proactivity, although this is a common pattern). In addition, the literature is clear that few people are simultaneously proactive in all possible domains of identity formation (e.g., occupational issues, religious beliefs, political leanings). It is also clear that proactivity does not always culminate in long-term commitments, because some experimentation does not work out (e.g., failed occupational plans).[39] As such, the identity literature suffers the same deficit as the self-esteem literature to the extent that measures of the "global" construct are less reliable than are measures of specific domains of that construct. Nevertheless, the following "portraits" of approaches to identity activities represent the results of studies that have attempted to estimate "global" approaches to the entire task, rather than approaches to specific identity domains.

- Adolescents and young adults who take a proactive approach—Resolvers—have been found, compared to the other approaches, to have: higher levels of personal agency,[40] higher achievement motivation, lower neuroticism and use of defense mechanisms, more robust cognitive processes (functioning better under stress, exercising more balanced thinking, being more planful, and demonstrating higher levels of moral reasoning and ego development),[41] and better interpersonal skills and mature interpersonal relationships (higher intimacy, self-disclosure, and most secure attachments).[42] They also tend to have strong relationships with family and friends (but are better able to resist peer pressure), greater self-efficacy, and are more reflexive and self-confident.[43] Importantly, and adding to the self-development literature, their self-esteem is more stable and less prone to contextual influences because of their greater capacity for internal self-regulation.[44]
- Compared with those who are proactive, those who are merely active in their identity formation—Guardians—have been found to have lower forms of developmental complexity associated with a conformist and obedient orientation, as evidenced by such tendencies as authoritarianism, closed-mindedness, and rigidity,[45] and over-identification with their parents.[46]
- Those who are reactive exhibit behaviors commonly associated with so-called storm and stress,[47] and indeed score highest on measures of anxiety and uncertainty.[48] Nevertheless, they exhibit higher levels of critical thinking, open-mindedness, and can generate more alternatives in choice-making situations, associated with the Searcher strategy.[49]
- Finally, those adolescents and young adults who are inactive in their identity formation—Drifters and Refusers—show a litany of characteristics associated with lower levels of functioning. They are at highest risk of numerous problems that interfere with identity development.[50] In terms of adaptability, they have lower levels of self-esteem, difficulties adapting to new environments (like university settings), and are more self-focused. Cognitively, they tend to have disorganized thinking, an external locus of control, and a tendency toward procrastination and defensive avoidance of issues. And, they score lowest on measures of moral reasoning and ego development.[51] Inactivity can become a permanent approach to identity formation, although some

people can pass through it as a temporary respite when they are not up to a particular developmental challenge or are confronted with an obstacle that precludes the formation of commitments.

It is apparent that this categorical approach to identity formation is more complex than the Eriksonian approach that more simply places inactive and proactive approaches along a single continuum.[52] This complexity may be due to the inadvertent introduction of nondevelopmental factors by those who attempt to empirically study identity, so for the sake of clarity and to maintain a compatibility with the self-development and moral reasoning literatures, the research synthesis to follow in the next chapter will follow the Eriksonian continuum approach that contrasts inactive with proactive identity formation, with the implicit assumption that reactive and active forms can be located somewhere to the center of this continuum. In the next chapter, therefore, we examine the contextual variations in this inactive–proactive continuum of identity formation.

Conclusion: The Developmental Benefits of Proactivity

The scientific literature on identity formation has burgeoned over the past 50 years to produce thousands of published, peer-reviewed studies. Consequently, approaching this field can be daunting for the novice and taxing for the expert who tries to keep up with the nuances of all of the different approaches and findings. In this chapter, we provided a simplified way of understanding identity formation in terms of several clusters or types of people regarding how inactive or proactive they are in self-development and identity formation. By all accounts, proactivity is the key to more effective functioning in late-modern societies; yet we should stress again that societal obstacles as well as some people's own personality structures formed in childhood may limit their ability to function in a proactive manner, while other people's personalities seem more suited to approaching identity formation proactively. In the next chapter, we examine further the extent to which proactivity in identity formation is enhanced or hindered, this time in terms of specific societal and interpersonal contexts.

8

CONTEXTS OF IDENTITY FORMATION IN LATE-MODERN SOCIETIES

"I don't blame the average seventeen-year-old punk-rock kid for calling me a sell-out. I understand that. And maybe when they grow up a little bit, they'll realize there's more things to life than living out your rock & roll identity so righteously."
Kurt Cobain[1]

Understanding how social contexts affect human development constitutes perhaps the greatest challenge facing researchers.[2] A problem has been that psychological approaches to development have tended to under-theorize "the social" in its broadest sense. Early studies adopting this approach have been devoted mainly to immediate context variables like family background and educational settings. More recently, interest has turned to more general issues that have occupied public policy agendas, particularly culture, ethnicity, and gender. It needs to be stressed, however, that "ethnicity" and "gender" are not social contexts per se. Rather, they are also social identities attributed to individuals by others that take on particular meanings within socially constructed cultural contexts; additionally, individuals experiencing these social identities have different subjective experiences of them in different contexts. In the case of social identity, then, contexts are not easily separated from identity formation because, with factors such as ethnicity and gender, the context is part of the developmental process.

Moreover, categories of social identities can compound each other, producing complex interaction effects, especially when social class is added to the mix. When viewed as variables, ethnicity, gender, and class each have multiple categories, so their combined effects are multiplicative. For example, even if ethnicity and class were restricted to three categories each, and gender to two, 18 specific social identities would need to be investigated (i.e., 2 genders × 3 ethnicities × 3 social classes = 18 specific social identity categories).

Thus, no one study can realistically examine the combined effects of all possible contexts. This helps to explain why there is little research examining the simultaneous effects of multiple contexts. Accordingly, in this chapter, we examine the influence of each context separately, with multiple effects noted only when there is research to report. At the same time, identity formation has been studied more in some contexts, and self-development studied more in other contexts. However, attempting to discuss the thousands of published studies of all of the contextual effects would be overly complex and fragmented. To contain the coverage of the identity formation literature in this chapter, only those studies of identity that pertain to the inactivity–proactivity dimension will be included.

Similarly, our review of the self-development literature focuses on those studies relevant to identity-based agency. In most cases, this literature involves self-esteem and self-efficacy, two key aspects of agency identified by the Identity Capital Model, as discussed in Chapter 6.

Societal Influences Regarding Who People Are and How They Feel About Themselves

Ethnicity

The study of ethnic identity has been one of the most popular areas of identity research, perhaps because of the multicultural nature of many late-modern societies. These societies participate in the globalization process and for the most part have liberal immigration policies, producing a variety of combinations and permutations of ethnic groups that render different societies quite distinctive in their ethnic mixes.

Unfortunately, early research into this topic did not get off to a good start. That research attempted to study how social contexts affect ethnic identity formation by operationalizing ethnicity in terms of respondents' ethnic group "membership." However, simply treating ethnicity as group membership fails to distinguish ethnicity from ethnic identity, confusing the social and psychological dimensions of identity.[3]

An illustration of this problem can be seen in the results of a study investigating self-perceived ethnicity among Aboriginal youth in British Columbia, which found that only half of these young people consistently self-identified as Aboriginal on a longitudinal survey from one point in time to the next. This anomaly is also found in the U.S. among Hispanic adolescents. Interestingly, those who consistently identified themselves as Aboriginal each year from grade seven and into high school were more likely to drop out of school than those who were less consistent in their Aboriginal self-identification. The authors of this study were hard-pressed to explain these findings, except to point to the finding that those who consistently self-identified as Aboriginal might have been inactive in their identity formation, not exploring aspects of it. Their data did not allow them to verify this, but the study underscores the fact that ethnic self-identification is more complex than it appears at first blush and that many people do not identify strongly enough with their ethnic origins for it to be a highly salient aspect of their identity.[4] This is especially the case for members of majority groups in a society, as well as those from ethnic groups that are not stigmatized and excluded from full participation in the economy.

Over time, several measures of racial and ethnic identity formation have been developed,[5] but the Multigroup Ethnic Identity Measure (MEIM) has been the most widely used in the study of adolescent development.[6] The MEIM comprises three dimensions: self-identification of a sense of belongingness to a particular group, ethnic affirmation and belonging, and ethnic "identity achievement." The model upon which this measure was developed defines ethnic identity as a self-constructed internalization of the meaning and implications of a person's group membership based on that person's attitudes and feelings toward his or her cultural background, ethnic heritage, and racial phenotype.[7] In this model, ethnic identity develops proactively through the processes of exploration and experimentation.

Ethnic identity formation involves resolving positive and negative understandings and feelings about the one's own group in relation to other relevant groups. During childhood, these understandings tend to be concrete and oriented to physical attributes like skin color and food preferences, but during adolescence they become more abstract, involving issues associated with ethnic group consciousness.

The MEIM model posits ethnic identity formation as a three-stage process. In the first stage, ethnicity remains unexamined, having been internalized from significant others in the family/community. The unexamined stage is more common in early adolescence.[8] It usually takes significant "encounter experiences" of prejudice or discrimination to make a person's ethnicity salient in identity formation by triggering the second stage—a period of exploration during which the person questions what it means to have that specific ethnicity in his or her society. A person who becomes proactive in this way will explore cultural differences between his or her ethnic group and the dominant group in the society, an exploration that implicates moral and ethical reasoning capacities.

In this model, this proactive period is optimally followed by a third stage involving people committing "to a particular way of being a member of their group."[9] Research based on the MEIM finds that there is significant movement through these three stages between ages 16 and 19, and that college/university students score higher than high school students.[10] However, only about one quarter of ethnic minority adolescents reach the third stage by the end of high school, and there appears not to be an increase in the proportion reaching this stage in young adulthood, even among those who attend college/university.[11]

Still, those who attend college/university are more likely to explore their ethnicity. And, those who proactively synthesize an ethnic identity are more likely to become involved in cultural activities that further strengthen their ethnic identity, while those with a weaker sense of ethnic identity may withdraw from these cultural activities and experience a further weakening of that identity.[12] Those who have proactively resolved these issues have also been found to have higher self-esteem[13] and self-efficacy,[14] as well as better psychological well-being in terms of coping ability, mastery, optimism, and lower levels of loneliness and depression.[15] In addition, they have more positive attitudes toward other groups, and more mature intercultural thinking,[16] along with the highest scores on psychological adjustment and ego identity.[17]

Finally, American research based on this model finds that the meaning and strength of ethnic identity differs among ethnic groups, with African Americans having the strongest ethnic identities, presumably in response to the negative stereotypes and discrimination they can face daily. Asians and Latinos also have strong ethnic identities, but score lower than African Americans. Americans of European descent have the lowest scores, even those living in diverse communities and attending mixed schools, reflecting the low salience associated with their majority group status.[18]

Another approach to studying identity and ethnicity comes from Canada in the study of suicide among the Aboriginal population. Suicide can be considered the ultimate "statement" in a severe and aggravated identity crisis that leads people to a sense of despair associated with a lack of purpose in, and control over, their life.[19] The general literature does indeed find that suicide rates are higher in stigmatized minority groups.[20] For example, the suicide rate for Native Canadian men aged 15 to 29 exceeds 100 per 100,000, one of the highest rates in the world,[21] a rate that is five to six times higher than non-Aboriginal Canadian youth.[22]

Conversely, those who do not feel as culturally disenfranchised have lower suicide rates.[23] For example, as highlighted in box 7.2 in the preceding chapter, Native Canadian youth who live in a tribal community with good employment and educational opportunities have significantly lower suicide rates. Thus even marginalized groups that provide a basis for their young people to develop viable senses of identity can mitigate one of the most deleterious effects of social anomie—the desire of a person who finds no purpose and meaning in life to end his or her existence. Box 8.1 illustrates some of the research applying the identity capital model to the area of ethnicity.

BOX 8.1   IDENTITY CAPITAL AND THE MANAGEMENT OF ETHNIC IDENTITIES

A variety of applications have been found for the identity capital model in the areas of personal and social identity formation. The management of ethnic identities has been investigated in several qualitative studies. A study of young South Asian Canadians observed how they used their available "ethnic identity capital" to strategically choose whether to "brown it up" or "bring down the brown," depending on the ethnicities of their audiences.[24] The author of this study concluded that their ethnic identities were multidimensional and flexible, and they possessed the resilience and agency to mediate their personal biographies and cultural attachments in multicultural contexts. Another Canadian study examined the identity capital deployment strategies among staff members in a Canadian multicultural immigrant-serving organization.[25] These researchers concluded that various forms of identity capital are strategically deployed as part of impression management through greetings, body language, finding connecting pieces and methods of communication in interactions with clients, colleagues and supervisors. Similarly, an American study explored how Black/White biracial American young adults deployed their identity capital resources in multiracial "identity markets."[26] Finally, a study from the UK explored the concept of transnational identity capital to examine the position of internationally mobile academic intellectuals, framing it within Georg Simmel's concept of the stranger (i.e., someone not committed to the specifics of the group, but having a special form of detached objectivity with respect to the group and its members).[27] This author argued that a number of generic competences were used by itinerate academics to forge and sustain social relations, thereby facilitating movement among diverse ethno-national groups and professional contexts.

Gender

There is a broad consensus in the literature that among contemporary Western youth, there are no significant differences in *how* and *when* females and males synthesize their overall sense of ego identity. In other words, scientists investigating this topic agree that there are no meaningful gender differences in *how* the psychological processes of identity come together or *when* they come together.[28]

In contrast, gender differences have been found in terms of several specific *identity domains* or content areas of identity issues representing different personal and social identities. It appears that females experience more proactive identity formation in the domains of sexuality,[29] family/career prioritizing,[30] and friendship,[31] but not on vocation, religious beliefs, sex roles, values, dating, and so forth. In other words, more females appear to be exploring issues related to certain interpersonal concerns, thereby increasing the breadth of their identity formation over that of males.[32]

Similarly, at the level of social identity, gender differences still emerge along the private versus public dimension (i.e., the home vs. the wider society) that has dominated late-modern societies. In terms of socialization tasks, more women than men are tackling issues in both the public and private spheres as they form their identities. Women who move into the public sphere, including occupational contexts, apparently find it necessary to balance issues associated with both the "private" and "public," often negotiating these issues with significant others as they go along.[33] The majority of men, in contrast, seem to have been less willing to interconnect the public and private domains, preferring the public; when they do sense links, they apparently deal with the two domains as separate issues. For these reasons, identity formation currently appears to be more complex for those women who attempt to form an identity based on participation within both spheres. This includes more breaks in their career trajectories and the need to be more flexible in the social roles that are salient in their overall sense of adult identity (e.g., a parenting role that is balanced with professional or occupational roles).[34]

Culture

Theories about cultural differences in identity formation were reviewed in Chapter 5, where the focus is on differences between independent and interdependent self-construals as they are related to the exercise of personal agency in individualistic and collectivist cultures, respectively. Here we focus on research into cultural differences in self-esteem and self-efficacy. As noted in box 5.3, the self-development literature is vulnerable to the criticism of ethnocentrism, or even "Ameri-centrism," to the extent that studies have been carried out largely in the U.S. Criticism can even find purchase in the narrow focus taken in studies conducted on adolescents in the U.S., to the extent that White, middle-class young people have been the focus of investigation. As noted in Chapter 5, there has been great concern that adolescent females have self-esteem problems, but more recent research suggests that this applies mainly to White females, and then only to the extent that they have modeled their behaviors after advertisements portraying unrealistic standards of beauty and sexuality.

These anxieties about the importance of high levels of self-esteem may be the result of a "self-esteem movement" that began in the 1960s, especially in schools.[35] This movement was based on the assumption that if young people value themselves more they will have better academic achievement and peer relations. Unfortunately, the relationship between self-esteem and behavior is more complex than this. For example, over the past several decades, especially at the secondary level, to entice students to become more academically engaged, educators increasingly targeted students' self-esteem with higher grades (thereby inadvertently producing grade inflation, which has had a ripple effect in creating other problems[36]). However, the recent research conducted on the relationship between self-esteem and academic achievement (grades) reveals a weak statistical relationship between the two.[37] Studies examining cause and effect between grades and self-esteem find that higher grades may temporarily increase self-esteem to a minor degree, but this minor gain in self-esteem does not have an effect on subsequent grades.

Indeed, studies that have simultaneously examined both self-efficacy and self-esteem have found that when self-efficacy is included in the statistical analyses, a significant and substantial effect on academic achievement is found, but self-esteem is not a significant predictor at all.[38] In other words, controlling for self-efficacy, self-esteem is not statistically related to academic achievement. At the same time, those who are low in self-efficacy will reduce their academic aspirations and exhibit more problem behavior, including internalization problems, such as depression. If this decline is not stemmed, occupational aspirations are lowered.[39] Recent studies show that the negative effects of low self-efficacy can be addressed and reversed with educational interventions.[40] It thus appears that educators' focus on increasing self-esteem without also first addressing self-efficacy has been a major error.

Self-efficacy appears to operate to produce favorable academic outcomes to the extent that past skill-demonstrating performances enhance academic motivations, with these motivations enhancing future achievements.[41] Those with higher levels of self-efficacy monitor their performances more and persist with task completion more, two activities that are likely to produce better outcomes. Nonetheless, certain school environments or educational experiences can undermine a student's sense of self-efficacy. The transition out of primary school can undermine a student's sense of self-efficacy if less supportive teachers are encountered and less effective grading methods are used, as can classroom environments that emphasize group competition over individual mastery. In general, learning environments that set goals and support attempts to reach those goals by focusing on each student's task mastery enhance self-efficacy. A progressive educational philosophy that supports these learning environments may produce the best outcomes.[42]

Turning to the broader issue of cross-cultural differences, the self-efficacy literature has reported on these since its outset. The findings indicate that adolescents in (Asian) collectivist cultures hold weaker self-efficacy beliefs than do those in (Western) individualistic ones in the domains of academic achievement, occupational attainment, and emotional independence. These findings are counterintuitive in the area of academic achievement, because Asian students do better as a group than Western students.[43]

One explanation for this paradox is that collectivist societies are places that (a) are more norm-oriented, (b) have larger power distances between teachers and students, and (c) where students are highly motivated to reduce uncertainty, so they judge their own performances in relation to "externals." These externals include in-group and authority feedback, as well as clear norms and rules from their families and schools. Accordingly, outcomes are less likely to be attributed to the (efficacious) self, and more to characteristics of the task and the context in which it is carried out. In contrast, individualistic societies are less norm-oriented, the power difference between teacher and student is smaller, and students are less motivated to reduce uncertainty. Consequently, it is proposed that attributing causality to the self is necessary in order to compensate for weak performance norms. Thus Western students would be more likely to judge their performances in relation to "internals," which involve reflecting on their own performance histories. Self-efficacious beliefs appear to be especially important in (Western) societal contexts in which (a) performance norms are ambiguous, (b) individual-ization is "compulsory," and (c) forms of personal agency take on a greater impor-tance in determining situational outcomes.

Social Class

Unfortunately, in spite of various theoretical formulations and common-sense understandings, there are few empirical studies that assess social class differences in identity formation. In the absence of an empirical base, the default assumption among researchers is that forms of discrimination and under-privilege create diffi-culties that hamper identity formation among the disadvantaged—everyone who is not middle class or above will encounter special and/or more severe problems. Regrettably, although some theoretical models have been proposed,[44] there are no comprehensive studies investigating these processes among the most seriously economically disadvantaged to test this assumption,[45] perhaps because of the dif-ficulty in studying poor young people who often leave school at an early age. In contrast, it is much more convenient to conduct research on mainstream young people in school systems.

In fact, a few studies have examined social class differences among univer-sity students. One study of American college students compared lower-income students attending an élite college with affluent students at that college, find-ing that the affluent students were more status conscious—aware of their struc-tural advantages for their future prospects.[46] In contrast, lower-income students developed ways of downplaying the stigmatizing aspects of their socio-economic background. This study also compared this group of lower-income students with lower-income students attending a state college, finding that the lower-income students in the élite school also engaged in more of this identity management than their counterparts at the state college. The authors of this study accounted for this finding by suggesting that the lower-income students in the élite school experienced a more salient sense of contrast with affluent students because they faced it on a daily basis, whereas the lower-income students in the state col-lege were less likely to encounter these social-class contrasts. These results parallel those discussed above concerning members of ethnic groups who have certain "encounter" situations that highlight their status differences with other groups, prompting them to engage in more identity formation.[47] Interestingly, both groups of lower-income students engaged in more proactive identity formation than the affluent students, perhaps out of necessity because they did not have parental affluence to fall back upon.

This last point—that those from less affluent backgrounds have more of an onus placed on them to act proactively—is supported by other research finding that university students from less affluent backgrounds "grow up" faster in terms of their adult identity formation.[48] The key factor appears to be the extent to which parents are willing to finance a prolonged transition for their children and/or micromanage their lives. When young adults (especially males) must pay their own way through higher education, they appear to resolve adult-identity issues earlier and do better in college.[49] Too much parental paving of their way keeps them in more of a childlike state[50] and creates a *moral hazard* with respect to the responsibility of taking advantage of the educational and developmental opportunities afforded by a higher education.

In contrast to the dearth of studies investigating social class differences in identity formation, there are more studies investigating social class and self-esteem. Early studies focused on socio-economic status (SES; a measure usually based on a young person's father's educational level and sometimes occupation), finding that it was unrelated to self-esteem in children, but that a (negative) relationship emerged in adolescence, and strengthened in adulthood.[51] The explanation was that children are not aware of their socio-economic disadvantages/advantages, but adolescents become more aware, and adults are fully aware.

More recent studies have taken a closer look at the day-to-day conditions of lower social-class life (e.g., whether on welfare, father unemployed, condition of the neighborhood) that might affect children's and adolescent's self-esteem, finding stronger effects on adolescents than children.[52] It appears that social class can have special "hidden injuries." Unlike other stigmatized groups such as minority ethnic groups, the blame for their disadvantage is more often placed on the individual than the group. That is, ethnic group membership can be protective when it is construed as a source of pride, sheltering self-esteem when the person identifies with the group's positive aspects. In contrast, poor young people cannot seek succor from others living in poverty in ways available to young ethnic group members. Consequently, poor adolescents tend to blame themselves for their economic circumstances more than do others.[53] This situation is worse in societies that are widely believed by the public to be "classless," such as the U.S.

Studies have not examined the effects of social class on self-efficacy in the same depth as self-esteem, but the effects on children's and adolescent's self-efficacy appear to be mediated by parental behaviors, and lower-income parents tend to be less encouraging of academic and occupational achievement in their offspring.[54] However, research is conclusive that children and adolescents from lower social-class backgrounds are pessimistic about the future and their chances in the opportunity structures of their society, feeling that their efforts and abilities will not be duly rewarded. Consistent with the *self-fulfilling prophecy* prediction from the self-efficacy literature, any educational and occupational aspirations they might have to improve their economic conditions are adversely affected.[55]

Special-Needs Youth

As noted in the preceding section, the majority of the self and identity research has been conducted on mainstream youth samples in school systems. However, a common-sense hypothesis is that young people with special needs such as physical, mental, or learning disabilities, and those with family-origin issues like adoption face unique challenges in identity formation.[56]

Although the empirical literature about special-needs youth is meager, there have been some findings that run counter to the common-sense hypothesis. For example, one study found no differences in identity formation between adopted adolescents and a comparison sample of non-adoptees.[57] In contrast, much of the clinical literature on the adjustment of adoptees reports that adoptees experience myriad developmental problems, including identity disturbances and self-esteem problems.

In addition, it appears that some young people can develop positive disability identities similar to that found with the three-stage ethnic identity formation MEIM model discussed previously. They can do so by constructing the disability as a positive resource for growth and engaging in the proactive processes of exploring and experimenting to develop this positive identity.[58] This self-fulfilling prophecy effect can be applied to all young people with a stigmatized social identity, including LGBT (gay) youth.

A good example of this self-fulfilling prophecy effect can be found in a recent study of Deaf youth advocating the embracement of "Deafhood."[59] Deafhood represents a positive identity based on the collective heritage of the culture of Deaf people. Identifying with this heritage provides a source of pride and positive self-esteem, while combatting "audist" attitudes that devalue Deaf culture. In this advocacy approach to youth development, the Deaf community constitutes a minority group that can be seen as a resource rather than a deficit to society.[60] This research identifies the importance of nurturing self-efficacy in addition to self-esteem to help young Deaf people to become more proactive in their development:

> parents, teachers, and counselors should highlight competencies rather than self-esteem. [Deaf] children need to know what they are good at and have that fostered rather than attempting to boost self-esteem by encouraging unrealistic expectation in areas of lesser competencies. Moreover, the Deaf community must have a proactive, authoritative role in Deaf education. Deaf children need to see successful Deaf adults as role models and mentors and need to see themselves and their life experience reflected in their curricula.[61]

Like the identity literature, the vast majority of the self literature has been focused on mainstream samples, especially those in the regular school system.

A problem facing researchers, though, is that there are many types of special-needs youth, and each type of special need could constitute a field of study in itself, so it is not possible to speak of this group as *one* category of young people. Moreover, within some categories, such as the Deaf, there are significant variations in needs that make any generalizations difficult. Consequently, there has been no systematic study of the self-development of special needs youth as a "group."

The practical problems associated with studying the various types of young people with special needs include communication issues and assessment limitations for those with cognitive disabilities (i.e., because of their mental age they are unable to understand questions or complete certain types of questionnaires). To make matters worse, the literature is sparse because some medical disciplines concerned with conditions like Down syndrome do not recognize adolescence or early adulthood as areas of study.[62]

Extrapolating from the mainstream literature, the general default hypothesis would be that young people with special needs (such as developmental disabilities[63]) and family-origin issues (like adopted children) would face special challenges with respect to maintaining higher levels of self-esteem and/or positive self-concepts. The literature on self-esteem suggests that certain cognitive impairments can protect the young people from negative self-concepts, depending on their physical appearance. With respect to personal agency, for those with developmental disabilities during adolescence and early adulthood, the research suggests that the early development of a sense of self-efficacy predicts better skills development over time, which in turn feeds the sense of self-efficacy. This greater sense of self-efficacy predicts better life-course outcomes, including employment opportunities. The opportunities for those with developmental disabilities appear to be improving in the U.S., with about 30 percent going on to post-secondary studies (compared to 41 percent for mainstream samples).[64]

The special-needs literature on self-efficacy is even sparser than that on self-esteem. Building a database of literature is impeded by the fact that self-efficacy is largely domain-specific; consequently, there are so many types of special needs in relation to myriad domains of self-efficacy that an incredibly large number of studies will have to be undertaken to shed light on this important subject.

However, one area has been studied in depth, revealing some rather counter-intuitive findings. The study of self-efficacy among those with learning disabilities (LD) finds consistently that these young people can often have unrealistically high self-efficacy. That is, compared to students without these disabilities, LD students tend to consistently overestimate how well they perform in writing, spelling, and reading. Researchers in this area conclude that many adolescents with LD are "unskilled and unaware of it," or "don't know what they don't know," but lack the reflexive judgment to appreciate this. As a result of their overconfidence, they tend to expend less effort than do non-LD students, studying less, and spending less time on reading and writing assignments. Teachers of these students are thus faced with dealing with over-confidence. However, self-efficacy beliefs must have a realistic basis, so simple praise and encouragement does not help (in fact, praise can harm students if it produces unrealistic levels of self-esteem, as noted earlier). Instead, teachers and counselors must figure out how to teach LD students to become reflexive about their skills, and to maintain a realistic awareness of their skill levels. If they do this, students are more likely to focus on the effort needed to increase those skill levels.[65]

How Family And Friends Influence Who People Are and How They Feel About it

Family Settings

Much of the research on family context has focused on *parenting styles*, and the extent to which parents grant *psychological autonomy* to their children; that is, thinking for themselves and exploring their potentials and social opportunities. This parenting style gives children more independence while at same time providing benign guidance. The research literature is quite consistent in finding that those granted psychological autonomy while they grow up show the best developmental outcomes.[66]

The most popular empirical model for studying parenting styles identifies two dimensions of parenting behavior: responsiveness and demandingness.[67] Responsiveness is the parents' sensitivity to their children's signals, needs, and states. Demandingness refers to parents' expectations about their children's maturity and the parents' demands for their children to comply with those expectations. Cross-tabulating the two dimensions, in "present/absent" terms, produces four parenting styles.[68] The *authoritative* parent is both responsive and demanding. Together, these parental behaviors facilitate the development of psychological autonomy in offspring. In contrast, the *authoritarian* parent is demanding of compliance but unresponsive to the child's feelings. The *indulgent* parent is not demanding but is highly responsive to the child's needs. And the *indifferent* parent is neither responsive nor demanding. Indulgent and indifferent parenting styles are both more commonly called *permissive parenting*.

Both the identity formation and self-development literatures report consistent findings that certain parenting styles are more nurturing of positive and proactive forms of development. Responsive behaviors such as parental warmth and support, as well as encouragement and companionship, have been found to be positively associated with proactive identity formation. However, excessively high levels of responsiveness can apparently impede proactive identity explorations if the parental warmth and support leads to problems in *individuation*. At the same time, moderate demandingness (more democratic parenting) can enhance developmentally positive forms identity exploration, while excessive parental attempts to control adolescent behaviors can discourage identity explorations.[69]

Authoritative parenting is clearly the most favorable type of parenting for identity formation outcomes because it encourages independent problem solving and critical thinking, and thus provides opportunities for young people to engage in the proactive exploration of ideas. One study assessed the relationship between parenting styles and adolescent employment of coping strategies, finding that those socialized by authoritative parents tend to employ adaptive, task-oriented strategies that are associated with prosocial identity formation.[70] Over- and under-controlled adolescents are more likely to engage in task-irrelevant or passive behaviors that characterize inactive identity formation. Indeed, the literature suggests that young people raised by parents employing permissive styles are not socialized to become self-regulating, and the result can be greater impulsivity and lower self-reliance and orientation to work.[71]

As one would expect, authoritarian parents can discourage the proactive exploration of ideas and independent problem solving, and instead encourage an unquestioning dependence upon their control and guidance. A study of delinquent adolescent females revealed relationships in which mothers invalidated the daughter's positive identity statements or contradicted the daughter's positive assertions about her identity. Consistently negative or ambiguous feedback from a parent reflects an unresponsive relationship and is unlikely to encourage identity exploration.[72]

In sum, the empirical literature shows that young people who are over-controlled by authoritarian parents or under-controlled by permissive parents are not provided with sufficient encouragement and opportunities to practice exploration of ideas and self-regulation of behavior. The result can be the adoption of maladaptive strategies to problem solving concerning personal goals. The literature suggests that a moderate degree of connectedness, reflected through shared affection and an acceptance of individuality, provides the psychological foundation and security for adolescents for proactive identity formation.[73] In contrast, weak affectionate bonding with parents and poor communication levels, reflected by rejection or psychological withdrawal by the parent, seems to provide an insecure or constricted psychological base for identity explorations and experimentation. In addition, extreme affection that blurs self/ego boundaries between young people and their parents and limits family tolerance for individuality can discourage proactive identity formation.

Turning to self-development, the research on parenting effects finds that higher self-esteem among children and adolescents is associated with authoritative parenting, as well as with acceptance and warmth provided by other family members.[74] Similarly, the active promotion of both the individuality of adolescents and positive relationships with parents is associated with more positive forms of self-development.[75] Lastly, some research suggests that adolescents in single-mother households have lower self-esteem, especially if both the adolescent and the single mother are relatively young, but authoritative parenting skills apparently can offset this effect.[76]

Although the literature on the family and self-efficacy is not as extensive as the self-esteem literature, the consensus is that children's and adolescent's self-efficacy is affected by their parental models. Parents who are themselves self-efficacious provide their offspring not only with a model for this attribute but also with information about how to build self-motivations and competencies. And parents who are authoritative in providing high but realistic challenges to their offspring, while counseling them through these challenges, can engender higher levels of self-efficacy.[77]

The preceding review of the parenting styles literature needs to be understood in the context of criticisms about the underlying model of the four parenting styles. For example, there appears to be more of a reciprocal effect between parents and their children than this model suggests, and investigations are now underway into how children shape their relationship with their parents.[78] Attempting to authoritatively parent a willfully rebellious child may be ineffective because that child will not discuss issues or try to engage in higher-order moral reasoning and perspective taking (see Chapter 4).[79] Critics of this parenting model have studied the strategies children use to circumvent various forms of monitoring practices by parents that ostensibly provide guidance.[80] These monitoring-avoiding practices have been found even among apparently well-behaving children who score high on authoritative scales.[81] Clearly, it is easier to conceptualize young people as *tabula rasa* to be shaped by parental practices and to carry out studies based on this assumption, because bidirectionality is difficult to deal with statistically, but the comprehensive understanding of the effects of parenting practices suffers as a result.[82]

Peer Influences

It is a basic assumption of the SIFT that people who are inactive in their identity formation tend to avoid making decisions for themselves and are thus more reliant on situational demands than self-determined actions. This tendency to conform to external demands can make them more easily influenced by peer pressure.[83] While peer pressure does not always result in negative outcomes, identity-inactive adolescents have fewer agentic resources to resist provocation from peers to engage in deviant or antisocial behaviors, including activities associated with health risks.[84] There is also a tendency to become over-involved in aspects of popular youth culture that can prolong the transition to adulthood because of the avoidance of activities that lead to adult roles.[85]

The young person's self-esteem is also vulnerable to peer acceptance, especially with respect to issues of popularity like physical attractiveness.[86] As one would expect, those with more supportive peer relationships have higher self-esteem.[87] Self-esteem vulnerability is thus an important issue during the transition to adulthood, and needs to be attended to by those whose guidance and direction matters to young people, especially to guard against negative or manipulative influences.

Recent research has found that "peer initiatives" can bolster self-esteem, along with a number of related issues, like positive health-promoting behaviors. These peer initiatives are designed to provide group and counseling opportunities for adolescents to feel competent and successful with their peers, which in turn helps them to develop effective coping strategies and receive social support. Ultimately, the adolescent can come to feel more self-efficacious in the peer domain, with all the benefits of higher levels of self-efficacy. The mutual social support that can result from good peer relations, and the social support derived from planned peer initiatives, can inoculate the adolescent from the negative stereotypes and social exclusion that go with the role of the "teenager" in contemporary Western societies.[88]

Peers can strongly influence each other's sense of self-efficacy through support and encouragement, but also through imitation. Peers observing each other's successes (and failures) can experience them vicariously. This effect is enhanced by the fact that adolescents tend to associate with peers who are similar in motivation and competence; thus, individual competencies can produce positive effects in other members of the peer group, as in the case of boosting academic achievement. Conversely, less competent peers can decrease the self-efficacy of others in the peer group, for example, pulling down their academic achievement.[89]

How Identity Formation Is Influenced by Educational Experiences

It is widely assumed that attending college or university has dramatic effects on personality development, including identity formation, and for several decades researchers have explored the ways in which these settings might stimulate forms of human development. Some early identity research suggested that the proportion of college/university students who engage in proactive identity formation doubles between first and fourth year, from about 20 percent to 40 percent.[90] However, in the largest review of these studies, it was concluded that the evidence of widespread (main effect) identity development that is directly attributable exclusively to college/university attendance is inconclusive, because few controls have been employed to account for maturation effects (i.e., whether comparable identity formation takes place among those not attending, as a result of normal maturational processes).[91] The same can be said for identity formation during secondary school attendance: there is evidence of change but how much happens as a result of maturation or other effects, and how much can be attributed to the educational contexts themselves, has not been established.

Thus, net of competing explanations like maturation effects, there has been little demonstrable effect of college/university attendance on identity formation. This may be because deep-seated characteristics underpinning identity are resistant to change during this period,[92] or simply that these factors are not targeted in any systematic way at most higher-educational institutions (whereas the cognitive variables are directly targeted, and conclusive evidence exists for changes in these areas), so expectations of substantive changes may be unrealistic.

Research based on the Identity Capital Model (ICM) sheds some light on these educational issues. This model shifts the focus to identity-based agency and its importance in late-modern contexts characterized by loose normative structures that open up the possibility of individualized adaptation strategies. With this model, we can identify potential interactions between educational context and the student (i.e., person-context interactions, as postulated by developmental contextualism). For example, there is evidence that university students who are more agentic in their identity formation make greater gains in subjectively feeling like, and being treated as, an adult while at university and afterward. These gains are associated with subsequently integrating into an adult community, with occupational benefits that carry over into their adulthood.[93]

Similarly, a series of studies published in the UK[94] shed light on the relevance of the ICM in understanding the influence of educational institutions in late-modern societies. These studies analyzed data generated by the British Birth Cohort Studies, which drew samples based on births in a single week in the three years 1946, 1958, and 1970. The chief finding is that the most recent cohort (born in 1970) needed more intangible identity capital resources than did the earlier cohorts, whose transitions were governed far more by the extant occupational opportunities and mainstream structures in the education-work transition. In the past, employment prospects were structured much more independently of these sorts of agentic qualities, whereas more recently people have needed to possess certain agentic characteristics if they were to make the transition at all. This research concludes that those without certain key agentic attributes increasingly face exclusion from, or precarious participation in, the labor force, whereas in the past some sort of transition could have been made independent of these attributes (including basic resources such as literacy and numeracy).

The increasing need for young people to take proactive approaches to the education-to-work transitions is of particular concern in Britain with respect to those young people who leave full-time education at the minimum age of 16 and then spend a substantial period not in education, employment, or training. Accordingly, British researchers call for counseling targeted at high-risk groups to help young people compensate for a lack of tangible and intangible identity capital in the transition to work and adult life.[95]

Similar results have been reported in the U.S., with researchers there concluding that the ICM helps to conceptualize "the deficiencies in guiding structures caused by dejobbing and disintegration of career paths in contemporary organizations"[96] that require planfulness among prospective employees, confirming the ICM's fundamental postulate that "planful competence in career development [is] related to greater realization of one's potential and a higher degree of social adjustment." A key ingredient of planfulness is what could be called a "life skill" for making choices. Remarkably, given the importance of the choices people have to make in late-modern societies in regulating their lives and to some degree being the "architects" of their identities, there is virtually no formal or informal preparation for this life skill, even in educational systems. Box 8.2 provides some socio-historical perspective on this problem and possible solutions by including an "education for choice" for young people as part of a life-skills curriculum.[97]

BOX 8.2 EDUCATION FOR CHOICE

Almost a century ago, the famous anthropologist Margaret Mead argued that Western societies need to provide their young people with a formal "education for choice" as they grow up.[98] Mead wrote that in comparison to modern Western societies (of the 1920s), in premodern societies (specifically Samoan culture, which she was studying at the time) young people had far less choice as they came of age regarding the specific content of their future adult identities, and she noted that this had the effect of eliminating much conflict from their lives: they did not have to choose among competing religions, political philosophies, or from among a bewildering array of adult occupations. In contrast, observing an earlier version of the individualization process we have been examining in the present book, Mead noted there was a virtual *requirement* in the U.S. that young people choose for themselves among myriad religious, political, and occupational options.

Of course, the answer to our educational problems today is not to revert to premodern social forms, which have their own sets of problems, but to advance to new ones that can realistically help us deal with these problems. What Mead's analysis does suggest is that we need to think of contemporary challenges in terms of a baseline found in tribal societies where identities are ascribed, rather than based on choice and individualization, because it appears that humans do not have an inherent capacity for make propitious choices. Rather, it appears that we need to be taught how to do so. Moreover, we now have little guidance for making even default choices, because the traditional models of adulthood have been eroded by economic changes, especially the more recent ones associated with neoliberal market policies that have put even more pressure on people to be autonomous, self-determining agents (see box 2.1 for more).

Mead advocated the development of critical thinking skills and out-group tolerance among young people as a way of making the freedom to choose more of a reality than an illusion. As it was in 1920s America, even in a society where freedom of choice was highly valued, the reality of the situation was that the freedom to choose was often an illusion that the average citizen could not see through. In Mead's words, young people "must be taught how to think, not what to think," and they must be "unhampered by prejudices" that cloud their thinking about the choices that might be available to them and others.[99]

Choices based on unreflective thought limit the effectiveness of those very choices in making a difference in a person's life; choices based on prejudice limit the breadth of the person's social radius as well as the effectiveness of choices in other people's lives to the extent that those choices create obstacles to others' life chances. In making these recommendations, Mead prefigured later thinking in educational and developmental psychology concerning post-conventional morality (Kohlberg) and ethical identities (Erikson). The likelihood of proactive, agentic action that overcomes social structural obstacles is diminished if choices are based on lower-order levels of cognition, morality, and ethics. Accordingly, we cannot expect the disadvantaged to rise above adversity if they are not equipped with the personal resources for doing so. And, even if social structural obstacles were suddenly magically eliminated, those who have lived their lives under constrained conditions would not have the agentic resources for functioning in unconstrained environments.

Unfortunately, since the time of Mead's writing, we have not developed the educational means by which to teach young people critical thinking skills and tolerance on a mass scale, even as the ideology of free choice has spread throughout societies around the world. Instead, only a small percentage of (young) people today develop these attributes, and then largely on their own and sometimes as part of a rebellion against the obtuseness and bigotry that they perceive in the adults who are ostensibly teaching them about life. While these advances in educational wisdom and technique did not come to fruition in the 20th century, perhaps they will in the 21st century. If they do, we can look forward to advanced societies where social cohesion is created and maintained among competent, goal-oriented, and ethically responsible citizens.

Identity Capital and Mass Higher Education

It is worth delving into the ICM in more detail here for three reasons. First, as we saw earlier, the general research on identity formation is inconclusive about the influence of school contexts—schools do not appear to "create a tide that raises all boats" for students' identity formation (i.e., there is no statistical main effect, net of control variables). Second, evidence from the ICM suggests that "some boats do rise"—some types of students do make developmental gains in specific contexts (i.e., there are interaction effects whereby certain students benefit in certain contexts). And third, the ICM directs us to examine the wider societal context—late-modernity—to look for influences that might make identity formation more difficult in general and require that identity-based agency be utilized in order for students to make gains.

Accordingly, the ICM suggests that a reason why identity formation may not flourish in contemporary school systems lies with the problematic nature of some types of educational systems. Part of the difficulties faced by students in many late-modern societies is that higher educational settings have become *massified*—expanded to include significant portions of the youth population while reducing per-student funding. The massification influence pushes more people—even reluctant ones—into schools for longer periods. The consequences of this massification trend are likely lower levels of educational, financial, and emotional support for many students. For many students in these mass systems, education is merely "sustaining" rather than "transformative."[100]

In many countries, the creation of mass higher-educational systems has led to the development of a "business model" at the university level based on efficiencies and accountability, both in terms of how universities are governed and how students are recruited and treated. The university student is often treated as a "consumer" in these mass systems. At the same time, more young people are "pushed" by external factors to attend because of parental pressures, a poor youth labor market, and credential inflation (i.e., successive cohorts of students have to earn higher degrees to qualify for jobs once performed by those with less education). Together, these influences signal to students that "education" is something to be "consumed" in the same fashion as other items common in late modernity. These students can then simply undertake default individualization strategies because they do not see higher education primarily as an opportunity to engage in developmental individualization.

The "student-as-consumer" model of education thus encourages various forms of intellectual and agentic passivity. In cases where some students expect to be "served," they are less likely to meet their educational environments "halfway" in bilateral, agentic relationships that would foster active academic engagement. Approaching education as something to be served and consumed encourages a hedonic, extrinsic motivation for participating, as opposed to an intrinsic "pull" motivation based on an appreciation of learning, self-discipline, and mastery of experience. Such a system apparently does not nurture identity-based agency among most students to a great degree. These issues have been recently discussed in two books written for the public.[101]

As noted earlier, the ICM is based on the developmental contextualism premise that optimal development requires a goodness of fit between the person and his or her contexts.[102] The implications of the investigations of the university context for the ICM are clear: only a minority of university students are fully engaged in their studies, with the majority either putting in a token effort or treating their studies like a part-time activity. This "culture of disengagement" context, implicitly condoned by many universities in countries like Canada, the U.S., and the UK, encourages a default individualization strategy of identity capital acquisition in this setting and thus does not encourage the use of, or nurture, agentic or integrative forms of identity capital. Graduates from this culture of disengagement will likely reap minimal personal benefits from their higher education, except from the possession of a (devalued) credential.

The various attitudes students take toward their university education have been studied by applying the goodness-of-fit concept to university learning contexts.[103] This research identifies *person-context interactions* where students' motivations and behaviors can be all-important in determining how university settings are experienced and what benefits are derived from them. Specifically, this research suggests that those who approach their higher-education studies in an agentic manner—with the primary goal of enhancing their own personal and intellectual development—experience these contexts and their mentors more favorably, and have better outcomes in terms of grades and learning, regardless of their socio-economic background. Non-agentic—inactive or perfunctory approaches—are not associated with these positive experiences and outcomes; indeed, excessive parental pressure can have negative effects, as can high levels of financial support from parents (i.e., students can be less engaged in their studies when their parents are paying for their education).

A questionnaire, the Student Motivations for Attending University (SMAU), was developed to measure the various reasons university students have for attending, identifying five "push-pull" motivations. The logic in developing this measure involved identifying the intangible resources associated with various motivations along with the beneficial person-context interactions that university students might experience in mass universities.

This research revealed that two "push" motivations are relatively common but passive approaches to learning among contemporary students: an "expectation driven" motivation, where students are attending in order to please their parents, and a "default" motivation, where students are attending because of a lack of perceived alternatives, yet are deriving little from their studies. These passive approaches generally show negative outcomes with respect to learning, as measured by skills acquired and grades attained.[104]

Three active "pull" approaches undertaken by undergraduate students are also identified: the "careerist materialist" approach, the "personal-intellectual development" drive, and the "humanitarian" motivation. Of these three active motivations, the personal-intellectual development motivation is the most beneficial in terms of acquiring academic skills and attaining higher grades, while the careerist-materialist approach yields fewer positive benefits, suggesting that those who are most willing to invest in their personal-intellectual development acquire more identity capital than those who are simply making career investments.[105]

This higher-educational research confirms the capitalizing role of agency, namely, that it is important for certain forms of development, and that these forms of development can lead to even further development of identity capital; for instance, academic skills associated with developmental individualization, and the grade/credentials necessary to move into higher spheres of functioning. The sequence in the capitalization on agency can be depicted as follows:

> Agency → active motivations → academic engagement → skills/grades … → further opportunities (including chances to exercise more complex forms of agency)

As noted, based on developmental contextualism, the ICM proposes that positive outcomes are predicted by a goodness of fit between the motivations students have in attending universities and the learning environments they encounter there. The ICM built on the goodness-of-fit proposition by adding the concept of agency; namely, that individual differences in personal agency help to account for how people can potentially influence this goodness of fit by being active participants in their own personal/intellectual development. This research also led to the identification of identity horizons and identity anxiety. Identity horizons vary along a narrow–broad dimension, with broader horizons including a greater variety of projections of future possible identities into educational and work contexts, thereby potentially broadening their social radius. Identity anxiety refers to a fear of experiencing the transformations associated with proactive identity formation and moving beyond current "comfort zones," especially the limited social radius provided by childhood friends and family. Questions used to measure this form of anxiety suitable for high school and college/university students include: "If I pursued a further education, I'm afraid that it would confuse me about 'who I am,'" and "I'm hesitant to pursue more education because it would create tensions with the people I grew up with."[106]

The empirical analysis of these concepts finds support for the "identity horizon effect." With this effect, first-generation undergraduate and graduate students (whose parents do not have college/university degrees or graduate/professional degrees, respectively), especially those without parental encouragement, have more limited perceptions of their future educational and occupational horizons. Those with limited horizons experience anxieties about potential identity changes. In turn, these anxieties can create inflated estimates of financial costs, which can then increase indecision about future educational plans. Ultimately, this can lead some secondary students to not pursue a post-secondary education at all, and some undergraduate students to not consider a graduate education, even though they may have the ability to progress further in their studies.

Research also suggests that the identity horizon model could be useful in studies of educational planning by students and parents, and in evaluations of potential programs that might address the problems associated with the restricted identity horizon effect. Given the deep-seated nature of identity horizons/anxieties, these interventions should start no later than early high school, especially among students whose parents did not go beyond secondary school. Of course, it is also the case that many people are, and can be, perfectly happy without undertaking these higher forms of education, so we must be careful not to "push" these people into something that is not a good fit for them. Indeed, as discussed earlier, our research demonstrates that pushing someone into higher-educational settings can be counterproductive for all concerned.

These recommendations are based on the assumption that early interventions should help those with restricted horizons and who are prone to identity anxiety (and thus lower levels of intangible identity capital) to become proactive in their own identity formation and develop more positive academic self-concepts upon which to expand their social radii. Their educational experiences would thus become "transformative" rather than merely "sustaining." These findings and recommendations are consistent with our other findings indicating that identity-based agency[107] is likely a relatively stable, deep-seated disposition, probably formed earlier in life, and that it may be too late to attempt to nurture it at the post-secondary level. They are also consistent with educational research based on the Matthew effect with respect to interventions with children who are poor readers.[108] The earlier these interventions are undertaken the better. Children who can read experience multiple positive ripple effects from these abilities and practices, whereas those who do not practice reading miss out on these developmental experiences. Children who are poor readers may never make up for their skills deficits later in life, and they can fall further behind their peers as "learning to read" is replaced by "reading to learn" as a developmental necessity. In short, the Matthew effect does not have to be zero-sum in all contexts; there is no reason why everyone cannot become "rich readers," or for that matter "rich" in identity-based agency.

Box 8.3 shows the various components of identity-based agency measured in research based on the ICM, highlighting the low levels of agency that can make progress through schools and into the workforce more precarious in late-modern societies.

BOX 8.3   TYPES AND LEVELS OF IDENTITY-BASED AGENCY

The identity capital model has been empirically evaluated with identity-based agency measured with the Multi-Measure Agentic Personality Scale (MAPS).[109] The MAPS is a composite scale based on the sum of measures of the character traits commonly called self-esteem, purpose in life, internal locus of control, and ego strength. Respectively, items measuring each trait represent the following types of content: "People usually follow my ideas," "My life is . . . running over with exciting good things," "What happens to me is my own doing," and "I enjoy difficult and challenging situations." The combination of these types of items makes a useful measure of identity-based agency that is particularly applicable to the identity *resources* relevant to the individualistic, late-modern, higher-educational context.

To give a better idea of the importance of these traits for identity-based agency, the following bullet points highlight what it is like to experience relatively low levels of each:

- *self-esteem*: context shy—not feeling worthy of moving up the stairways of maturity and responsibility;

- *purpose in life*: a lack of connection between inner potentials and needs and outer opportunities;
- *internal locus of control*: waiting for direction and guidance from others;
- *ego strength*: inability to complete tasks and a lack of focus; vulnerability to distraction and a need for immediate impulse gratification.

The consequences of having low levels of each—having low levels of functional identity capital—are obvious in cultures where proactivity is the norm for the more successful adult identities. Thus far, this scale has been successfully translated into Finnish, Italian, Japanese, and Turkish,[110] showing acceptable reliability and validity in all of these versions.

Conclusions: Proactivity and Context

The results are consistent for both identity formation and self-development that proactivity is linked in late-modern social contexts to many forms of positive development. Proactive identity formation associated with explorations and experimentations leading to goal setting and social commitments are consistently positive across a variety of social contexts, including the education-to-work settings. Factors such as broad identity horizons are also important, as are various means of diminishing identity anxieties among those who are intimidated by, or unprepared for, the complex transformations now required of people during the transition to adulthood.

The research findings on self-esteem, in contrast, are less clear, both developmentally and when applied to subgroups of the adolescent population. This area of research remains controversial from the point of view of some psychologists who feel that self-esteem is a mere epiphenomenon (a by-product of mental activity that has little subsequent causal influence on behavior), and not the "vaccine" for positive development that some have contended.[111] Instead, empirical research shows that high self-efficacy is a far more important attribute promoting academic achievement than is high self-esteem, and that high self-esteem is more likely a *consequence* of circumstances than a *cause* of behavior, so interventions to increase self-esteem without first engendering self-efficacy will be of limited success.

In contrast to the limited benefits of self-esteem, self-efficacy has been found to be empirically associated with: higher learning outcomes and academic aspirations and accomplishments; the ability to manage school transitions and poor teachers; the consideration, and pursuit of, a wider array of career options and greater persistence in pursuing chosen career paths (although there are gender differences in this realm in favor of boys); lower levels of risky sexual behaviors and other high-risk activities; the ability to resist peer pressure; and more involvements in civic and prosocial activities. The value of self-efficacy has also been demonstrated in both individualistic and collectivist societies, although the mechanisms by which it develops and is exercised, as well as its purposes, may vary.[112]

9

IDENTITY FORMATION AND THE POTENTIALS OF HUMAN DEVELOPMENT

"The best way to find yourself is to lose yourself in the service of others."

Mahatma Gandhi[1]

In the first part of this concluding chapter, we summarize the most robust findings regarding the relationships among forms of proactive self-development, identity formation, and moral reasoning. In the second part, we examine some attempts to practically apply these findings. We end the chapter and book with our reflections about promising future methodological and theoretical directions.

Factors Affecting Development

The empirical literature on self-development and identity formation is clear in terms of the findings concerning the personal and contextual factors associated with the respective positive forms of development. There are also clear conclusions to be drawn from the literature regarding moral reasoning and positive development.

Self-Development

The literature suggests that self-esteem increases over adolescence and into early adulthood and can be an important developmental factor, but its importance has been over-estimated. At the same time, the importance of self-efficacy, a form of agency, appears to have been overlooked by early researchers. Self-esteem can be unstable and subject to situational influences, especially during adolescence, but self-efficacy is more stable and less affected by situational factors. Self-esteem needs to have a firm basis in reality if it is to be stable, and if it is based on false premises, can set the person up for serious personal disappointments and misdirected trajectories into adulthood.

For example, if a young person with low or average academic abilities is continually given false feedback that s/he is a top student and internalizes that designation as a self-concept, that person will eventually discover the truth if s/he goes far enough in the educational system. Along the way, this misled student may experience considerable anxiety and depression as it becomes increasingly difficult to maintain the illusion. Eventually, he or she will be disillusioned, which can be the source of an intense personal crisis. This crisis can include the realization by the person of having gone further and further in an educational/occupational direction for which s/he is not well suited.

In contrast, a student who bases his or her academic self-esteem on a sense of self-efficacy—meaning that s/he is actually talented in one or more academic areas—subsequent educational experiences will be rewarding and less stressful, and are more likely to take the person on a realistic trajectory through the educational system and into the labor force, providing a firm foundation for the transition to adulthood and the formation of an adult identity.[2]

High self-esteem is thus not the "inoculation" for positive forms of development as some have claimed, and in fact, can place the person at risk if it has an unrealistic basis. Nevertheless, low levels of self-esteem can be associated with poor adjustment and antisocial behavior, although the cause and effect relationships among these factors are not clear. For example, increasing someone's self-esteem may not make him or her better adjusted or less delinquent; low self-esteem may be a realistic consequence of poor adjustment.

However, it appears that the extreme importance that has been attributed to self-esteem in the West is largely a product of the form of individualism prevalent in the U.S. To the extent that young people hinge their self-concepts and identities on peer approval and popular cultural models as sources of self-esteem, they are more vulnerable to the vicissitudes of situational factors and unrealistic goals for their sense of well-being. This can create a precarious situation for their mental health (especially in terms of anxiety, depression, and proneness to suicide) and identity formation, especially if they internalize unrealistic ideals. For example, as noted, these unrealistic ideals might be associated with academic and career goals as a result of certain hyper-nurturing but misleading educational experiences. Self-efficacy appears to be a much more robust and positive attribute.

Identity Formation

The empirical literature is clear that adolescence is a critical time when many people become active in varying degrees in their identity formation, basing it in part on the self-concept development of childhood and early adolescence, in part on the social roles available to them in their immediate community, and in part on the age-status expectations of their culture. There are clear distinctions found in the research conducted in late-modern societies between those who become proactive and those who do not. Inactivity is related to most forms of maladjustment and lower functioning, especially if it persists into early adulthood. Proactivity is associated with the opposite characteristics, and is thus the model to be used in researching and promoting *positive youth development*, even if the young person chooses goals outside mainstream education-to-work institutional settings (e.g., pursuing alternative lifestyles and alternative careers in music, or arts and crafts). Most people eventually become sufficiently active in their identity formation to develop a functional adult identity and become productive members of society, in some context of their choosing, although the process seems to be taking longer for more young people than it did in the past, lasting into their 20s. Box 9.1 highlights the findings on the relationship between identity capital resources and mental health/social functioning.

BOX 9.1 IDENTITY CAPITAL RESOURCES AND MENTAL HEALTH/SOCIAL FUNCTIONING

It is axiomatic in Erikson's theory that positive forms of identity formation are associated with better mental health. This axiom is based on the assumption that, as people gain a more secure sense of ego identity (i.e., temporal-spatial continuity) during their progress through the identity stage, overall mental functioning improves. Several studies have confirmed this axiom with respect to identity capital acquisition. Based in part on the empirical measure highlighted in box 8.1, identity-based agency has been found to be statistically associated with mental health and higher levels of daily functioning.[3] These findings are compatible with the Matthew effect; namely, those who begin their adult-identity formation with sufficient resources will struggle less in the transition to adulthood than those who do not have adequate resources. Indeed, it appears that those who enter their 20s with a poorly synthesized ego identity are more likely to experience problems in their late 20s in developing a sense of adult identity and to experience chronic identity confusion at sub-clinical levels (some 20 percent of the sample had this level of identity confusion).[4]

These results provide further support for the postulate that young people need a sufficient level of certain intangible resources for the now-prolonged transition to adulthood. In this case, higher levels of ego identity in the late teens/ early 20s appear to be related to later gains in forms of adult identity, whereas those with lower levels of ego identity can have a more problematic transition to adulthood, with the transition impeded by chronic identity confusion.

It is also true that late-modern societies tend to place much of the onus on individuals to direct their own development, creating some unique difficulties for those with different cultural ancestries and ethnicities. Surprisingly, schools, including those at the post-secondary level, seem to contribute little on average to identity formation, at least in terms of the inactivity–proactivity dimension. The effects of educational settings are found mainly in terms of the content of the occupational identities they confer through the sorting of students by ability type/level and the awarding of credentials. Families appear to play a larger role in identity development, with the authoritative-type parenting style seeming to provide the best support and stimulus for proactive development.

Moral Reasoning Development

In most contemporary Western societies, and the non-Western societies studied thus far, it appears that the majority of both male and female late adolescents and young adults are capable of conventional forms of moral reasoning. Still, substantial arrests are evident among those who do not develop a sufficient capacity for empathy and perspective taking and/or who do not have the social stimuli to encourage them to exercise their cognitive capacities.

By early adulthood, however, only a minority of the population moves on to post-conventional reasoning, and this development is more likely to take place among those who experience a post-secondary education. At the same time, a minority may still be exercising pre-conventional reasoning even in adulthood. Primary- and secondary-level educational systems do not seem to provide consistent models or stimuli for higher forms of moral reasoning and instead encourage lower forms of reasoning with their authoritarian practices. Peers and parents appear to be the most influential, especially in families where parents practice an authoritative style of parenting.

Intervention and Counseling Applications

There are many obstacles to taking self/identity/moral-reasoning research into the applied realm, especially in individualistic societies where ideas of freedom of choice are virtually sacred. Given the increasingly choice-based nature of identity formation in late-modern societies, an obvious obstacle to be overcome is in proposing viable applications that influence people's choice-making. For example, we know that there are considerable drawbacks in late-modern contexts to inactive forms of development in terms of school failure, health-risk behaviors, mental health problems, and poor psychological functioning. However, given the "rights" of people to adopt whatever stances they like to their own personal development, how might these insights be applied in ways that do not interfere with people's sense of self-determination? Although this might seem like an intractable problem for modern democracies, it needs to be recognized that modern democracies *have* developed and *continue to* support institutions that directly and deliberately affect people's choices, most notably educational systems.

Nonetheless, the empirical literature suggests that our current educational systems do little to enhance the forms of (self/identity/moral) development examined in this book, at least in terms of the most important psychological process associated with the highest levels of functioning for all three, namely, proactivity. Few educational experiences are "transformative," while most are merely "sustaining" of the person's existing developmental capacities.[5] Education systems also vary in quality, and much mass education has become perfunctory, even at the tertiary level.[6] There appears to be ample room in the curriculum to experiment with innovations that yield returns in certain non-academic aspects of people's lives, including their self/identity formation and moral reasoning development.

Such efforts would need to be informed by a sophisticated view of choice-making itself. Some recent work in psychology helps to bring to light the difficulties associated with unrestrained choice options,[7] just as early work identified the potentially negative consequences of unguided self-determination.[8] This recent work argues that people in individualistic societies face a "tyranny of choice" by the very nature of excessive choice-making requirements for which they are not necessarily equipped. Certainly, there are liberating potentials to be gained from a greater freedom of choice, but ostensibly unconstrained choice can be paradoxically constraining, as in situations of having too many choices with too little information, living with the consequences of poor choices, and experiencing the various negative psychological consequences routinely associated with facing numerous choices on a daily basis.[9] Box 9.2 highlights the idea of the tyranny of choice, providing some useful examples of the problems that emerge, and how applying some principles of the Identity Capital Model might rectify them.

BOX 9.2 THE TYRANNY OF CHOICE, AND ITS IMPLICATIONS FOR IDENTITY CAPITAL IN LATE-MODERN EDUCATIONAL SYSTEMS

Psychologist Barry Schwartz recently presented the argument that Western societies have been so determined to provide unlimited choices through the market economy that they have created a "tyranny of freedom" and "a paradox of choice" for many people that actually decreases their quality of life and happiness, and to some extent, diminishes their life chances.[10] Although some people may flourish with the choices available, others suffer from indecision or a sense of being overwhelmed, which can lead to feelings of stress, regret, anxiety, depression, and self-blame. For example, consumer research shows that too many choices of a product line (e.g., shampoos, wine, computers) can actually reduce sales, as people walk away unable to select a product from shelves stocked with dozens of choices. People avoid choices for a variety of reasons. Paramount is the fear of being wrong and the ensuing anxiety about missing opportunities because the wrong decision was made. When choices are more limited, the fear and anxiety is mitigated because the person does not have to accept as much blame for the wrong decision.

Providing a familiar example for readers of this book, this psychologist argues that American college students experience "choice overload" in their curriculum to the point where they find it more difficult to finish college, and to even have an idea of what to do with their lives if they do graduate. Paradoxically, these students are taking longer and longer to finish their studies and many are finding that they eventually drift into occupations anyway, with no grand plan to direct them. Stress levels, depression, anxiety, and eating disorders are all on the rise among these student populations.

In approaching this problem with the Identity Capital Model, the distinction between default and developmental individualisation is useful when formulated in terms of the decision points that are faced on a daily basis. Each decision point can represent the difference between taking a more difficult, effort-based, potentially transformative, growth experience or the easier path of least resistance and effort that merely sustains existing levels of development. Of course, people do both, but what is needed to undertake the developmental route of individualization is to choose more of the growth-enhancing options over the least-effort ones. This sort of choice training is lacking in many educational systems today as highlighted above in box 9.2. In fact, there is evidence that public school systems in some countries, notably in the U.S., actually facilitate the path of least effort for many of their students and are therefore in effect training them to engage in default individualisation. Schools may encourage default individualisation for a variety of reasons, ranging from poor funding and over-crowded classes to trying to cajole students not to drop out by not presenting them with any challenges that might produce a sense of failure, thereby dumbing down the curriculum and making the situation worse.

From the perspective of identity capital acquisition, this is exactly the wrong approach to take because it simply fosters default individualisation, leaving young people vulnerable to attempts to manipulate their identities. What schools need to do is to provide some sort of training for choice-making and life-project planning, both of which are central tasks of the individualization process. This requires that guiding structures be put in place to facilitate choice-making, in part by showing the realistic limits to the choices available. Both choice training and life-project planning techniques would be essential building blocks of identity capital acquisition. If young people received, as part of their education, the skills to self-reflect and strategize about their lives and the roles they will play in their communities, this should help widen the radius of the person's experience and thinking from the local toward the global in a moral-ethical manner, while at the same time expanding their identity horizons.

In looking for ways to improve developmental support systems in schools, we can draw on research from the past couple of decades that has identified how support systems for positive youth development[11] can be created or enhanced at the community level,[12] as well as at the societal level, with opportunities for student exchanges, volunteer work abroad and at home, experiences with faith communities,[13] and so forth.[14] In addition, the literature indicates that the positive benefits of authoritative parenting, with its guided-nurturance encouragement of mature behaviors, extend to other institutions, such as schools, community centers, and the workplace.[15] Moreover, models have been developed for various forms of interventions to enhance identity formation and moral reasoning, and these could become part of school/community support infrastructures.[16] The Nordic countries lead the world in the latter types of opportunities for young people, premising such efforts on the (authoritative) view that young people constitute positive resources for society who deserve to participate in meaningful ways.[17]

Unfortunately, when we attempt to move from theory to specific applications, we find that our knowledge concerning how to effectively intervene when identity problems are evident is sparse. Indeed, as a field, identity intervention is in its infancy. Part of the problem lies in the "normality" of many identity problems, especially those experienced by young people during the transition to adulthood. In most cases, aberrations associated with identity crises are simply tolerated, or they are ignored, on the assumption that they will pass, which they may do in time. But not only do we know little about how to help young people through a stage-specific identity crisis, we know even less about how to deal with the more serious identity problems, disorders, and pathologies discussed in Chapter 2. In individualistic societies, as noted earlier, where the right to freely choose regardless of possible negative consequences is highly revered, it is difficult to convince many people of the need to be prudent about how to govern their lives. At the personal level, intervening can be seen as interfering, and adult concern can be mistaken for intergenerational prejudice. And, at the social level, communities can be seen as oppressive and reactionary, while programs and policies can be mistaken for authoritarian paternalism.

There is also the problem of developing a consensus about just what constitutes an identity problem, and how severe it might be before an intervention is undertaken. Some people just live with it, while others seek help. Erikson, himself, was quite cautious in this regard, in spite of his extensive clinical experience in dealing with identity pathologies. In his view, most people could work through their youthful identity crises, often in a growth-producing, self-therapeutic manner. He thought that the adult community should step back and ignore some forms of deviance associated with most identity crises. On the one hand, there is the potential of permanently labeling the young person and thereby setting up a self-fulfilling prophecy of a negative outcome.[18] On the other hand, he did not think that we know enough about identity crises to intervene in most cases. When directly asked about this, Erikson replied that "we would play engineers, without the necessary mathematics for engineering." For Erikson, intervention was appropriate in severe cases of obvious harm to the person or others, or when a person asked for it.

Fortunately, a useful research program is underway that combines the Eriksonian approach to identity formation with one from general psychiatry, taking the diagnostic criteria specified in the *Diagnostic and Statistical Manual of Mental Disorders* (DSM-III) discussed in Chapter 2 to develop a 10-item scale that can be easily and quickly administered in a variety of settings, ranging from clinical ones to large-scale online surveys. Following the DSM III's identification of identity disorder, and the DSM IV's symptomatology of the less severe identity problem, the Identity Distress Survey (IDS)[19] also provides a continuous measure of "identity distress."[20]

Thus far, the prevalence of identity disorder based on the IDS is estimated at between 8 and 12 percent for high school and college students in the U.S. and 16 percent among at-risk high school students.[21] The (less severe) identity problem is estimated at 14 percent for high school students,[22] 34 percent for at-risk high school students,[23] and 23 percent for adolescents (ages 11 to 20) receiving services from a community mental health center.[24]

With respect to the general construction of identity distress, this research suggests that it may be on the rise.[25] Higher levels of identity distress are correlated with poor adjustment to academic, social, and emotional conditions and lower levels of ego strength,[26] poor body image,[27] internalizing *and* externalizing symptoms,[28] and recent experiences of trauma.[29] Identity distress is also associated with "normal" identity explorations and is responsive to interventions.[30] Researchers in a number of countries around the world are currently using the IDS.[31]

In the meantime, other identity researchers have studied and experimented with interventions seeking to increase the extent to which a person explores commitment-related alternatives associated with choice-making.[32] The targets of these interventions are mainly identity diffused/confused young people, who by definition have not actively sought out alternatives to their current life-course trajectory. The results of empirical evaluations of these interventions show moderate levels of success in stimulating the exploration of various commitments, but as noted above there are also reasons to be cautious about pushing people into courses of action for which they are not prepared.

One particularly promising intervention model has emerged out of the empirical literature.[33] This is a "co-constructivist model" that seeks to increase the agentic capacity of the young person (e.g., positive aspects of development, such as self-regulation and self-transformation) by teaching critical skills associated with the exploration of alternatives (e.g., problem-solving skills such as creativity, critical valuation, and a suspension of judgment). Using small groups of peers in which mutual criticism is encouraged, critical discussions are generated regarding real-life problems that can help young people learn from each other about how to conceptualize their current situation and to imagine alternatives to it. This model has been effective among marginalized youth in helping them deal with real-life problems associated with numerous risk factors. Clearly, those interested in advancing the intervention field should make special note of these techniques.[34]

Coming from another perspective, clinical psychologist Meg Jay has based her treatment of troubled "twenty-somethings" in part on the identity capital model. She has laid her approach and clinical case studies out in her book, *The Defining Decade: Why Your Twenties Matter—And How to Make the Most of Them*,[35] and presented these in a TED talk, which has had over seven million views at the time of writing.[36] In this talk, she implores young people to "forget about having an identity crisis and get some identity capital. . . . Do something that adds value to who you are. Do something that's an investment in who you might want to be next." By this, she means that the 20s are a time for consolidating identities, not putting off the proactivity required to synthesize the various elements of identity and to find a way to integrate these into a career and family life. Her clients tend to be the more affluent youth who believe they *ought to be* delaying adulthood, putting off goals and adult roles. She sees this as a growing problem, fed by some academic theories such as Arnett's theory of *emerging adulthood*, which claims that all young people in Western-type societies now go through (yet) another developmental stage between adolescence and early adulthood lasting at least six years, from about 18 to 25.[37] Theories like Arnett's have serious logical and evidential problems, a discussion of which is beyond the scope of the present book, but they appeal to the public because of their "pop" simplicity.[38] Observers such as Jay are alarmed that pop-psychology explanations for social structural changes are being accepted and young people are enticed to believe that they *ought to* delay the assumption of adult roles, producing a variety of personal problems that are aggravated by a self-blame for failures and wasted opportunities.

Similarly, personal mentor and life coach Drew Lichtenberger draws on the Identity Capital Model to help his "twenty-something" clients cope with and rise above "the Twenties BeatDown," during which they have found themselves stuck or lost in the transition to adulthood and are perplexed as to why. He writes that

> common manifestations include wondering if you're not meeting your potential, questioning if you're on the right path, trying to figure out your purpose in life, or who you are. Alternatively, it could be the foreboding sense one gets when facing major life-decisions about the future.[39]

Lichtenberger has developed the "Prepare a Future Developmental Individualization Curriculum" to help people find ways to change their individualization process from the default one described above to a developmental one in which they engage in self-examination processes that help them to discover their unique potentials, clarify their values, and align themselves with a set of prioritized goals toward which they take concrete steps.[40]

Identity Capital Therapies

Based on the formulations developed above regarding the three levels of identity and their interrelationships, in conjunction with the material on identity capital and the emerging interventions based on the Identity Capital Model, we believe that there is sufficient justification for recommending that those undertaking identity interventions consider basing their efforts in part on the distinctions among social identity, personal identity, and ego identity. In doing this, attention should be drawn to the fact that identity formation and maintenance processes are different for each type of identity. Forming and maintaining social identities is a difficult and long-term task in late-modern societies. Finding an appropriate niche and securing validated roles in an adult community has become an increasingly prolonged task. An implication of this is that many adolescents and, increasingly, young adults are institutionally denied sources of meaningful adult social identities; hence they often rely mainly on personal identities for sources of meaning and validation. Unfortunately, among recent cohorts, personal identities have been targeted and penetrated by mass culture influences that seek to push and pull the young person in various directions.

The fluid and unstable nature of late-modern influences can be a source of concern and anxiety for the young person. Those who enter the period of youth with a relatively strong sense of ego identity, bolstered by well-developed ego-synthetic and executive functions, can likely endure the assaults on, and insecurities about, their personal and social identities. However, those who have weaker ego processes will probably encounter greater difficulties in dealing with the deficits in their social identities and assaults on their personal identities. Therapeutic interventions need to recognize this, and therapists need to let young people experiencing difficulties in their identity formation know that it may be the nature of contemporary society and not them personally that is at the heart of their distress. This does not remove responsibility from the young person for learning how to cope with the vicissitudes of late-modern societies, but giving a patient knowledge of contrasts with other societies, and how their lives might be different, might help relieve some of their self-blame and anxiety. Therapist and patient alike should recognize that the identity problems associated with the compulsory individualization process were not found in earlier types of societies, where social identities were ascribed and personal identities were not manipulated for profit.

With this sort of "reality therapy,"[41] attention can be focused on the young person's subjective and objective identity components to determine whether discrepancies between them are a source of difficulty. As argued earlier, the greater the discrepancy between the two, the more difficulty the person will have in relating to others and the more their identity formation progress may be affected, including identity capital acquisition. This sort of reality therapy can help the young person adjust both to his or her peer group and its pressures and to the adult community and its expectations. Maintaining accurate bearings on these social markers should facilitate the transition to membership in an adult community. Indeed, sustaining a realistic view of one's position in society has been the mark of adjustment in all societies, especially premodern ones that demanded a high level of conformity. We are not recommending blind conformity here; instead, people need the ability to realistically assess a situation and judge their chances for, and means of, achieving certain goals.

With a more aligned sense of reality, and of his or her "objective" locations in the larger community, the person should be in a much better position to engage in the identity capital acquisition process. Instead of squandering opportunities for growth and development by engaging in high-risk behaviors (as up to one half of American youth apparently do)[42] or following a default individualization trajectory, efforts can be made to build a solid future based on the deliberate building of personal strengths and social networks that will ultimately pay off for the person and the community. The waste in potential among the young that is currently the norm in many communities is shameful, and to the extent that the adult community sits by and ignores it—or worse yet, endorses it—is even more shameful. At the beginning of the current millennium, with the technological wonders that afford so much wealth and opportunity, we should be far more socially advanced than we are. Learning more about optimal identity formation and our generative responsibility for nurturing future generations may help us close the gap between our technical sophistication and social parochialism.

Moving Forward

In recent years, there have been a number of developments that promise to help guide further theory development, the testing of those theories, and their application. In this section, we first suggest a methodological framework, then present some recent theoretical initiatives that might improve the lives of young people while optimizing their developmental outcomes.

A Methodological Model: Applied Developmental Science

Richard Lerner argues that university-based academic research, as is found in Western countries, has tended to be disengaged from the realities and problems of local communities and civil society, preferring instead to validate itself in terms of pure research defined by rigid interdisciplinary boundaries.[43] Too much academic knowledge is a product of career scholars who are working independently, with the result that much decontextualized knowledge is being produced. These practices have led to a deficit of knowledge that can be used as a basis for policy and program endeavors. Clearly, this is unfortunate, given the breadth and magnitude of problems facing the citizens of developed and developing countries.

Lerner has pioneered *Applied Developmental Science* (ADS), an approach that explicitly seeks to rectify the above hiatus between pure and applied knowledge.

This approach promotes "scholarship that seeks to advance significantly the integration of developmental science and actions that address the pressing human problems of our world. As such, a key goal (intended impact) of applied developmental research is the enhancement of the life chances of the diverse individuals, families, and communities served by such scholarship."[44] More specifically, he defines ADS as

> the synthesis of research and applications to promote positive development across the lifespan. Applied developmental scientists use descriptive and explanatory knowledge about human development in order to provide preventive and/or enhancing interventions. The conceptual basis of ADS reflects the view that individual and family functioning is a combined and interactive product of biology and the physical and social environments that continuously evolve and change over time. ADS emphasizes the nature of reciprocal person-environment interactions among people and across settings. Within a multidisciplinary approach, ADS stresses the variation of individual development across the lifespan—including both individual differences and within-person change—and the wide range of familial, society, cultural, physical ecological, and historical settings of human development.[45]

This humanistically oriented research agenda is compatible with our SIFT, and we believe would receive endorsement from Erikson. For example, the moral-ethical, neo-Eriksonian approach of the SIFT matches the inherent humanism of the ADS approach, as is evident with its call for applied developmental scientists to

> develop ethical sensibilities that enhance both scientific and social responsibility, and that frame in collaborations with community members useful understanding of the forces that shape their development. . . . Put simply, a scholar's knowledge must be integrated with the knowledge that exists in communities in order to understand fully the nature of human development and, based on this co-constructed knowledge, to develop and sustain ethical actions that advance civil society.[46]

In addition, ADS is an implicit endorsement of the personality and social structure perspective that has guided the development of the SIFT. For example, Lerner writes that

> person-context relations provide both opportunities for, and constraints on, change across life, and thus constitute a basis for relative plasticity in development across the lifespan. . . . This stress on the dynamic relationship between the individual and his/her context results in the recognition that a synthesis of perspectives from multiple disciplines is needed to understand the multilevel (e.g., person, family, community) integrations involved in human development.[47]

Given that the SIFT postulates a multidimensional theory of identity formation that is trans-contextual and trans-historical, and identifies the emergent problems associated with the challenges to identity formation in late-modern societies, the applied developmental science approach is clearly compatible with our approach, so much so that we wholeheartedly recommend it as a masthead with which to direct future research efforts in the scientific approach to identity studies.

Promising Theoretical Directions

Identity Economics

George Akerlof, the winner of the 2001 Nobel Prize in Economics, has laid the basis for a new approach to identity research that should open up a variety of new avenues of application.[48] This approach—*identity economics*—should also lend more legitimacy to the field of identity studies by highlighting its scientific potential. In this approach, Akerlof adds psychological and sociological ideas to some basic principles of economics, demonstrating how people's personal and social identities influence important priorities in their lives above and beyond economic incentives. He makes the case that different types of people facing the same economic circumstances make choices that can be accurately predicted on the basis of knowledge of their perceptions of "who they are" and "who they want to be." He thus contends that people's self-conceptions and identity-related aspirations affect their work values and spending habits more so than various economic incentives. The contribution of this new field is described as follows:

> *Identity Economics* bridges a critical gap in the social sciences. It brings identity and norms to economics. People's notions of what is proper, and what is forbidden, and for whom, are fundamental to how hard they work, and how they learn, spend, and save. Thus people's identity—their conception of who they are, and of who they choose to be—may be the most important factor affecting their economic lives. And the limits placed by society on people's identity can also be crucial determinants of their economic well-being.[49]

As one would expect from an economist, the relevant theoretical ideas can be expressed in equations. The basic formula of this field is as follows:

social identity + identity norms + identity utility = choice/decision

Social identities are defined in the standard ways discussed throughout this book, including broad categories such as ethnicity and gender, and more specific categories like student and punk rocker. Identity norms stem from the cultural rules that apply to specific social identities, as in the case of high levels of academic engagement among "good students." And, identity utility designates the sense people have of the gains and losses when their choices conform to identity norms. Together, these predict the choices and decisions people make in a wide range of areas, from purchasing certain items, through joining specific groups, and pursuing various goals.

In their journal article introducing this theory to economics, Akerlof notes its bridging potential:

> Many standard psychological and sociological concepts—self-image, ideal type, in-group and out-group, social category, identification, anxiety, self-destruction, self-realization, situation—fit naturally in our framework, allowing an expanded analysis of economic outcomes. This framework is then perhaps one way to incorporate many different nonpecuniary motivations for behavior into economic reasoning, with considerable generality and a common theme.[50]

Akerlof makes a good case about a number of choice-based behaviors, including educational ones. For example, he cites anti-school and anti-learning norms among some high school students that result in lower learning and less socialization into a more intellectual mind-set. Students who identify with such norms (which can originate with peer cultures) will be less likely to graduate and advance to a higher education.

But what happens if/when students change their minds about their goals or are forced to because of a lack of other opportunities? For example, in the current poor youth labor market, young people are told to stay in school as long as possible. Most students who have disengaged academically during high school may not have the requisite resources to advance, or to succeed even if they are advanced. Schools face the collective problems of cultures of opposition and cultures of disengagement from such students who find normative support from each other in their oppositional and disengaged identities.[51] Macro remedies require a sea change in societal attitudes about how to deliver mass education in ways that shelter this system from influences that feed opposition and disengagement.[52]

However, we would add that micro remedies could be found at the individual level in ways suggested by the identity capital model. That is, some of those exposed to cultures of opposition and disengagement may *not* actually have the wherewithal to make the decision to go on to a higher education or to figure out how to succeed in that context. Thus, we would add a fourth term to the equation, as follows, with identity capital referring to the ability of people to strategize on the basis of their present or desired resources:

social identity + identity norms + identity utility + identity capital = choice/decision

In the case of high school students, some may have developed certain academic abilities and study habits even while playing along with their disengaged peers (e.g., by not appearing too smart or achieving grades that were too high) and/or they may have postponed becoming fully academically engaged until they find a curriculum that is challenging and interesting to them. This appears to be what happens for many students in the American school system, for example, among those who balance competing norms from peers, parents, and the future antici-pated job market.[53] Of course, there are also (a) good students who (b) identify with academic norms of engagement because (c) they find them rewarding, and therefore have an easy choice about going on to a higher education. But in adding (d) identity capital resources to the equation, we would predict that these students would tend to be much better prepared and do much better at the post-secondary level by merit of their accumulated identity capital resources. Following the Mat-thew effect, they would advance faster and with less effort than their peers men-tioned above who played both sides of the academic engagement coin, feigning the disengagement of their peers while putting in a perfunctory performance for their teachers. With the addition of the identity capital model, therefore, identity economics is also extended into the realm of human development theory.

Identity-Based Motivations

This addition of identity capital resources to the identity-economics equation finds empirical support in the work of Daphna Oyserman, who has researched the efficacy of *identity based motivations* (IBM). Oyserman's work also enhances the developmental value of Akerlof's theory because it theorizes that personal and social "identities are dynamically constructed in context."[54] Like Akerlof's theory, the IBM model proposes that people take into account their current identities and assess future possible actions in terms of how congruent or incongruent they are to those current identities. In cases of identity-congruent actions, people are willing to expend more effort and to see their actions as meaningful. Conversely, identity-incongruent actions are perceived as "pointless and 'not for people like me'."[55] Oyserman has tested and found support for this model in a variety of contexts, especially educational ones, where efforts (academic engagement) and aspirations (future possible identities involving further education among minority group members) are increased by a variety of interventions. In fact, she claims to have developed "small interventions with big effects" by making "foreign" or "distant" future identities seem more real to people through group counseling ses-sions.[56] This involves changing the perceived salience of certain identities as well as the perceived difficulty in adopting more adaptive identities. In one experiment, by manipulating their perceptions of future possible identities, students could be enticed "to focus on academic possible identities, allocate more time to studying, and [be] less tempted to drink and use drugs."[57] Her model essentially takes us in the same direction as the identity capital model, with its postulates of identity horizons affecting how willing people are to move from their comfort zones into situations that challenge their previous identities, raising certain anxieties (see

Chapter 8). If the sense of identity anxiety is too great, especially among those with narrow identity horizons, various options will be avoided and choices made that keep the person in his/her comfort zone.

A related approach to identity motives comes from Vivian Vignoles, who argues that that there are "at least six identity motives—for self-esteem, continuity, distinctiveness, meaning, efficacy, and belonging."[58] Readers will recognize the three first principles of human identity in belonging, distinctiveness, and continuity, which form the basis of the SIFT as explained in Chapter 1. Self-esteem, meaning, and efficacy are also recognizable as forms of identity capital, as outlined in Chapter 6. Vignoles argues that these are human universals that vary in their intensity in relation to cultural norms, and that knowledge of how they operate in different contexts should help us understand, predict, and improve outcomes associated with various identities.

Conclusion: Improving Outcomes for All

As a final word, we wish to summarize the main message of our book. The scientific community, as well as the community at large, is in need of a developmental science applied to the study of identity similar to that proposed by Lerner for the field of developmental psychology. This is a science with an explicit set of humanistic values whose objective is the improvement of the human condition and the life chances of every human. The misconception that science is a neutral enterprise needs to be abandoned if we hope to move beyond the current state of affairs, the political economy of which often favors a few at the expense of the many. Importantly, this false sense of scientific neutrality dovetails with a false sense of economic and political neutrality. The educated élites, many of whom are trained in the rudiments of the scientific method, and who have taken the helm of contemporary Western societies, have not fully met their obligation to assume the type of leadership needed; instead, they have tended to take their wealth and shield themselves from the world in large houses and gated communities.[59]

The possibility that the identity formation of our educated élites has predominantly followed a trajectory dictated by a technological ethos over a humanistic ethos is supported by observations of the difficulties many members of the élites have had as they moved through their adulthoods, as evidenced by how many have mishandled their ethical-identity formation.[60] Clearly, we need to find ways to reinstitutionalize the adult stages of intimacy, generativity, and integrity—stages that Erikson argued are crucial to intergenerational responsibility and continuity—if we are to steer our course back to the path wherein communities have as top priorities stable civil societies and intergenerational justice. While the right to "freely choose" has been the result of hard-fought battles, with rights must come responsibilities.[61] In this historical era, these responsibilities are to the entire human species as an "in-group," not solely to parochially and selfishly defined in-groups. We need, therefore, to teach people, beginning with our youngest, how to proactively engage in activities that promote a developmental individualization trajectory for themselves, especially in ways that benefit others. The key to this optimal form for development lies in expanding everyone's social radius of involvements. Adults need to take up this generative challenge in order to guide and protect not just their offspring, but also future generations that will face the difficult task of forging viable adult identities in late-modern societies, with their attendant diversions, risks, and rewards that lead people away from the formation of ethical identities.

In this generative, explicitly ethical spirit, we want to reiterate that neither the natural nor the social sciences are morally neutral; in fact, they often have serious moral-ethical consequences, even if the effects are indirect (e.g., medicine eradicating diseases, but only among wealthy nations; economics increasing affluence, but mainly among those who are already rich). It has been increasingly fashionable in this age of relativism to dismiss approaches that identify both the "good and bad" as "normative." So-called normative theories have elements of prescription and judgment in them. Some behaviors are identified as "better" than others for certain reasons. Although there are dangers in such approaches, when they are couched in the type of ethical awareness Erikson identified and the moral reasoning logic Kohlberg so thoroughly studied, the justifications for making such judgments are not simplistically "moralistic" or "ideological," but move beyond these parochial limitations in ways that promise to help us develop a collective identity as a species in which all humans are considered as part of the same "in group." As Erikson and Kohlberg—and others through the millennia, including the Buddha—have framed this challenge, until we learn how to develop these universalistic identities, humans will continue to suffer needlessly at the hands of other humans as well as from their own hubris about "themselves," a point that takes us back to the first box insert in this book (box 1.1).

GLOSSARY OF SIFT TERMINOLOGY

The concepts defined here are central to the Simplified Theory of Identity Formation (SIFT). In the text above, they are presented in bold and characterized following their first usage. The definitions here are sometimes more specific than the characterization found in the text. More generic concepts are presented in italics in the text on first use. If readers need further elaboration of these more common concepts, Google searches should lead to adequate introductory definitions.

Agency (also personal agency): The capacity for intentional, self-directed behavior, especially in face of obstacles such as a lack of opportunity or discrimination. **Identity-based agency** involves the use of this capacity in forming new identities and maintaining established identities, and has been empirically associated with such attributes as a sense of purpose in life, self-esteem, self-efficacy, and an internal locus of control.

Continuity (of identity): The third basic principle of human identity, experienced subjectively as a sense of a meaningful past in one's life, which gives significance to the present, and purpose in the future. Objectively, continuity is evident in the stability of the roles and commitments held by members of a community.

Default individualization: An individualized life course that follows paths of least resistance and effort, essentially allowing options to be determined by inaction, rather than an active engagement of oneself in a deliberate decision-making process.

Developmental individualization: An individualized life course that follows active, growth-enhancing decisions and paths while resisting various pressures to follow default options.

Differentiation (of identity): The second principle of human identity, experienced subjectively as a sense of uniqueness/individuation from others and observable objectively in people's specific niche in a community. Optimally, the sense of differentiation is balanced with the sense of **integration**.

Early-modern society: See **late-modern society**.

Ego identity: A sense of temporal-spatial continuity that allows people to sustain an experience of themselves as agents with a past and future, which are optimally meaningful and purposeful. This psychological capacity is necessary for the continuity of personal and social (identity) functioning, namely, that long-term goals and commitments developed at one point in time are reasonably sustained at future points in time.

Ego-executive functions/abilities: The mental processes associated with putting thoughts into action, producing behaviors such as self-presentations in interpersonal situations. These abilities range from weak to strong.

Ego-synthetic functions/abilities: The mental processes with which information is synthesized by the person and thus how a person thinks—constructs reality. These abilities range from weak to strong.

Executive functions: See **ego-executive functions/abilities**.

Identity anxiety: The distress associated with thinking about possible future personal and social identities beyond a person's current "comfort zones," especially those provided by friends and family. Associated with narrow identity horizons and a reticence to engage in proactive identity formation.

Identity capital portfolio: The net **intangible** and **tangible resources** a person has at a given point in time that can be "exchanged" for gaining membership access to certain contexts and roles, including those in the workplace.

Identity capital: The personal resources that can be acquired developmentally that help people move among, fit into, and gain acceptance in various social contexts. These resources are those relevant to interpersonal "exchanges" in interactive contexts, whereby people engage in mutually benefiting identity validations (e.g., group memberships, with their attendant benefits such as employment and salaries) (see **intangible** and **tangible resources**).

Identity confusion: The antithesis of ego identity, associated with low levels of temporal-spatial continuity and the attendant behavioral disarray. A possible cause or consequence of a disruption of a person's social roles and place in a community/society wherein the senses of "fitting in" and "who one is" are in question. This subjective experience can range from mild to severe, and although a lifelong possibility, is more likely a developmental aspect of the transition to adulthood. When persistent, identity confusion can precipitate a severe and aggravated **identity crisis**.

Identity crisis: A potential phase of identity formation characterized by a sense of identity confusion and a disruption of a person's behavior patterns and commitment to socially sanctioned roles. Normally, the identity crisis is a developmental feature of the transition to adulthood during which the young person is reworking childhood identifications and self-concepts into those more appropriate with the adulthood of his/her culture. Most people do not experience this as a severe disruption, but for some it can be prolonged and aggravated because viable resolutions cannot be established.

Identity diffusion (also **diffuse identity**): A mental state involving the avoidance of forming goals and commitments that would help a person synthesize a coherent adult identity.

Identity formation: The multidimensional process in which the sense of temporal-spatial continuity (**ego identity**) is developed and embedded in stable behavior patterns, interpersonal relationships, shared belief systems, social roles, and societal commitments (**personal and social identities**). The process varies considerably among individuals along an inactive–proactive continuum. Inactive identity formation is characterized by a reticence to think ahead, experiment and explore, or to commit to future personal and social identities (synonymous with identity diffusion), whereas proactive identity formation involves a willingness to think ahead in one's life in a planning and purposeful manner, and to explore and experiment with future possible selves and identities. Two other types of identity formation have been identified: "active" approaches characterized by a willingness to commit to courses of action based on mainstream personal and social identities, but an unwillingness to explore identities that might possibly provide a better fit for the person in his/her society; and "reactive" approaches, during which a person intensively explores goals and belief systems, often accompanied by identity confusion and an identity crisis (see also **identity strategies**).

Identity horizons: A person's sense of his/her future possible personal and social identities (e.g., in educational systems and the workplace), which varies along a narrow–broad dimension. Associated with variations in the experience of **identity anxiety**.

Identity strategies: A working typology of the approaches people can take to their identity formation and maintenance in **late-modern societies** in response to the variety of ways in which adult identities can be formed as part of the **individualization process**. Five types have been identified: Refusers, Drifters, Searchers, Guardians, and Resolvers.

Individualization process: The life-course process of developing one's self as an "individual" in **late-modern societies**. This process becomes necessary to the extent that collective norms for life-course trajectories have been de-structured, leaving people more to their own devices in the transition to adulthood and beyond. The process works best when people have a reflexive self-awareness with which to make life-altering decisions and to choose courses of action from a range of options. (To be distinguished from "individuation," which involves developing an emotional distance from one's parents.)

Intangible (identity capital) resources: Mental capacities people have, or can acquire, that enable them to engage in interpersonal "exchanges" involved in negotiating various identity-related opportunities and obstacles.

Integration (of identity): The first principle of human identity, experienced subjectively as a sense of cooperative relationships with others, and observable objectively in people's adaptation to, and acceptance in, a community, fitting into available roles and statuses. Optimally, the sense of integration is balanced with the sense of **differentiation**.

Late-modern society (late modernity): The current historical phase of Western societies. Whereas the basis of social solidarity in **premodern societies** was based on primary-group relations (largely in terms of familial and intergenerational obligations), and in (early-)**modern** societies it was based on secondary-group relations (social bonds are more voluntary and based more on rational self-interest), in late-modern societies secondary relations have evolved to greater self-interest, especially through recent developments in capitalism. At the same time, because of a decline in collective supports, social contexts can be fragmented and anomic, challenging people to compensate in various ways, including engaging in the **individualization process**.

Modern society: The transformation from premodern to modern involved a shift in the basis of social solidarity from one of primary-group relations to one of secondary-group relations. In secondary-group relations, social bonds are more voluntary and based more on rational self-interest, rather than largely on familial and intergenerational obligation.

Moratorium period (of identity): A period of time sanctioned as a permissible delay of adult commitments that some societies grant young people who need to take more time in the transition to adulthood.

Personal agency: See **agency**.

Personal identity: A person's (subjective) sense of him/herself at the level of daily interactions with others, as well as how others (objectively) define them in terms of those interactions. Personal identities thus include the way people present themselves to others in normal interactions and how others perceive them as a result of those self-presentations in terms of reputation and inferred personality/ behavioral characteristics.

Premodern society: Often distinguished from early-modern societies with homologies such as folk vs. urban society, agrarian vs. industrial, or *Gemeinschaft* vs. *Gesellschaft*. In most Western societies, this transformation was largely completed during the nineteenth century, but considerable variation can be found.

Self-concept(s): A subjective sense of "who one is," as reflected in participation in various situations, activities, and roles.

Self-efficacy: The sense that one's actions can produce certain predictable outcome, such as in certain school subjects, languages, or sports. It is based on a belief that is matched with a realistic outcome (e.g., believing that one is good at math, matched with actually doing well in mathematics). Importantly, the belief can influence the outcome, because if one does not try to be good at something, one does not practice; and if one does not even try in the first place, one cannot by definition be successful at something.

Social identity: A person's social location in terms of key characteristics, like ethnicity and gender. The term is used to describe how a person experiences his/ her specific location in society as well as how others define and treat that person because of inferred key characteristics. It thus has subjective and objective aspects.

Synthetic functions: See **ego–synthetic functions/abilities**.

Tangible (identity capital) resources: The concrete statuses, possessions, and observable behaviors/attributes that people have, or can acquire, that enable them to engage in interpersonal "exchanges" involved in negotiating various identity-related opportunities and obstacles.

ENDNOTES

Chapter 1

1 www.brainyquote.com/quotes/quotes/a/aristotle148472.html#3QWyWf7BDVSb 20Ay.99

2 Riesman, D. (1950). *The lonely crowd: A study of the changing American character*. New Haven, CT: Yale University Press.

3 Weigert, A.J., Teitge, J.S., & Teitge, D.W. (1986). *Society and identity: Toward a sociological psychology*. Cambridge, MA: Cambridge University Press.

4 Identity politics can be defined in terms of various contestations of the political rights and advantages of different groups based on social identities, such as race/ethnicity, gender, sexual orientation, and so forth. The term is often used to describe the strategies and positions used to gain an upper hand in social movements, like the feminist and gay rights movements, or more generally in improving the material conditions of the oppressed. The focus of the political approach is therefore on intergroup relations and not human development, so its overlap with our developmental approach to identity is minimal.

5 Simon, B. (2004). *Identity in modern society*. Oxford: Blackwell.

6 It was common in these types of cultures to enforce out-migration when villages reach this size; Côté, J.E. (1994). *Adolescent storm and stress: An evaluation of the Mead-Freeman controversy*. Hillsdale, NJ: Lawrence Erlbaum Associates.

7 See, e.g., MacDonald, K. (2006). *How to mediate: A practical guide*. Boston: Wisdom Publications.

8 Brewer, M.B. (1999). Multiple identities and identity transition: Implications for Hong Kong. *International Journal of Intercultural Relations*, 23, 187–97, p. 188.

9 Leonardelli, G.J., Pickett, C.L., & Brewer, M.B. (2010). Optimal distinctiveness theory: A framework for social identity, social cognition and intergroup relations. In M. Zanna & J. Olson (Eds.), *Advances in experimental social psychology* (Vol. 43, pp. 65–115). New York: Elsevier.

10 Vignoles, V.L. (2011). Identity motives. In S. Schwartz, K. Luyckx, & V. Vignoles (Eds.), *Handbook of identity theory and research* (pp. 403–32). New York: Springer.

11 James, W. (1948). *Psychology*. Cleveland, OH: World Publishing. (Original work published in 1892); Cooley, C.H. (1902). *Human nature and the social order*. New York: Scribner's; Mead, G.H. (1934). *Mind, self, and society*. Chicago: University of Chicago Press.

12 See, e.g., Baumeister, R.F., Tice, D.M., & Hutton, D.G. (1989). Self-presentational motivations and personality differences in self-esteem. *Journal of Personality*, 57, 547–79; Brown, J.D. (1993). Motivational conflict and the self: The double-bind of low self-esteem. In R. Baumeister (Ed.), *Self-esteem: The puzzle of low self-regard* (pp. 117–30). New York: Plenum.

13 Mead, 1934.

14 Dusek, J.B., & McIntrye, J.G. (2003). Self-concept and self-esteem development. In G.R. Adams & M.D. Berzonsky (Eds.), *Blackwell handbook of adolescence* (pp. 290–309). Malden, MA: Blackwell Publishing.

15 Baumeister, R.F. (1998). The self. In D.T. Gilbert, S.T. Fiske & G. Lindzey (Eds.), *The handbook of social psychology* (4th ed.) (pp. 680–740). New York: McGraw-Hill.

16 Bandura, A. (1997). *Self-efficacy: The exercise of control*. New York: Freeman.

17 Holden, G. (1991). The relationship of self-efficacy appraisals to subsequent health related outcomes: A meta-analysis. *Social Work in Health Care*, 16, 53–93; Holden, G., Moncher, M.S., Schinke, S.P., & Barker, K.M. (1990). Self-efficacy of children and adolescents: A meta-analysis. *Psychological Reports*, 66, 1044–6; Multon, K.D., Brown, S.D., & Lent, R.W. (1991). Relation of self-efficacy beliefs to academic outcomes: A meta-analytic investigation. *Journal of Counseling Psychology*, 38, 30–8; Stajkovic, A.D., & Luthans, F. (1998). Self-efficacy and work-related performance: A meta-analysis. *Psychological Bulletin*, 124, 240–61.

18 Bandura, A. (2001). Social cognitive theory: An agentic perspective. *Annual Review of Psychology*, 52, 1–26.

19 Bandura, A. (2006). Toward a psychology of human agency. *Perspectives on Psychological Science*, 1, 164–80.

20 Leary, M. (2004). What is the self? A plea for clarity. *Self and Identity*, 3, 1–3, p. 1.

21 Hoyle, R. (n.d.). What is the Self? *International Society for Self and Identity*. www.psych.neu.edu/ISSI/daily.htm—this link is now dead, but the portal to this Society is now www.issiweb.org.

22 Freud, S. (1975). *The ego and the id*. London: Hogarth Press. (Original work published in 1923)

23 Erikson, E.H. (1968). *Identity: Youth and crisis*. New York: Norton, pp. 216–21.

24 In turn, these five stages are linked with adult development. During the sixth stage, young adults face the challenge of developing a sense of intimacy (vs. isolation), while during the seventh stage mature adults face the problem of nurturing a sense of generativity or caring for others, instead of being drawn into a sense of self-absorption and stagnation. In the last stage, usually entered in old age, individuals must evaluate and come to terms with the overall quality of their lives. Here the major alternatives are integrity or despair. Considered together, the eight stages in Erikson's model represent accumulated developmental capacities; better resolutions of earlier stages facilitate better resolutions of later stages. Moreover, understanding the endpoint of life-cycle development in terms of what Erikson called "wisdom" helps to identify the waypoints earlier in life that can lead people toward a sense of integrity in old age or away from it to despair. It is within this context that we can appreciate the importance of the ego

strengths gained with earlier stage resolutions, as well as higher-order capacities for perspective taking and moral reasoning. See, e.g., Erikson, 1968.

25 Côté, J.E. (1996a). Identity: A multidimensional analysis. In G.R. Adams, R. Montemayor, & T. P Gullotta (Eds.), *Psychosocial development during adolescence: Progress in developmental contextualism* (pp. 130–80). Thousand Oaks, CA: Sage.

26 For a detailed discussion of Erikson's writings on these two interrelated concepts, see Côté, J.E., & Levine, C. (1987). A formulation of Erikson's theory of ego identity formation. *Developmental Review, 9,* 273–325.

Chapter 2

1 Wheelis, A. (1958). *The quest for identity.* New York: Norton, p. 18.

2 Giddens, A. (1991). *Modernity and self-identity: Self and society in the late modern age.* Stanford, CA: Stanford University Press. Giddens argues that in late-modernity "the self becomes a reflexive project" for the entire lifespan. This is due in part to the degree of institutional de-structuring (in habits and customs), and in part to continual institutional restructuring and differentiation, which require continual monitoring by people (pp. 32–3).

3 American Psychiatric Association. (1980). *Diagnostic and statistical manual of mental disorders* (3rd ed.). Washington, DC: Author.

4 American Psychiatric Association. (1994). *Diagnostic and statistical manual of mental disorders* (4th ed.). Washington, DC: Author.

5 American Psychiatric Association. (2013). *Diagnostic and statistical manual of mental disorders* (5th ed.). Washington, DC: Author.

6 Task Force on DSM-IV. (1991). *DSM-IV options book: Work in progress.* Washington, DC: American Psychiatric Association.

7 Berman, S.L., & Montgomery, M. (2014). Problematic identity processes: The role of identity distress. *Identity: An International Journal of Theory and Research,* 14, 1–5.

8 Buchmann, M. (1989). *The script of life in modern society: Entry into adulthood in a changing world.* Chicago: University of Chicago Press.

9 Côté, J.E. (2000). *Arrested adulthood: The changing nature of identity and maturity in the late-modern world.* New York: New York University Press; Côté, J.E. (2014a). Towards a new political economy of youth. *Journal of Youth Studies,* 17(4), 527–43.

10 The term "corporate capitalist" would be more fitting, but explaining why would require a complex account that would divert our attention from the current focus on identity formation. For an analysis of the impact of capitalism on the transition to adulthood, see, e.g., Côté, 2014a.

11 This part of the framework generally follows Giddens, 1991.

12 Bourdieu, P., & Passeron, J.C. (1977). *Reproduction in education, society and culture.* Beverly Hills, CA: Sage.

13 Côté, J.E., & Allahar, A. (2007). *Ivory tower blues: A university system in crisis.* Toronto: University of Toronto Press.

14 Identity displays refer to the physical objects and images that adorn the person, which currently range from tattoos and body piercings to the latest technological gadget such as smart phones. See, e.g., Quart, A. (2001). *Branded: The buying and selling of teenagers.* New York: Perseus.

15 Goffman, E. (1956). *The presentation of self in everyday life.* New York: Doubleday; Goffman, E. (1963). *Stigma: Notes on the management of spoiled identity.* New York: Prentice-Hall.

16 Koughan, F. (writer), Rushkoff, D. (writer), & Berman, J. (director of photography). (2014). Generation Like [Television series episode]. In D. Rushkoff & F. Koughan (producers), *PBS Frontline*. Boston, MA: WGBH. www.pbs.org/wgbh/pages/frontline/generation-like/

17 Sennett, R. (1998). *The corrosion of character: The personal consequences of work in the new capitalism.* New York: Norton, p. 10.

18 Josselson, R. (1996). *Revising herself: The story of women's identity from college to midlife.* New York: Oxford University Press.

19 See, e.g., Jones, R.M. (1992). Identity and problem behaviors. In G.R. Adams, T.P. Gullotta, & R. Montemayor (Eds.), *Adolescent identity formation: Advances in adolescent development* (pp. 216–33). Newbury Park, CA: Sage.

20 Kroger, J. (2003). Identity development during adolescence. In G.R. Adams & M.D. Berzonsky (Eds.), *Blackwell handbook of adolescence* (pp. 205–26). Malden, MA: Blackwell Publishing.

21 Kroger, J., Martinussen, M., & Marcia, J.E. (2010). Identity status change during adolescence and young adulthood: A meta-analysis. *Journal of Adolescence, 33,* 683–98.

22 Steinberg, M., & Schnall, M. (2000). *The stranger in the mirror: Dissociation—The hidden epidemic.* New York: Cliff Street Books.

23 Erikson, E. (1963). *Childhood and society* (2nd ed.). New York: Norton; Steinberg and Schnall, 2000.

24 Steinberg and Schnall, 2000.

Chapter 3

1 www.brainyquote.com/quotes/quotes/c/cwrightmi388772.html#xez2IWi5vfJt MGpz.99

2 Wetherell, M. (Ed.). (2009). *Theorizing identities and social action.* Houndmills, UK: Palgrave MacMillan, p. 2.

3 Rattansi, A., & Phoenix, A. (2005). Rethinking youth identities: Modernist and post-modernist frameworks. *Identity: An International Journal of Theory and Research, 5,* 97–123, pp. 104 and 101, respectively.

4 Turner, R.H. (1976). The real self: From institution to impulse. *American Journal of Sociology, 81,* 989–1016.

5 Babbitt, C.E., & Burbach, H.J. (1990). A comparison of self-orientation among college students across the 1960s, 1970s and 1980s. *Youth and Society, 21,* 472–82.

6 House, J.S. (1977). The three faces of social psychology. *Sociometry, 40,* 161–77.

7 See, for example, Secord, P.F., & Backman, C.W. (1974). *Social psychology* (2nd ed.). New York: McGraw Hill.

8 Côté, 2014a.

9 Talaga, T. (1999, Feb. 3). Uniforms would cramp their style. *The Toronto Star,* A20.

10 CBC News. (2014, May 22). Teen claims school's bodysuit ban is about gender identity. Retrieved from www.cbc.ca/news/canada/toronto/teen-claims-school-s-bodysuit-ban-is-about-gender-identity-1.2650746

11 Kuhn, M.H., & McPartland, T.S. (1954). An empirical investigation of self-attitudes. *American Sociological Review, 19,* 68–76.

12 Cf. Côté, 2014a.

13 For example, see journals such as *IEEE Transactions on Intelligent Transportation Systems* and *Accident Analysis and Prevention.*

14 To expand this illustration, we could review studies that examine the effects of driver subjectivity on traffic behavior and congestion, as in the cases of, for example, aggressive drivers tailgating in small gaps between cars in heavy traffic, thereby slowing down the cars behind them trying to keep safe distances; road rage, which can bring traffic to a stop with sometimes tragic consequences; or "rubber-necking," which slows traffic as drivers try to look at accident scenes.

Chapter 4

1 www.brainyquote.com/quotes/quotes/m/mahatmagan109075.html#BVjtPjlr4Lt1q BFg.99

2 Mumford, L. (1944). *The condition of man*. New York: Harcourt, Brace, and World, pp. 162–3.

3 Kohlberg, L. (1984). *The psychology of moral development: Moral stages and the life cycle*. San Francisco: Harper and Row.

4 LaBouvie-Vief, G. (2006). Emerging structures of adult thought. In J.J. Arnett & J. L. Tanner (Eds.), *Emerging adults in America: Coming of age in the 21st century* (pp. 59–84). Washington, DC: American Psychological Association, p. 64.

5 Kohlberg, L., Boyd, D., & Levine, C. (1990). The return of stage 6. In T.E. Wren (Ed.), *The moral domain: Essays on the ongoing discussion between philosophy and the social sciences* (pp. 151–81). Cambridge, MA: MIT Press.

6 Lapsley, D.K. (1990). Continuity and discontinuity in adolescent cognitive development. In R. Montemayor, G.R. Adams, & T.P. Gullotta (Eds.), *From childhood to adolescence: A developmental period?* (pp. 183–204). Newbury Park, CA: Sage.

7 See, e.g., Arendt, H. (1968). *Eichmann in Jerusalem: A report on the banality of evil*. New York: Viking; Milgram, S. (1974). *Obedience to authority: An experimental view*. New York: Harper Collins.

8 See, e.g., Damon, W. (1988). *The moral child: Nurturing children's natural moral growth*. New York: Free Press.

9 Damon, 1988.

10 Selman, R.L. (1980). *The growth of interpersonal understanding*. New York: Academic Press.

11 Muuss, R. (1996). *Theories of adolescence* (6th ed.). New York: McGraw Hill.

12 Arnett, J.J. (2004). *Adolescence and emerging adulthood: A cultural approach* (2nd ed.). Upper Saddle River, NJ: Prentice Hall.

13 Damon, 1988.

14 Higgins-D'Alessandro, A., & Pafford, C. (2003). Moral development. In J.R. Miller, R.M. Lerner, & L.B. Schiamberg (Eds.), *Human ecology: An encyclopedia of children, families, communities, and environments* (pp. 502–7). Santa Barbara, CA: ABC-Clio.

15 Labouvie-Vief, 2006.

16 Dawson, T.L. (2002). New tools, new insights: Kohlberg's moral judgment stages revisited. *International Journal of Behavioral Development*, 26, 154–66.

17 Colby, A., Kohlberg, L., Gibbs, J., & Lieberman, M. (1983). A longitudinal study of moral judgment. *Monographs of the Society for Research in Child Development*, 48 (1–2, Serial no. 200); Dawson, 2002; Eisenberg-Berg, N. (1979). The development of children's prosocial moral judgment. *Developmental Psychology*, 15, 128–37. Note that these are for mainstream samples. Figures are not available for those in conflict with the law or other socially excluded young.

18 Hoffman, M.L. (1981). Perspectives on the difference between understanding people and understanding things: The role of affect. In J.H. Flavell & L. Ross (Eds.), *Social cognitive development: Frontiers and possible futures* (pp. 67–81). Cambridge, UK: Cambridge University Press; Hoffman, M.L. (2000). *Empathy and moral development*. Cambridge, UK: Cambridge University Press.

19 Eisenberg, N., Sheffield M.A., McDaniel, B., & Spinrad, T.L. (2009). Moral cognitions and prosocial responding in adolescence. In R.M. Lerner & L. Steinberg (Eds.), *Handbook of adolescent psychology* (3rd ed.) (pp. 229–65). Hoboken, NJ: Wiley.

20 See, e.g., Marcia, J.E. (1980). Identity in adolescence. In J. Adelson (Ed.), *Handbook of adolescent psychology* (pp. 159–87). New York: Wiley.

21 Weinreich, H.E. (1974). The structure of moral reasoning. *Journal of Youth and Adolescence*, 3, 135–40.

22 Eisenberg et al., 2009.

23 Lerner, R., Brown, J.D., & Kier, C. (2005). *Adolescence: Development, diversity, context, and application*. Toronto: Pearson Education Canada.

24 Higgins-D'Alessandro & Pafford, 2003.

25 Shweder, R.A., Goodnow, J., Hatano, G., Levine, R.A., Markus, H., & Miller, P. (1998). The cultural psychology of development: One mind, many mentalities. In W. Damon (Ed.), *Handbook of child development* (5th ed., Vol. 1, pp. 865–937). New York: Wiley.

26 Arnett, 2004.

27 Gibbs, J.C., Basinger, K.S., Grime, R.L., & Snarey, J.R. (2007). Moral judgment development across cultures: Revisiting Kolhberg's universality claims. *Developmental Review*, 27, 443–500.

28 Snarey, J.R., Reimer, J., & Kohlberg, L. (1985). Development of social-moral reasoning among kibbutz adolescents: A longitudinal cross-cultural study. *Developmental Psychology*, 21, 3–17.

29 Arnett-Jensen, L. (2008). Through two lenses: A cultural-developmental approach to moral psychology: Theoretical and methodological considerations. *Developmental Review*, 28, 289–315.

30 Blatt, M., & Kohlberg, L. (1975). The effects of classroom moral discussion upon children's level of moral judgment. *Journal of Moral Education*, 4, 129–61.

31 Hickey, J.E. (1972). The effects of guided moral discussion upon youthful offenders' level of moral judgment. *Dissertation Abstract International*, 33 (4-A), 1551.

32 Speicher, B. (1994). Family patterns of moral judgment during adolescence and early adulthood. *Developmental Psychology*, 30, 624–32; Weinreich, 1974.

33 Pascarella, E.T., & Terenzini, P.T. (2005). *How college affects students: Volume 2; A third decade of research*. San Francisco: Jossey-Bass; Speicher, 1994.

34 Muuss, 1996.

35 Pascarella & Terenzini, 2005. The caveat with these findings, as with most findings on the effects of higher education, is that there may be a pre-selection factor such that those who attend university may possess characteristics that predispose them to higher forms of development independent of educational experiences; that is, they would have advanced to these levels even had they not attended a university. It is impossible to carry out a study in which people are randomly assigned to attend university or not, so there may always be some unknown factor at work producing the change in spite of educational experience.

36 Pascarella & Terenzini, 2005, pp. 368–71.

37 Walker, L.J., & Taylor, J.H. (1991). Family interactions and the development of moral reasoning. *Child Development*, 62, 264–83.

38 See, e.g., Walker, L.J., & Henning, K.H. (1999). Parenting style and the development of moral reasoning. *Journal of Moral Education*, 28, 359–74.

39 Speicher, 1994.

40 Damon, 1988.

41 Eisenberg et al., 2009.

42 Côté, J.E., & Allahar, A. (2006). *Critical youth studies: A Canadian focus*. Toronto: Pearson Educational Publishing.

43 See especially Erikson, E.H. (1975). *Life history and the historical moment*. New York: Norton; Côté & Levine, 1987; and Côté, J.E., & Levine, C. (1988). The relationship between ego identity status and Erikson's notions of institutionalized moratoria, value orientation state, and ego dominance. *Journal of Youth and Adolescence*, 17, 81–99.

44 Côté & Levine, 1988.

45 Nunley, T., & Snarey, J. (1998). Erik Erikson's value orientation stages: A longitudinal study of ethical identity development among kibbutz adolescents. *International Journal of Educational Research*, 27(7), 629–41.

Chapter 5

1 http://refspace.com/quotes/Albert_Einstein/Q697

2 House, 1977, citing Durkheim's work.

3 Burrell, G., & Morgan, G. (1979). *Sociological paradigms and organisational analysis*. London: Heinemann.

4 Arnett, J.J. (2006). Emerging adulthood in Europe: A response to Bynner. *Journal of Youth Studies*, 9, 111–23, p. 115.

5 Emirbayer, M., & Mische, A. (1998). What is agency? *American Journal of Sociology*, 103, 962–1023.

6 Emirbayer & Mische, 1998, p. 970.

7 Lerner, R.M., & Kauffman, M.B. (1985). The concept of development in contextualism. *Developmental Review*, 5, 309–33; Lerner, R.M., Lerner, J.V., & Tubman, J. (1990). Organismic and contextual bases of development in adolescence: A developmental contextual view. In G.R. Adams, R. Montemayor, & T.P. Gullotta (Eds.), *Biology of adolescent behavior and development* (pp. 11–37). Newbury Park, CA: Sage.

8 For an examination of these issues, see Côté, J.E. (2014b). *Youth studies: Fundamental issues and debates*. Houndmills, UK: Palgrave MacMillan.

9 For a critique of this general approach, see Sukarieh, M., & Tannock, S. (2011). The positivity imperative: A critical look at the 'new' youth development movement. *Journal of Youth Studies*, 14, 675–91.

10 Turcotte, M. (2011, Winter). Intergenerational education mobility: University completion in relation to parents' education level. *Canadian Social Trends*, 38–44.

11 Blanden, J., Gregg, P. & Machin, S. (2005). *Intergenerational mobility in Europe and North America: A report supported by the Sutton trust*. London: Centre for Economic Performance.

12 Frenette, M. (2007). *Why are youth from lower-income families less likely to attend university? Evidence from academic abilities, parental influences, and financial constraints*. Analytical Studies Branch Research Paper Series, Catalogue Number 11F0019MIE—Number 295. Ottawa: Statistics Canada.

13 Finnie, R., Lascelles, E., & Sweetman, A. (2005). *Who goes? The direct and indirect effects of family background on access to post-secondary education*. Analytic Studies Branch Research Paper Series, Catalogue Number 2005237e. Ottawa: Statistics Canada.

14 See, e.g., Bernstein, B.B. (1975). *Class, codes, and control: Towards a theory of educational transmissions*. New York: Routledge; Bourdieu & Passeron, 1977.

15 Cf. Ryan, J., & Sackrey, C. (1985). *Strangers in paradise: Academics from the working class*. Boston: South End Press.

16 See, e.g., Wright, E.O. (1982). Class boundaries and contradictory class locations. In A. Giddens & D. Held (Eds.), *Classes, power, and conflict: Classical and contemporary debates* (pp. 112–29). Berkeley: University of California Press.

17 See, e.g., Hughey, M.W. (2008). Tripping the White fantastic: Navigating the politics of dislocation and bicultural authenticity in academe. In D.M. Rutledge (Ed.), *Biculturalism, self identity and societal transformation* (Research in Race and Ethnic Relations, Vol. 15, pp. 131–58). Bingley, UK: Emerald Group Publishing.

18 See, e.g., Blanden, J., Gregg, P. & Machin, S. (2005). *Intergenerational mobility in Europe and North America: A report supported by the Sutton trust*. London: Centre for Economic Performance.

19 Côté & Allahar, 2007; Côté, J.E., & Allahar, A. (2011). *Lowering higher education: The rise of corporate universities and the fall of the liberal arts*. Toronto: University of Toronto Press.

20 For evidence and arguments about how this applies to conditions in countries like South Africa, India, and China, see chapters in Helve, H., & Evans, K. (Eds.). *Youth, work transitions and wellbeing*. London: Tufnell Press, 2013.

21 Evans, K. (2002). Taking control of their lives? Agency in young adult transitions in England and the new Germany. *Journal of Youth Studies*, 5, 245–69.

22 For a further discussion of these issues, see Côté, 2000.

23 Jordan, J.V. (1997). A relational perspective for understanding women's development. In J.V. Jordan (Ed.), *Women's growth in diversity: More writings from the Stone Center*. (pp. 9–24). New York: Guilford Press, p. 9.

24 Lytle, L.J., Bakken, L., & Romig, C. (1997). Adolescent female identity development. *Sex Roles*, 3/4, 175–85, p. 184.

25 E.g., Tavris, C. (1992). *The mismeasure of woman*. New York: Touchstone.

26 Josselson (1996) traced the identity development of a group of thirty women over a twenty-two year period from the end of their college years in the early 1970s through to their mid-years in 1993.

27 Josselson, 1996, pp. 178, 241.

28 Markus, H.R., & Kitayama, S. (1991). Culture and the self: Implications for cognition, emotion, and motivation. *Psychological Review*, 98, 224–53.

29 Schwartz, S.J., Montgomery, M.J., & Briones, E. (2006). The role of identity in acculturation among immigrant people: Theoretical propositions, empirical questions, and applied recommendations. *Human Development*, 49, 1–30.

30 Mageo, J.M. (1997). The reconfiguring self. *American Anthropologist*, 97, 282–96.

31 Oyserman, D., Coon, H.M., & Kemmelmeier, M. (2002). Rethinking individualism and collectivism: Evaluation of theoretical assumptions and meta-analyses. *Psychological Bulletin*, 128, 3–72.

32 Taras, V., Sarala, R., Muchnisky, P., Kemmelmeier, M., Singelis, T. M., Avsec, A., . . . Sinclair, H. C. (2014). Opposite ends of the same stick? Multi-method test of the dimensionality of individualism and collectivism. *Journal of Cross-Cultural Psychology*, 45, 213–45.

33 Takata, T. (2007). Independent and interdependent self-schema in Japanese adolescents and elders. *Japanese Journal of Psychology*, 78, 495–503.

34 Sugimura, K., & Mizokami, S. (2012). Personal identity in Japan. *New directions for child and adolescent development*, 138, 123–43.

35 Sugimura & Mizokami, 2012, p. 124.
36 Sugimura & Mizokami, 2012, p. 130.
37 Sugimura & Mizokami, 2012, p. 131.
38 Erikson, 1975.
39 Email communication with Shinichi Mizokami, July 14, 2014.
40 Sugimura & Mizokami, 2012.
41 Furlong, A. (2008). The Japanese hikikomori phenomenon: Acute social withdrawal among young people. *The Sociological Review*, 56, 309–25.
42 Parker, S., Nichter, M., Vuckovic, N., Sims, C., & Ritenbaugh, C. (1995). Body image and weight concerns among African American and White adolescent females: Differences which make a difference. *Human Organization*, 54, 103–14; Twenge, J.M. & Crocker, J. (2002). Race and self-esteem: Meta-analyses comparing Whites, Blacks, Hispanics, Asians, American Indians and comment on Gray-Little and Hafdahl. *Psychological Bulletin*, 128, 371–408.
43 Takata, T. (2007). Independent and interdependent self-schema in Japanese adolescents and elders. *Japanese Journal of Psychology*, 78, 495–503.

Chapter 6

1 www.brainyquote.com/quotes/quotes/k/karlmarx402889.html#ELT1IXFzbLji2A2O.99
2 Hewitt, J.P. (2000). *Self and society: A symbolic interactionist social psychology* (7th ed.). Boston: Allyn and Bacon.
3 Côté, J. E. (2013). A stranger in paradise: Fitting in, managing identities, and reaching out. In J. Brooks-Gunn, R. M. Lerner, A. C. Petersen, and R. K. Silbereisen (Eds.), *The developmental science of adolescence: History through autobiography* (pp. 97–103). New York: Psychology Press.
4 Lerner and Kauffman, 1985.
5 Côté, J.E., & Levine, C. (1997). Student motivations, learning environments, and human capital acquisition: Toward an integrated paradigm of student development. *Journal of College Student Development*, 38, 229–43.
6 Turcotte, M. (2011, Winter). Intergenerational education mobility: University completion in relation to parents' education level. *Canadian Social Trends*, 38–44.
7 Lehmann, W. (2007). "I just didn't feel like I fit in": The role of habitus in university drop-out decisions. *Canadian Journal of Higher Education*, 37, 89–110.
8 This sociological concept is different than the psychological concept of "individuation," the process involving the boundary between self and other; see Côté, J.E., & Schwartz, S.J. (2002). Comparing psychological and sociological approaches to identity: Identity status, identity capital, and the individualization process. *Journal of Adolescence*, 25, 571–86.
9 Merton, R.K. (1968, January 5). The Matthew effect in science. *Science*, 159, 56–63.
10 Côté, J.E. (2006). Emerging adulthood as an institutionalized moratorium: Risks and benefits to identity formation. In: J.J.Arnett & J.Tanner (Eds.), *Emerging adults in America: Coming of age in the 21st century*. Washington, DC: American Psychological Association; Roberts, S. & Côté, J.E. (2014). The identity issues inventory: Identity stage resolution in the prolonged transition to adulthood. *Journal of Adult Development*, 21(4), 225–38.
11 Jay, M. (2012). *The defining decade: Why your twenties matter—And how to make the most of them*. New York: Twelve.

12 Cf. Woodward, I. (2007). *Understanding material culture*. Los Angeles: Sage.

13 Woodward, 2007, p. 137.

14 Apropos to the Internet, this particular blog is no longer live. Perhaps the blogger has moved on to other forms of impression management. http://charlenecroft.wordpress. com/2007/05/20/virtual-capital/

15 Côté, J.E. (1996b). Sociological perspectives on identity formation: The culture-identity link and identity capital. *Journal of Adolescence*, 19, 419–30; Côté, J.E. (1997a). An empirical test of the identity capital model. *Journal of Adolescence*, 20, 421–37.

16 Note that the measurement of parental financial "investments" in their children is not perfectly correlated with social class—some affluent parents want their children to make their own way in life, and some children themselves insist on doing so.

17 Côté, 1997a; Côté, J.E. (2002). The role of identity capital in the transition to adulthood: The individualization thesis examined. *Journal of Youth Studies*, 5, 117–34.

18 Cf. Schuller, T., Preston, J., Hammond, C., Brassett Grundy, A., & Bynner, J. (2004). *The benefits of learning: The impact of education on health, family and social capital*. London: Routledge Farmer Press.

19 For some studies investigating these ideas, see Luyckx, K., De Witte, H., & Goossens, L. (2011). Perceived instability in emerging adulthood: The protective role of identity capital. *Journal of Applied Developmental Psychology*, 32, 137–45; Luyckx, K., Schwartz, S.J., Goossens, L., & Pollock, S. (2008). Employment, sense of coherence, and identity formation: Contextual and psychological processes on the pathway to sense of adulthood. *Journal of Adolescent Research*, 23, 566–91; Schwartz, S.J. (2006). Predicting identity consolidation from self-construction, eudaimonistic self-discovery, and agentic personality. *Journal of Adolescence*, 29, 777–93; Schwartz, S.J. (2007). The structure of identity consolidation: Multiple correlated constructs or one superordinate construct? *Identity: An International Journal of Theory and Research*, 7, 27–49.

20 Hall, R.M., & Sandler, R. (1982). *The classroom climate: A chilly one for women?* Washington, DC: Association of American Colleges, Project on the Status and Education of Women.

21 E.g., Lerner, Lerner, & Tubman, 1990. Regardless of "climate" issues, there is much evidence that being an attractive woman is a potent asset in a number of contexts, including educational settings.

22 Cf. Côté & Levine, 1997.

23 This diagram borrows from Schuller et al., 2004.

24 Some people may not think of self-esteem as a "skill," but when a realistic sense of self-esteem (vs. an artificially inflated one) is under consideration, it is something to be learned by experiencing both successes and failures, and then reflecting on these experiences (vs. acquiring self-esteem mindlessly through simple positive and negative reinforcements).

25 Malcolm Gladwell wrote of a man he interviewed who had an IQ of 200, but had spent his life working in low-skilled jobs. This man had the misfortune of being born into a troubled, low-income family and did not have the opportunities to develop the types of soft skills discussed here. Gladwell argues being "smart enough" is sufficient if it is supplemented with other factors, including the opportunity to integrate those smarts with other skills, citing evidence that IQ scores alone above 120 do not predict achievement. Gladwell, M. (2008). *Outliers: The story of success*. New York: Little, Brown and Company.

26 Cf. Heckman, J.J., & Kautz, T. (2012). *Hard evidence on soft skills*. NBER Working Paper no. w18121. http://ssrn.com/abstract=2073161

27 This type of logic is the basis of the work on the benefits of social capital proposed by Putnam and others, but it may be that adding identity capital and moral-ethical reasoning to the equation will reveal even more benefits to cooperation among highly resourced people. For example, Putnam remarked, "[T]he more interesting question is not whether leaders affect the stock of social capital, but rather what affects the stock of leaders." Putnam, R.D. (2002). *Democracies in flux: The evolution of social capital in contemporary society*. New York: Oxford University Press, p. 17.

Chapter 7

1 www.brainyquote.com/quotes/authors/w/woody_allen.html
2 In contrast, the life course approach that has become popular emphasizes mainly the development of the individual as related to specific events in the person's life, and not the intergenerational interweaving of people's lives.
3 Erikson, 1968, p. 17.
4 For a quick discussion of these procedures, see http://en.wikipedia.org/wiki/AVPU
5 Events that disrupt previously nurturant and harmonious social forms, such as a nuclear family, provide good micro examples of what happens with other–other relations breakdown. Children of divorce can suddenly experience potentially disruptive ego–other relationships that can create difficulties for their sense of ego identity. See, e.g., Amato, P.R., & Keith, B. (1991). Parental divorce and the well-being of children: A meta-analysis. *Psychological Bulletin*, 110(1), 26–46.
6 Côté, J.E. (1997). A social history of youth in Samoa: Religion, capitalism, and cultural disenfranchisement. *International Journal of Comparative Sociology*, 38, 217–34.
7 Chandler, M. (2001). The time of our lives: Self-continuity in Native and non-Native youth. In W. Reese (Ed.), *Advances in child development and behavior* (pp. 175–221). New York: Academic Press.
8 See, e.g., Steinberg, L. (2001). We know some things: Parent-adolescent relationships in retrospect and prospect. *Journal of Research on Adolescence*, 11, 1–19.
9 Cf. Erikson's (1968) concept of the negative identity.
10 Goossens, L., & Phinney, J.S. (1996). Identity, context, and development. *Journal of Adolescence*, 19, 491–6; Marcia, J.E. (1989). Identity diffusion differentiated. In M.A. Luszcz & T. Nettlebeck (Eds.), *Psychological development: Perspectives across the life-span* (pp. 289–94). North-Holland: Elsevier Science Publishers B.V.
11 Klapp, O. (1969). *Collective search for identity*. New York: Holt, Rinehart and Winston.
12 For studies of those who engage in long-term ruminations over identities, see Luyckx et al., 2008, 2011.
13 Cf. the literature on authoritarian parenting; Steinberg, 2001.
14 Cf. Josselson, 1996.
15 Cf. Côté, J.E., & Levine, C. (1992). The genesis of the humanistic academic: A second test of Erikson's theory of ego identity formation. *Youth and Society*, 23, 387–410. See also the literature on authoritative parenting; Steinberg, 2001.
16 E.g., Standing, G. (2011). *The precariat: A dangerous new class*. London: Bloomsbury Academic; Sum, A., Khatiwada, I., McLaughlin, J., & Palma, S. (2011). No country for young men: Deteriorating labor market prospects for low-skilled men in the United States. *The ANNALS of the American Academy of Political and Social Science*, 635, 24–55.
17 This latter point is further supported by the fact that the empirical measures of identity do not work well in early adolescence, suffering especially in terms of internal

consistency estimates, presumably because identities are not sufficient consolidated to produce acceptable intercorrelations among scale items.

18 Coopersmith, S. (1967). *The antecedents of self-esteem*. San Francisco: Freeman.

19 Fitts, W.H. (1965). *The Tennessee Self-Concept Scale*. Nashville: Counsellor Recordings and Tests.

20 Dusek & McIntrye, 2003.

21 These comparisons are based on population norms derived from a database of over 400 studies using the Tennessee Self-Concept Scale; see Fitts, 1965.

22 Harter, S. (1986). Processes underlying the enhancement of the self-concept of children. In J. Suls & A. Greenald (Eds.), *Psychological perspectives on the self* (Vol. 3, pp. 137–81). Hillsdale, NJ: Erlbaum.

23 Harter, S. (1997). The personal self in context: Barriers to authenticity. In R.D. Ashmore & L. Jussim (Eds.), *Self and identity: Fundamental issues* (pp. 81–105). New York: Oxford University Press; Harter, S. Waters, P.L., & Whitesell, N.R. (1997). Lack of voice as a manifestation of false-self behavior among adolescents: The school setting as a stage upon which the drama of authenticity is enacted. *Educational Psychologist, 32*, 153–73.

24 Palh, K., Greene, M., & Way, N. (2000, April). *Self-esteem trajectories among urban, low income, ethnic minority high school students*. Poster presented at the biennial meeting of the Society for Research on Adolescence, Chicago, IL.

25 Dusek & McIntyre, 2003.

26 Ramey, H.L., Busseri M.A., Khanna, N., & Rose-Krasnor, L. (2010). Youth engagement and suicide risk: Testing a mediated model in a Canadian community sample. *Journal of Youth and Adolescence, 39*, 243–58.

27 Rosenberg, M. (1986). Self-concept from middle childhood through adolescence. In J. Suls & A. Greenwald (Eds.), *Psychological perspectives on the self* (Vol. 3, pp. 107–36). Hillsdale, NJ: Erlbaum.

28 Baumeister, R. (Ed.) (1993). *Self-esteem: The puzzle of low self-regard*. New York: Plenum Press; Baumeister, R., Campbell, J., Krueger, J., & Vohs, K. (2005). Exploding the self-esteem myth. *Scientific American, 292.1*, 84–91; Zimmerman, B.J., & Cleary, T.J. (2006). Adolescents' development of personal agency: The role of self-efficacy beliefs and self-regulatory skill. In F. Pajares & T. Urdan (Eds.), *Self-efficacy beliefs of adolescents* (pp. 45–69). Greenwich, CT: Information Age Publishing.

29 Marcia, 1980.

30 Pajares, F. (2006). Self-efficacy during childhood and adolescence: Implications for teachers and researchers. In F. Pajares & T. Urdan (Eds.), *Self-efficacy beliefs of adolescents* (pp. 339–67). Greenwich, CT: Information Age Publishing.

31 It is estimated that only about 20–30 percent of adolescents experience a prolonged period of emotional turmoil: Offer, D., & Offer, J. (1975). *From teenage to young manhood: A psychological study*. New York: Basic Books.

32 Côté, 1994; Côté, J.E. (2009). Identity and self development. In R.M. Lerner & L. Steinberg (Eds.), *Handbook of adolescent psychology* (3rd ed.) *Volume 1: Individual bases of adolescent development* (pp. 266–304). Hoboken, NJ: Wiley.

33 When Erikson wrote in the 1950s, far fewer people extended their identity formation by attending post-secondary institutions. Prior to that period, even fewer did so, but Erikson noted some examples, as in his book on Martin Luther, and his extended identity formation; Erikson, E.H. (1958). *Young man Luther*. Norton: New York.

34 Côté, 2006.

35 Kroger, J., Martinussen, M., & Marcia, J.E. (2010). Identity status change during adolescence and young adulthood: A meta-analysis. *Journal of Adolescence, 33*, 683–98.

36 Kroger et al., 2010; Côté, 2009.

37 The "identity status paradigm" modified Erikson's bipolar continuum by proposing that additional dimensions are involved in resolution of the identity stage (e.g., Marcia, 1980). Although this approach has spawned hundreds of studies, primarily in the U.S., it appears to have muddied the waters somewhat in terms of clearly mapping the developmental trajectories in the formation of coherent adult identities. The complexities of this debate are beyond the purview of this research synthesis, but for articles on one round of this debate, see: Berzonsky, M.D., & Adams, G.R. (1999). Reevaluating the identity status paradigm: Still useful after thirty-five years. *Developmental Review*, 19, 557–90; van Hoof, A. (1999). The identity status field re-reviewed: An update of unresolved and neglected issues with a view on some alternative approaches. *Developmental Review*, 19, 497–556; Waterman, A.S. (1999). Identity, the identity statuses, and identity status development: A contemporary statement. *Developmental Review*, 19, 591–621.

38 The technical terminology used in the identity status research that roughly corresponds to these four types of identity formation is, respectively, identity achievement, identity foreclosure, identity moratorium, and identity diffusion.

39 See, e.g., Fadjukoff, P., & Pulkkinen, L. (2005). Identity processes in adulthood: Diverging domains. *Identity: An International Journal of Theory and Research*, 5, 1–20.

40 Côté & Schwartz, 2002. Agency is measured in terms of self-esteem, internal locus of control, ego strength, and purpose in life (see box 8.3).

41 Boyes, M.C., & Chandler, M.J. (1992). Cognitive development, epistemic doubt, and identity formation in adolescence. *Journal of Youth and Adolescence*, 21, 277–304.

42 See, e.g., Côté & Schwartz, 2002; Dyk, P.H., & Adams, G.R. (1990). Identity and intimacy: An initial investigation of three theoretical models using cross-lag panel correlations. *Journal of Youth and Adolescence*, 19, 91–110; Kroger, J. (2003). Identity development during adolescence. In G.R. Adams & M.D. Berzonsky (Eds.), *Blackwell handbook of adolescence* (pp. 205–26). Malden, MA: Blackwell Publishing; Orlofsky, J.L., Marcia, J.E., & Lesser, I.M. (1973). Ego identity status and the intimacy versus isolation crisis of young adulthood. *Journal of Personality and Social Psychology*, 27, 211–19.

43 Marcia, J.E., Waterman, A.S., Matteson, D.R., Archer, S.L., & Orlofsky, J.L.E. (Eds.). (1993). *Ego identity: A handbook for psychosocial research*. New York: Springer-Verlag; Jakubowski, T.G., & Dembo, M.H. (2004). The influence of self-efficacy, identity style, and stage of change on academic self-regulation. *Journal of College Reading and Learning*, 35, 5–22.

44 Marcia, J.E. (1993). The ego identity status approach to ego identity. In J.E. Marcia, A.S. Waterman, D.R. Matteson, S.L. Archer, & J. L Orlofsky (Eds.), *Ego identity: A handbook for psychosocial research* (pp. 3–41). New York: Springer-Verlag

45 Marcia, 1980; Berman, A.M., Schwartz, S.J., Kurtines, W.M., & Berman, S.L. (2001). The process of exploration in identity formation: The role of style and competence. *Journal of Adolescence*, 24, 513–28.

46 Adams, G.R., Bennion, L., & Huh, K. (1987). *Objective measure of ego identity status: A reference manual*. Unpublished manuscript: Guelph, Ontario, Canada; Côté, J.E., & Levine, C. (1983). Marcia and Erikson: The relationships among ego identity status, neuroticism, dogmatism, and purpose in life. *Journal of Youth and Adolescence*, 12, 43–53.

47 Kidwell, J.S., Dunham, R.M., Bacho, R.A., Pastorino, E., & Portes, P.R. (1995). Adolescent identity exploration: A test of Erikson's theory of transitional crisis. *Adolescence*, 30, 185–93.

48 Meeus, W. (1996). Studies on identity development in adolescence: An overview of research and some new data. *Journal of Youth and Adolescence*, 25, 569–98; Meeus, W.,

Iedema, J., Helsen, M., & Vollebergh, W. (1999). Patterns of adolescent identity development: Review of literature and longitudinal analysis. *Developmental Review*, 19, 419–61.

49 Berman et al., 2001.

50 See, e.g., Jones, 1992.

51 Kroger, 2003.

52 See, e.g., Côté & Schwartz, 2002.

Chapter 8

1 www.brainyquote.com/quotes/quotes/k/kurtcobain574681.html#Q6hkiUv9MK0 wtgKZ.99

2 Lerner, R. (2002) *Concepts and theories of human development* (3rd ed.). Mahwah, NJ: Lawrence Erlbaum.

3 Phinney, J.S. (1989). Stages of ethnic identity development in minority group adolescents. *Journal of Early Adolescence*, 9, 34–49.

4 Hallett, D., Want, S.C., Chandler, M.J., Koopman, L.L., Flores, J.P., & Gehrke, E.C. (2008). Identity in flux: Ethnic self-identification, and school attrition in Canadian Aboriginal youth. *Journal of Applied Developmental Psychology*, 29, 62–75.

5 See, e.g., Cross, W.E. Jr. (1991). *Shades of Black: Diversity in African-American identity*. Philadelphia: Temple University Press; Helms. J. (1990). *Black and White racial identity: Theory, research, and practice*. New York: Greenwood Press.

6 Phinney, 1989.

7 Phinney, J.S. (2006). Ethnic identity exploration in emerging adulthood. In J.J. Arnett & J.L. Tanner (Eds.), *Emerging adults in America: Coming of age in the 21st century* (pp. 117–34). Washington, DC: American Psychological Association.

8 Phinney, J. S., & Rosenthal, D. A. (1992). Ethnic identity in adolescence: Process, context, and outcome. In G. R. Adams, T. P. Gullotta, & R. Montemayor (Eds.), *Adolescent identity formation: Advances in adolescent development* (pp. 145–72). Newbury Park, CA: Sage.

9 Phinney & Rosenthal, 1992, pp. 150–1.

10 Phinney, 1992.

11 Phinney, 2006. Phinney, J.S. (2005). Ethnic identity development in minority adolescents. In C.B. Fisher & R.M. Lerner (Eds.), *Encyclopedia of Applied Development Science* (Vol. 1, pp. 420–2). Thousand Oaks, CA: Sage.

12 Phinney, 2006.

13 Phinney. J.S., & Alipuria, L. (1990). Ethnic identity in college students from four ethnic groups. *Journal of Adolescence*, 13, 171–84.

14 Phillips-Smith, E., Walker, K., Fields, L., Brookins, C.C., & Seay, R.C. (1999). Ethnic identity and its relationship to self-esteem, perceived efficacy and prosocial attitudes in early adolescence. *Journal of Adolescence*, 22, 867–80.

15 Roberts, R.E., Phinney, J.S., Masse, L.C., Chen, Y., Roberts, C.R., & Romero, A. (1999). The structure of ethnic identity of young adolescents from diverse ethnocultural groups. *Journal of Early Adolescence*, 19, 301–22.

16 Phinney, J.S., Jacoby, B., & Silva, C. (2007). Positive intergroup attitudes: The role of ethnic identity. *International Journal of Behavioral Development*, 31, 478–90.

17 Kroger, 2003.

18 Phinney, 2005.

19 Côté, J.E. (1997b). A social history of youth in Samoa: Religion, capitalism, and cultural disenfranchisement. *International Journal of Comparative Sociology*, 38, 217–34.

20 Stockard, J., & O-Brien, R.M. (2002). Cohort effects on suicide rates: International variations. *American Sociological Review*, 67, 854–72.

21 Beneteau, R. (1988, Winter). Trends in suicide. *Canadian Social Trends*, 22–24.

22 Almey, M., & Normand, J. (2002). *Youth in Canada* (3rd ed.). Ottawa: Minister of Industry.

23 Nielsen, L. (1991). *Adolescence: A contemporary view* (2nd ed.). Fort Worth, TX: Harcourt Brace Jovanovich.

24 Sundar, P. (2008). "Brown it up" or to "bring down the brown" Identity and strategy in second-generation, South Asian-Canadian youth. *Journal of Ethnic & Cultural Diversity in Social Work: Innovation in Theory, Research & Practice*, 17(3), 251–78.

25 Ho, M. & Bauder, H. (2010). "We are chameleons": Identity capital in a multicultural workplace (Ryerson University, CERIS Working Paper No. 77). www.ceris.metropolis.net/wp-content/uploads/pdf/research_publication/working_papers/wp77.pdf

26 Brunsma, D.L., & Delgado, D.J. (2007). *Identity as resource: Identity capital and identity markets*. Presentation to the Southern Sociological Society, Atlanta, GA.

27 Kim T. (2010). Transnational academic mobility, knowledge, and identity capital. *Discourse: Studies in the Cultural Politics of Education*, 31(5), 577–91.

28 See. e.g., Sorell, G.T., & Montgomery, M.J. (2001). Feminist perspectives on Erikson's theory: Its relevance for contemporary identity development research. *Identity: An International Journal of Theory and Research*, 1, 97–128; Waterman, A.S. (1993). Developmental perspectives on identity formation: From adolescence to adulthood. In J.E. Marcia, A.S. Waterman, D.R. Matteson, S.L. Archer, & J. L Orlofsky (Eds.), *Ego identity: A handbook for psychosocial research* (pp. 42–68). New York: Springer-Verlag; Kroger, 2003.

29 Waterman, C.K., & Nevid, J.S. (1977). Sex differences in the resolution of the identity crisis. *Journal of Youth and Adolescence*, 6, 337–42.

30 Archer, S.L. (1989). Gender differences in identity development: Issues of process, domain and timing. *Journal of Adolescence*, 12, 117–38.

31 Thorbecke, W., & Grotevant, H.D. (1982). Gender differences in interpersonal identity formation. *Journal of Youth and Adolescence*, 11, 479–92.

32 Waterman, A.S. (1992). Identity as an aspect of optimal psychological functioning. In G.R. Adams, T.P. Gullota, & R. Montemayor (Eds.), *Adolescent identity formation* (pp. 50–72). Newbury Park, CA: Sage.

33 Côté, 2000; Kroger, J. (1983). A developmental study of identity formation among late adolescent and adult women. *Psychological Documents*, 13, (Ms. No. 2527).

34 E.g., Archer, 1989.

35 Côté & Allahar, 2007.

36 Côté & Allahar, 2011.

37 Dusek & McIntyre, 2003.

38 Zimmerman & Cleary, 2006.

39 Zimmerman & Cleary, 2006.

40 Pajares, 2006; Zimmerman & Cleary, 2006.

41 Schunk, D.H., & Meece, J.L. (2006). Self-efficacy development in adolescence. In F. Pajares & T. Urdan (Eds.), *Self-efficacy beliefs of adolescents* (pp. 45–69). Greenwich, CT: Information Age Publishing.

42 Schunk & Meece, 2006.

43 See, e.g., Oettingen, G., & Zosuls, K.M. (2006). Culture and self-efficacy in adolescents. In F. Pajares & T. Urdan (Eds.), *Self-efficacy beliefs of adolescents* (pp. 245–65). Greenwich, CT: Information Age Publishing; Stajkovic, A.D., & Luthans, F. (1998). Self-efficacy and work-related performance: A meta-analysis. *Psychological Bulletin*, 124, 240–61.

44 Phillips, T.M., & Pittman, J.F. (2003). Identity processes in poor adolescents: Exploring the linkages between economic disadvantage and the primary task of adolescence. *Identity: An International Journal of Theory and Research*, 3, 115–29; Yoder, A.E. (2000). Barriers to ego identity status formation: A contextual qualification of Marcia's identity status. *Journal of Adolescence*, 23, 95–106.

45 Rotheram-Borus, M.J., & Wyche, K.F. (1994). Ethnic differences in identity formation in the United States. In S.L. Archer (Ed.), *Interventions for adolescent identity development* (pp. 62–83). Thousand Oaks, CA: Sage.

46 Aries, E., & Seider, M. (2007). The role of social class in the formation of identity: A study of public and elite private college students. *The Journal of Social Psychology*, 147, 137–57.

47 For a study of class consciousness among university students, see Thomas, V., & Azmitia, M. (2014). Does class matter? The centrality and meaning of social class identity in emerging adulthood. *Identity: An International Journal of Theory and Research*, 14, 195–213.

48 Côté, 2002, 2006.

49 Hamilton, L.T. (2013). More is more or more is less? Parental financial investments during college. *American Sociological Review*, 78, 70–95.

50 Lareau, A. (2011). *Unequal childhoods: Class, race, and family life. Second edition with an update a decade later*. Berkeley, CA: University of California Press.

51 Rosenberg, M., & Pearlin, L. (1978). Social class and self-esteem among children and adults. *American Journal of Sociology*, 84, 53–77.

52 Wiltfang, G., & Scarbecz, M. (1990). Social class and adolescents' self-esteem: Another look. *Social Psychology Quarterly*, 53, 174–83.

53 McLoyd, V.C., Kaplan, R., Purtell, K.M., Bagley, E., Hardaway, C.R., & Smalls, C. (2009). Poverty and socioeconomic disadvantage in adolescence. In R.M. Lerner & L. Steinberg (Eds.), *Handbook of adolescent psychology* (3rd ed., pp. 444–91). Hoboken, NJ: Wiley.

54 Schunk & Meece, 2006.

55 McLoyd et al., 2009.

56 See, e.g., Most, T., Wiesel, A., Blitzer, T. (2007). Identity and attitudes towards cochlear implant among deaf and hard of hearing adolescents. *Deafness & Education International*, 9, 68–82.

57 Stein, L.M., & Hoopes, J.L. (1985). *Identity formation in the adopted adolescent: The Delaware family study*. New York: Child Welfare League of America.

58 Hauser-Cram, P., Wyngaarden Krauss, M., & Kersh, J. (2009). Adolescents with developmental disabilities and their families. In R.M. Lerner & L. Steinberg (Eds.), *Handbook of adolescent psychology* (3rd ed., pp. 589–617). Hoboken, NJ: Wiley.

59 Small, A., & Cripps, J. (2012). On becoming: Developing an empowering cultural identity framework for deaf youth and adults. In A. Small, J. Cripps, & J.E. Côté, *Cultural space and self/identity development among deaf youth* (pp. 29–41). Toronto: Canadian Cultural Society of the Deaf.

60 See, e.g., Most et al., 2007.

61 Small, A., Cripps, J., & Côté, J.E. (2012). *Cultural space and self/identity development among deaf youth*. Toronto: Canadian Cultural Society of the Deaf, p. 45.

62 Hauser-Cram et al., 2009.

63 Hauser-Cram et al. (2009) define developmental disabilities as "biologically based delays or impairments in one or more areas of development" (p. 589).

64 Hauser-Cram et al., 2009.

65 Klassen, R.M. (2006). Too much confidence? The self-efficacy of adolescents with learning disabilities. In F. Pajares & T. Urdan (Eds.), *Self-efficacy beliefs of adolescents* (pp. 181–200). Greenwich, CT: Information Age Publishing.

66 Adams, G.E., Côté, J.E., & Marshall, S. (2002). *Parent/adolescent relationships and identity development: A literature review and policy statement*. Ottawa: Division of Childhood and Adolescence, Health Canada; Steinberg, 2001; Steinberg, 2001.

67 This typology is based on Baumrind, D. (1968). Authoritarian vs. authoritative control. *Adolescence*, 3, 255–72. It was later extended by Maccoby, E.E., & Martin, J.A. (1983). Socialization in the context of the family: Parent-child interaction. In P.H. Mussen (Series Ed.) & E.M. Hetherington (Vol. Ed.), *Handbook of child psychology: Vol. 4 Socialization, personality, and social development* (4th ed. pp. 1–101). New York: Wiley.

68 Of course, these exist as continua rather than dichotomies, but the present/absent criterion is useful for illustrating and testing concepts.

69 See, e.g., Adams, Côté, & Marshall, 2002.

70 Aunola, K., Stattin, H., & Nurmi, J. (2000). Parenting styles and adolescents' achievement strategies. *Journal of Adolescence*, 23, 205–22.

71 Lamborn, S., Mounts, N., Steinberg, L., & Dornbusch, S. (1991). Patterns of competence and adjustment among adolescents from authoritative, authoritarian, indulgent, and neglectful homes. *Child Development*, 62, 1049–65.

72 Kerpelman, J.L., & Smith, S.L. (1999). Adjudicated adolescent girls and their mothers: Examining identity perceptions and processes. *Youth and Society*, 30, 313–47.

73 See, e.g., Grotevant, H.D. (1983). The contribution of the family to the facilitation of identity formation in early adolescence. *Journal of Early Adolescence, 3*, 225–37.

74 Dusek & McIntyre, 2003; Luster, T., & McAdoo, H.P. (1995). Factors related to self-esteem among African-American youths: A secondary analysis of the High/Scope Perry Preschool data. *Journal of Research on Adolescence*, 5, 451–67.

75 Cooper, C.R., Grotevant, H.D., & Condon, S.M. (1983). Individuality and connectedness in the family as a context for adolescent identity formation and role-taking skill. *New Directions in Child Development*, 22, 43–59; Grotevant, H.D., & Cooper, C.R. (1985). Patterns of interaction in family relationships and the development of identity exploration in adolescence. *Child Development*, 56, 415–28.

76 Dusek & McIntyre, 2003.

77 Schunk & Meece, 2006.

78 Kuczynski, L., Marshall, S., & Schell, K. (1997). Value socialization in a bi-directional context. In J.E. Grusec & L. Kuczynski (Eds.), *Parenting and the internalization of values: A handbook of contemporary theory* (pp. 23–50). Toronto: John Wiley & Sons.

79 See, e.g., Adams, Côté, & Marshall, 2002.

80 See, e.g., Marshall, S.K., Tilton-Weaver, L.C., & Bosdet, L. (2005). Information management: Considering adolescents' regulation of parental knowledge. *Journal of Adolescence*, 28, 633–47.

81 Harris, J.R. (2009). *The nurture assumption: Why children turn out the way they do* (Revised and updated). New York: Free Press.

82 Cf. Marshall, S.K., Young, R.A., Tilton-Weaver, L.C. (2008). Balancing acts: Adolescents' and mothers' friendship projects. *Journal of Adolescent Research*, 23, 544–65.

83 Adams, G.R., Munro, B., Doherty-Poirer, M., Munro, G., Petersen, A., and Edwards, J. (2001). Diffuse-avoidance, normative, and informational identity styles: Using identity theory to predict maladjustment. *Identity: An International Journal of Theory and Research*, 1, 305–18.

84 See, e.g., Jones, R.M., & Hartmann, B.R. (1988). Ego identity: Developmental differences and experimental substance use among adolescents. *Journal of Adolescence*, 11, 347–60.

85 See, e.g., Côté, 2000.

86 Harter, S. (1993). Self and identity development. In Feldmann, S.S. and Elliott, G.R. (Eds.). *At the threshold: The developing adolescent.* Cambridge, MA: Harvard University Press.

87 Robinson, N.S. (1995). Evaluation of the nature of perceived support and its relation to perceived self-worth in adolescence. *Journal of Research on Adolescence*, 5, 253–80.

88 Turner, G. (1999). Peer support and young people's health. *Journal of Adolescence*, 22, 567–72.

89 Schunk & Meece, 2006.

90 Waterman, A.S., Geary, P.S., & Waterman, C.K. (1974). Longitudinal study of changes in ego identity status from the freshman to the senior year at college. *Developmental Psychology*, 10, 387–92.

91 Pascarella, E., & Terenzini, P.T. (1991). *How college affects students: Findings and insights from twenty years of research.* San Francisco: Jossey-Bass. In their recent update to this research review, Pascarella & Terenzini (2005) still could not identify any "studies that examined the extent to which such development could be attributed to the college/university experience rather than to other maturational or sociocultural forces" (p. 228).

92 Côté, J.E., & Levine, C. (2000). Attitude versus aptitude: Is intelligence or motivation more important for positive higher educational outcomes? *Journal of Adolescent Research*, 15, 58–80.

93 Côté, 2002.

94 Bynner, J. (1998). Education and family components in the transition to work. *International Journal of Behavioural Development*, 22, 29–53.

95 Bynner, J., & Parsons, S. (2002). Social exclusion and the transition from school to work: The case of young people not in education, employment, or training (NEET). *Journal of Vocational Behavior*, 60, 289–309.

96 Savickas, M.L., Briddick, W.C., & Watkins, C., Jr. (2002). The relation of career maturity to personality type and social adjustment. *Journal of Career Assessment*, 10, 24–41, p. 35.

97 For a summary of research that suggests ways of scientifically studying the "true self" or daimon, see Waterman, A.S. (2004). Finding someone to be: Studies on the role of intrinsic motivation in identity formation. *Identity: An International Journal of Theory and Research*, 4, 209–28. Following Aristotelian thought, Waterman's research investigates how choices and goals are "better" when they follow one's inner potentials and talents.

98 Mead, M. (1928). *Coming of age in Samoa: A psychological study of primitive youth for Western Civilization.* New York: Morrow Quill Paperbacks.

99 Mead, 1928, p. 246.

100 Cf. Schuller et al., 2004.

101 Côté and Allahar, 2007, 2011.

102 Côté, J.E. (2005). The identity capital model. In C. Fisher & R.M. Lerner (Eds.), *Applied developmental science: An encyclopedia of research, policies, and programs (ADSE).* Thousand Oaks, CA: Sage.

103 Côté & Levine, 1997; Côté, J.E., & Levine, C. (2000). Attitude versus aptitude: Is intelligence or motivation more important for positive higher educational outcomes? *Journal of Adolescent Research*, 15, 58–80.

104 Côté & Levine, 1997.

105 Côté, J.E., Skinkle, R., & Motte, A. (2008). Do perceptions of costs and benefits of postsecondary education influence participation? *Canadian Journal of Higher Education*, 38, 73–93.

106 Côté, J. E., Mizokami, S., Roberts, S. E., Nakama, R., Meca, A., & Schwartz, S. J. (2015). *The role of identity horizons in education-to-work transitions: A cross-cultural validation study in the United States and Japan.* Manuscript submitted for publication.

107 Côté, 1997a.

108 Stanovich, K.E. (1986). Matthew effects in reading: Some consequences of individual differences in the acquisition of literacy. *Reading Research Quarterly*, 21, 360–407.

109 Côté, 1997a.

110 Atak, H., Kapci, E.G., & Cok, F. (2013). Evaluation of the Turkish version of the Multi-Measure Agentic Personality Scale. *The Journal of Psychiatry and Neurological Sciences*, 26, 36–45.

111 DuBois, D.L., & Tevendale, H.D. (1999). Self-esteem in childhood and adolescence: Vaccine or epiphenomenon? *Applied and Preventative Psychology*, 8, 103–17.

112 Bandura, A. (2006). Adolescent development from an agentic perspective. In F. Pajares & T. Urdan (Eds.), *Self-efficacy beliefs of adolescents* (pp. 1–43). Greenwich, CT: Information Age Publishing.

Chapter 9

1 www.brainyquote.com/quotes/quotes/m/mahatmagan150725.html#P30O2VbP5BQo0X50.99

2 See, e.g., Murray, C. (2008). *Real education: Four simple truths about bringing America's schools back to reality.* New York: Crown Forum; Twenge, J.M. (2006). *Generation me.* New York: Free Press.

3 See, e.g., Burrow, A.L. & Hill, P.L. (2011). Purpose as a form of identity capital for positive youth adjustment. *Developmental Psychology*, 47, 1196–206; Schwartz, S.J., Forthun, L.F., Ravert, R.D., Zamboanga, B. L., Umaña-Taylor, A. J., . . . Hudson, M. (2010). Identity consolidation and health risk behaviors in college students. *American Journal of Health Behavior*, 34, 214–24; Schwartz, S.J., Zamboanga, B.L., Weisskirch, R.S., & Rodriguez, L. (2009). The relationships of personal and ethnic identity exploration to indices of adaptive and maladaptive psychosocial functioning. *International Journal of Behavioral Development*, 33, 131–44; Weems, C.F., Costa, N.M., Dehon, C., & Berman, S.L. (2004). Paul Tillich's theory of existential anxiety: A preliminary conceptual and empirical examination. *Anxiety, Stress & Coping*, 17, 383–99.

4 Côté, 2006.

5 Work in this area has already begun in England through the efforts of the British government in funding the Centre for the Wider Benefits of Learning: see Schuller et al., 2004.

6 Côté & Allahar, 2007.

7 Schwartz, B. (2000). Self-determination: The tyranny of freedom. *American Psychologist*, 55, 79–88; Schwartz, B. (2004). *The paradox of choice: Why more is less.* New York: Harper Collins.

8 Cf. Erikson, E.H. (1959). Late adolescence. In D.H. Funkenstein (Ed.), *The student and mental health: An international view* (pp. 66–106). Cambridge, MA: Riverside Press.

9 These circumstances can lead some young people to "disengage" psychologically and behaviorally, with unfortunate consequences. See, e.g., Ramey, H.L., Busseri M.A., Khanna, N., & Rose-Krasnor, L. (2010). Youth engagement and suicide risk: Testing a

mediated model in a Canadian community sample. *Journal of Youth and Adolescence*, 39, 243–58.

10 Schwartz, B. (2004). *The paradox of choice: Why more is less*. New York: Harper Collins.

11 See, e.g., Lerner, R.M., Fisher, C.B., & Weinberg, R.A. (2000). Applying developmental science in the 21st century: International scholarship for our times. *International Journal of Behavioral Development*, 24, 24–9; Lerner, R.M., Lerner, J.V., von Eye, A., Bowers, E.P., & Lewin-Bizan, S. (2011). Individual and contextual bases of thriving in adolescence. *Journal of Adolescence*, 34, 1107–14.

12 Benson, P. (1997). *All kids are our kids: What communities must do to raise caring and responsible children and adolescents*. San Francisco: Jossey-Bass.

13 For an evaluation informed by the ICM of the Christian Inter-Varsity program, see Lederleitner, M. (2014). *Transition journeys in emerging adulthood as Inter-Varsity students seek to connect with faith communities after graduation: A qualitative study with educational and sociological implication* (Unpublished doctoral dissertation). Trinity International University, Deerfield, IL.

14 The Katimavik program in Canada provides an excellent example of this type of experience. See Lerner et al., 2005, p. 10.

15 Steinberg, 2001; Lamborn et al., 1991.

16 See, e.g., Berman, S.L., Kennerley, R.J., & Kennerley, M.A. (2008). Promoting adult identity development: A feasibility study of a university-based identity intervention program. *Identity: An International Journal of Theory and Research*, 8, 139–50; Ferrer-Wreder, L., Montgomery, M.J., Lorente, C.C. (2003). Identity promotion, adolescence. In T.P. Gullotta & M. Bloom (Eds.), *Encyclopedia of primary prevention and health promotion* (pp. 600–6). New York: Kluwer Academic.

17 See Chapter 7 of Côté & Allahar, 2006.

18 Erikson, E.H., & Erikson, K.T. (1957). On the confirmation of the delinquent. *Chicago Review*, 10, 15–23.

19 Berman, S., Montgomery, M., & Kurtines, W. (2004). The development and validation of a new measure of identity distress. *Identity: An International Journal of Theory and Research*, 4, 1–8.

20 Respondents are asked: "To what degree have you recently been upset, distressed, or worried over any of the following issues in your life?" Seven content areas are assessed: Long-term goals, career choice, friendships, sexual orientation and behavior, religion, values or beliefs, and group loyalties. Using this scale, an identity problem is diagnosed if at least three of the seven items are rated as *severe* or *very severe*, and if respondents also indicate high level of overall discomfort about these symptoms or their interference with their lives. If respondents who meet the criteria for identity problem rate the distress as having lasted for more than three months, they are also diagnosed with identity disorder.

21 Berman et al., 2004; Berman, S.L., Weems, C.F., & Petkus, V. (2009). The prevalence and incremental validity of identity problem symptoms in a high school sample. *Child Psychiatry and Human Development*, 40, 183–95.

22 Berman, Weems, & Petkus, 2009.

23 Hernandez, L., Montgomery, M.J., & Kurtines, W.M. (2006). Identity distress and adjustment problems in at-risk adolescents. *Identity: An International Journal of Theory and Research*, 6, 27–33.

24 Wiley, R.E., & Berman, S.L. (2013). Adolescent identity development and distress in a clinical sample. *Journal of Clinical Psychology*, 69, 1299–304.

25 Berman, S.L., & Wilson, J. (2010, March). *Changing individuals in a changing world: Recent trends in identity development.* Paper presented at the meeting of the Society for Research on Identity Formation, Philadelphia, PA.

26 Gfellner, B.M., & Cordoba, A.I. (2011). Identity distress, psychosocial maturity, and adaptive functioning among university students. *Identity: An International Journal of Theory and Research*, 11, 136–54.

27 Kamps, C.L., & Berman, S.L. (2011). Body image and identity formation: The role of identity distress. *Revista Latinoamericana de Psicología*, 43, 63–73.

28 Hernandez, Montgomery, & Kurtines, 2006.

29 Wiley, R.E., Berman, S.L., Marsee, M.A., Taylor, L.K., Cannon, M.F., & Weems, C.F. (2011). Age differences and similarities in identity distress following the Katrina disaster: Theoretical and applied implications of Erikson's theory. *Journal of Adult Development*, 18, 184–91.

30 Berman, Weems, & Petkus, 2009.

31 Berman & Montgomery, 2014.

32 E.g., Archer, S.L. (Ed.). (1994). *Interventions for adolescent identity development.* Newbury Park, CA: Sage.

33 Kurtines, W.M., Montgomery, M.J., Eichas, K, Ritchie, R., Garcia, A., Albrecht, R., Berman, S., Ferrer-Wreder, L., & Lorente, C.C. (2008). Promoting positive development in troubled youth: A Developmental Intervention Science outreach research approach. *Identity: An International Journal of Theory and Research*, 8, 125–38.

34 For a review, see Eichas, K., Meca, A., Montgomery, M.J., and Kurtines, W.M. (2014). Identity and positive youth development: Advances in developmental intervention science. In K.C. McLean & M. Syed (Eds.), *The Oxford handbook of identity development* (pp. 337–54). New York: Oxford University Press.

35 Jay, 2012.

36 www.ted.com/speakers/meg_jay

37 Arnett, J.J., & Tanner, J.L. (2011). Themes and variations in emerging adulthood across social classes. In J.J. Arnett, M. Kloep, L.B. Hendry, & J.L. Tanner (Eds.), *Debating emerging adulthood: Stage or process?* (pp. 31–50). New York: Oxford University Press.

38 Côté, J.E. (2014c). The dangerous myth of emerging adulthood. *Applied Developmental Science*, 18(4), 177–88.

39 http://drewlichtenberger.com/twenties-beatdown/

40 http://prepareafuture.com

41 Cf. the technique of *veridical attribution therapy*; e.g., Fiske, S., & Taylor, S.E. (1991). *Social cognition* (2nd ed.). New York: McGraw-Hill.

42 Lerner, R.M. (1995). *America's youth in crisis: Challenges and options for programs and policies.* Thousand Oaks, CA: Sage.

43 Lerner, Fisher, & Weinberg, 2000.

44 Lerner, Fisher, & Weinberg, 2000, p. 24.

45 Lerner, Fisher, & Weinberg, 2000, p. 25.

46 Lerner, Fisher, & Weinberg, 2000, p. 27.

47 Lerner, Fisher, & Weinberg, 2000, p. 26.

48 Akerlof, G.A., & Kranton, R.E. (2010). *Identity economics: How our identities shape our work, wages, and well-being.* Princeton, NJ: Princeton University Press.

49 Akerlof & Kranton, 2010. (From the blurb on the dust cover.)

50 Akerlof, G., & Kranton, R. (2000). Economics and identity. *Quarterly Journal of Economics*, CVX (3), 715–53, p. 749.

51 Côté & Allahar, 2011.

52 Akerlof gives the example of Comer's school reform, which included parents in their children's education to help them understand that teachers are allies, not enemies, thereby fostering identification with the school as a place they belong.

53 In a study of some twenty thousand American high school students, Steinberg found that peer culture tends to demean academic success as something for "brains," so the highest-achieving students—10 percent of the student body—often find themselves marginalized from peer culture. Another 20 percent report that they do not try to get higher marks because they are afraid of what their friends will think of them. He estimates that about 40 percent of American high school students are disengaged, meaning that they are simply "going through the motions" at school. See Steinberg, L. (1996). *Beyond the classroom: Why school reform has failed and what parents need to do*. New York: Simon & Schuster.

54 Oyserman, D., & Destin, M. (2010). Identity-based motivation: Implications for intervention. *The Counseling Psychologist*, 38, 1001–43, p. 1001.

55 Oyserman & Destin, 2010, p. 1001.

56 Oyserman & Destin, 2010, p. 1104.

57 Oyserman, D., & James, L. (2010). Possible identities. In S. Schwartz, K. Luyckx, & V. Vignoles (Eds.), *Handbook of identity theory and research* (pp. 117–45). New York: Springer, p. 139.

58 Vignoles, 2011.

59 E.g., Lasch, C. (1995). *The revolt of the elites: The betrayal of democracy*. New York: Norton; Standing, 2011.

60 Côté, 2000.

61 Cf. Fromm, E. (1955). *The sane society*. Greenwich, CT: Fawcett Publications.

INDEX